D0467847

METALWORKING

A MANUAL OF TECHNIQUES

Mike George

The Crowood Press

First published in 1987 as *The Complete Guide to Metalworking* by
The Crowood Press Ltd
Ramsbury, Marlborough
Wiltshire SN8 2HR

This impression 1996

British Library Cataloguing in Publication Data

George, Mike, *1941*-
Metalworking. — Rev. ed.
1. Metalworking
I. Title II. George, Mike, *1941*-. The complete guide to metalworking
684′.09

ISBN 1 85223 497 0

Acknowledgements

Line illustrations by Andrew Mackintosh

Typeset by Alacrity Phototypesetters
Banwell Castle, Weston-super-Mare, Avon
Printed and bound in Great Britain by
BPC Consumer Books Ltd
A member of
The British Printing Company Ltd

Contents

Introduction

One of my earliest memories as a child is of screwing a heavy lathe chuck off its spindle and being frightened when it plummeted to the ground a few inches from my foot. I was living with my mother in my grandfather's house while my father served in the RAF, and grandfather's workshop was a wonderland of machines, tools and materials which he used to produce my first toy railway engine.

The tools, however, soon became more fascinating than the toys they could produce, and, although I was later to become a journalist rather than follow the family engineering tradition, engineering never lost its fascination. In fact, I have been a lucky amateur who has always had links with the professional scene – because my mother ran the administration side of an engineering training department, while my sister is a technical translator for a huge European machine tool manufacturer.

The idea for this book was born out of a visit to a very advanced machine shop where the operators sat at computer keyboards, controlling complex machine tools through millions of pounds worth of electronics. I was greatly impressed, but I was left with the feeling that enjoyment and a sense of achievement are no longer the professional engineer's reward.

In a home workshop it is different. A few square yards of space serves as machine shop, forge, foundry, drawing office, and much more besides. If you do not have the correct tools for a job, you either make your own or improvise; if you cannot tackle something the 'correct' way, you invent a means of doing it with available tools and materials – and that is both enjoyable and rewarding.

In writing this book, I have assumed that you will want to begin with a few simple hand tools and, if you are bitten by the bug, you will eventually want to spend £100 or so on a drilling machine and maybe up to £1,000 on a metal-working lathe. However, there is an easy way of developing your skills first by spending only a few pounds. Many secondary schools and technical colleges run evening classes where you can get first-class instruction and access to some very accurate, specialist machinery. Several years ago, before I had my own workshop, I did just that, and it helped to develop an interest which has given thousands of hours of pleasure.

Finally, try to keep one point in mind: this is engineering for fun, not for profit. You may save yourself, and your friends, a little money by making things that you need, but the profit is measured in enjoyment rather than hard cash. If you want to make money out of engineering, try to get a job in a factory. Personally, I wouldn't push those computer buttons for all the tea in China!

MEASUREMENTS

At the time of writing, the imperial standard of measurements still exists in British industry, and the metric standard has not completely taken over, as was once predicted. This leads to some confusion, since although most teaching is now done using the metric standard, many imperially-calibrated tools are still available. On the second-hand market you are more likely to obtain imperially-calibrated tools than metric.

For this reason, and because imperial measurements are more readily understood than metric by most people over the age of twenty-five or so, imperial standards have been mainly used throughout this book. In all cases, however, metric measurements are listed in brackets.

Except in cases where absolutely precise conversion has been necessary, metric measurements have been rounded to the nearest convenient millimetre. For example, a measurement quoted as 'about 2in' is converted as 'about 50mm', whereas the correct conversion would be 50.8mm.

When in doubt, convert inches to millimetres by multiplying by 25.4. Convert millimetres to inches by multiplying by 0.03937.

SAFETY

It has to be acknowledged that some metalworking tools are potentially dangerous. In a home workshop it is not always possible or practical to conform to all aspects of industrial safety legislation, and neither is it a legal requirement for a person using his own tools. While every care has been taken to recommend safe procedures, neither the writer nor the publisher can accept responsibility for any accident or injury caused by following the advice given.

1 Where to Work

George Washington's slight embarrassment was with a cherry tree; with me it was the corner of the kitchen table. I did not saw it off – well, not right off – but filler failed to hide the damage and with the hacksaw in my hand I could not tell a lie. Metalworking activities were banished to the garden shed, and I have been working in various sheds for more than thirty years.

That boyhood experience highlighted a problem that all of us home metalworkers have – that of where to work. In the average suburban house there are, fortunately, several options which I will look at one by one, and later will discuss some ideas for people who live in smaller premises such as flats and bed-sits.

LARGER PREMISES

The Garage

On the face of it this sounds like a good idea, but suitability depends on the size of the building and what you are using it for already. If, like most people's, your garage is full of lawnmowers and junk while the car stands on the drive, you have no problem. Just have a good clear out and you are ready to start. If, however, the garage fulfils its intended purpose and houses the car, you have a problem, no matter how much spare space there may be.

The trouble with cars is that they get wet when it rains and even a small car, when wet, will bring the best part of a gallon of water indoors with it. Naturally you will want some sort of heating when you work in cold weather, and in the heat that gallon of water slowly evaporates, remaining suspended in the atmosphere until you turn the heat off. When the temperature is allowed to fall again, all that water condenses on cold surfaces. Much of it will find its way back on to the car, but an awful lot of it will end up on your tools and work, and you will find yourself fighting a constant battle against rust. You only win when you get rid of the car.

That problem apart, a garage has a lot of advantages. Garages are usually quite solidly built and they generally have concrete floors that are stressed to bear the weight of a heavy car. That is not very significant if you simply want to work with hand tools, but it will be very important if you ever expand your horizons and buy a lathe or milling machine of a reasonable size.

In some ways workshop floors are the most important part of the working area, because when you begin metalworking you never know how involved you are eventually going to become. A move from one working area to another, simply because you have decided to buy a machine tool, can be very awkward, so on the whole it is best to set up in the right place first.

Before we go any further, perhaps fuller explanation is in order. People who make the very large machine tools that are used in industry usually stipulate the requirements for the floors on which they are to be mounted, and I know of some that have to be stood on up to sixteen feet (five metres) of solid concrete. This not so much to bear the weight, as to ensure that the foundations *never* move by even a tiny fraction of an inch, because if they did, the accuracy of the machine would be affected.

Coming down the scale of machine tools the foundation requirements become less stringent, but retain their importance. Any machine tool, right down to a comparatively small lathe of the type you may one day consider buying, is only as good as the surface to which it is attached. A few inches of concrete under your feet when you start can be a good investment for the future.

The Garden Shed

This is another area with a rust problem, but one that can be beaten by a little work on weatherproofing and a sensible heating policy, which will be discussed later. There may also be a problem with the floor, but fortunately concrete is relatively cheap. You will need an electricity supply, and the ease or difficulty with which this problem is dealt with, is largely dictated by the distance the building is from the house. One important point: electricity *must* be safe, and I rate its installation a job for professionals. Do not play with it, because lashed-up wiring endangers both you and your property.

Inside the House

There is one home I know where you could be excused for thinking that a door off the downstairs hall leads into a small cloakroom or study. Open that door and you will find a big toolroom lathe, a milling machine, a bench, and racks containing almost every hand tool you could imagine.

Such a set up is obviously fine if you have both the money and an understanding partner. The room has a specially stressed floor, it has been very carefully but unobtrusively soundproofed, and it is heated on the house central heating system. There are no problems with dampness and rust, the workshop is always warm when you go in, and over all it is probably the best home workshop I have ever seen in my life.

Most of us have to settle for something a little less ostentatious, but mentioning this example does serve to highlight the obvious advantages of having a workshop that is part of the house. If you have an unused room, however small, where a little noise will create no problem, or can be contained by a little judicious panelling with softboard, you are in luck.

PLANNING A WORKSHOP

Seven years ago, when I moved into my present home, there was nowhere, either indoors or out, that would serve as a workshop. I had to start from scratch and build my own, and I tell the story in full because, even if you end up modifying an existing working space, the solution to some of the problems I encountered may be of help. Of course, initially you may not want to do everything that I mention, but eventually you may.

The first factor I had to consider was size, and I worked out that the minimum I would need would be 8ft × 12ft (2·5m × 3·7m). You may not need anything that large for a start, but I had a lot of tools that had been inconveniently stored all over the house.

I looked at the cost of building in brick, but I could not afford it, so I started looking at prefabricated wooden buildings – in other words, sheds. Some were cheap and looked it; others were expensive for no apparent reason, but I eventually found what I was looking for. It was exactly the required dimensions, had a ridged roof rather than a flat one, and it was made of treated wood that was guaranteed against rot for fifty years. This latter point was important, because in the only place where I could erect it, I would never be able to get at the back with a creosote brush.

The site was the corner of a concreted yard which leads out to the garden behind my house. One wall of the shed would almost touch the wall of the outside lavatory which contains the electricity meter and the main electrical distribution board for the house. When the house had been rewired I had made sure there were spare circuits available through this board, so I anticipated no problem in that direction.

One problem, however, was the foundations. The concrete sloped so that rainwater ran off on to the garden, and probing with a tungsten-tipped drill proved that it varied between two and four inches thick, with a substantial amount of hard-packed rubble underneath. I made up some wooden shuttering and poured an 8 × 12ft (2·5 × 3·7m)

The author's workshop viewed from the outside. Construction is of timber, and the building stands on a robust concrete base.

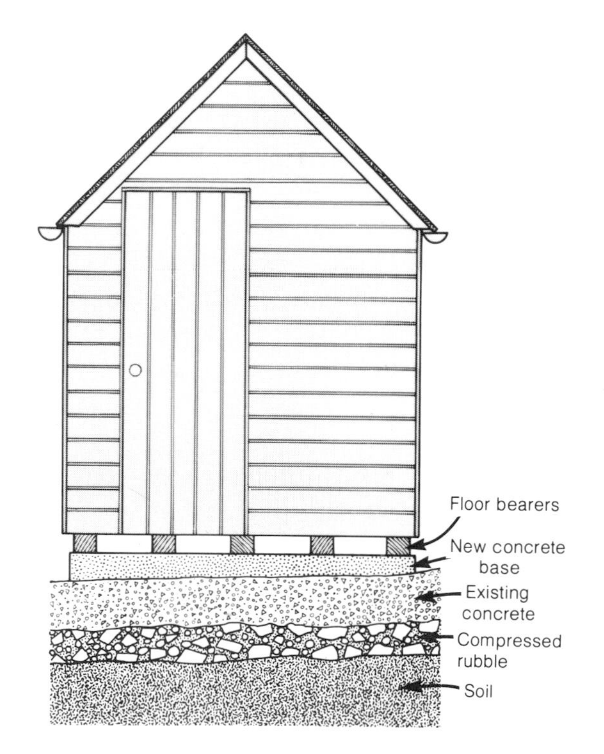

This is how I built my workshop on a firm foundation. Should the need arise, the base will bear extremely heavy weights.

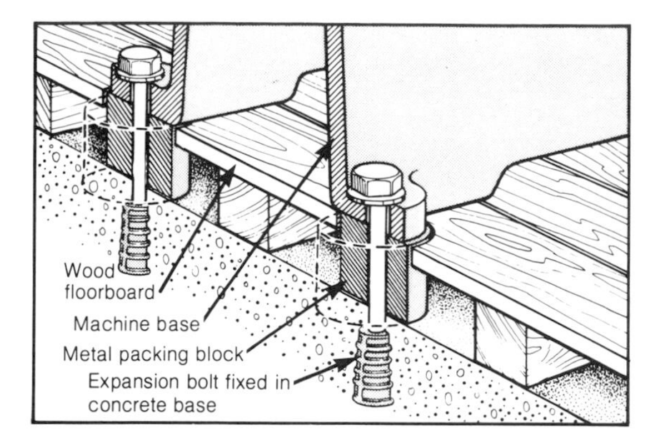

This was the method used to mount heavy precision machinery directly on to the concrete base.

concrete raft, with a level top, that averages about four inches (ten centimetres) thick, so that any machine tool that can be dragged through the door can be assured of an adequate foundation.

The shed, when erected, stood clear of this concrete base on 2in square (5cm square) timber runners. This has the advantage of providing a good circulation of air so that the floor timbers do not go rotten, but it also means that machine foundations must be cut through the wooden floor, and packing inserted to bring them up level with it. (*See* Chapter 10 on installing a lathe.)

The next move was to get the electricity on, so I made a sketch plan of the interior layout I wanted and called the

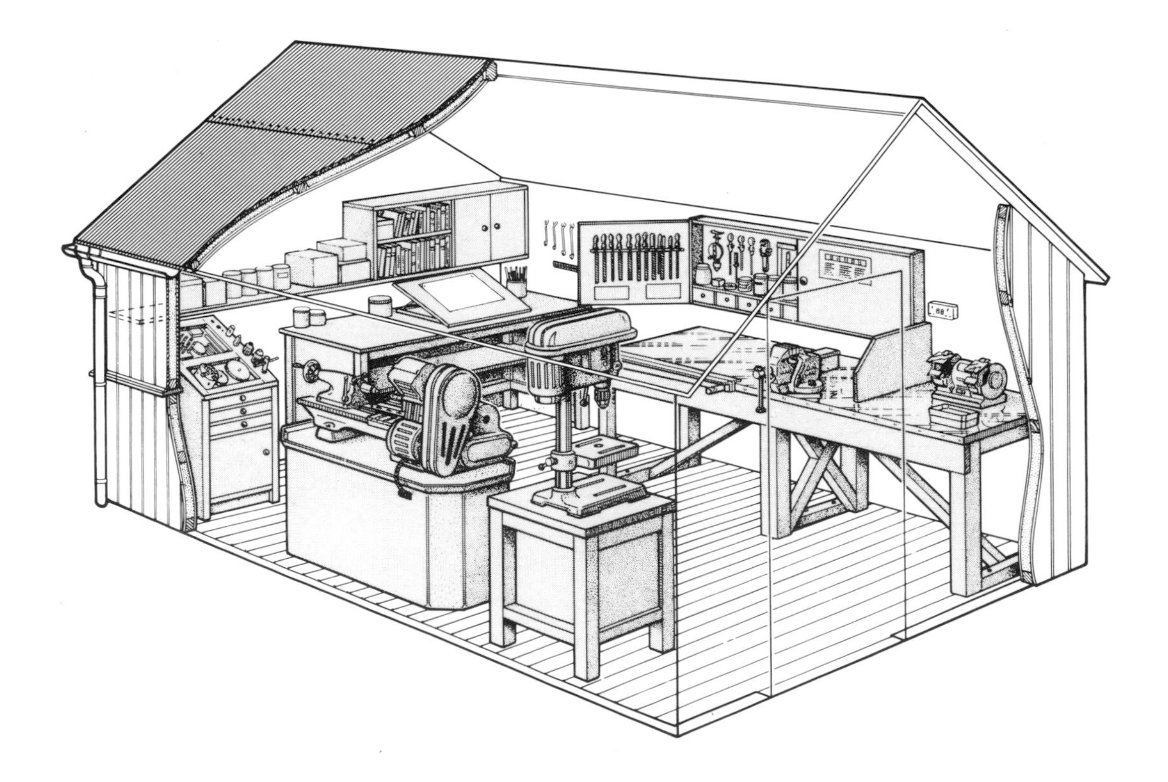

This layout has proved to be a good one for an 8ft × 12ft workshop, although some of the furniture shown is what I would like rather than what I actually have.

electrician. With the house main fuse block only about a foot away (although on the other side of a brick wall) there were no problems that could not be solved with a powerful electric drill.

When making my sketch I had been surprised to find I wanted no less than seven power sockets. Frankly, I now wish I had put in ten, because electrical requirements grow year by year and the most dangerous thing in a workshop is a lot of trailing wiring. Anyway, as I said before, I am happy to leave electricity to the professionals, and I ended up with an assurance that I was in no danger of overloading the circuit.

From my discussion with the electrician an interesting point emerged which you might like to bear in mind if you feel competent to tackle your own wiring. Single-phase electric motors of the type that power amateurs' machine tools do not draw a lot of power, but electric heating does. Make adequate provision for it when you make your calculations.

Lighting

For most metalworking operations you will need to work in quite a bright light, and strip lights are the cheapest to run. However, if you are using any form of

Strip lights inside the workshop are supplemented with spotlamps like this wall-mounted Anglepoise, which is essential when rotating machinery is in use.

rotating machinery, strip lights on their own can be dangerous because the light they give is delivered in the form of a very high speed flicker. Under this flickering light, a rotating component can look as if it is standing still. It may sound ridiculous, but I once saw a strip light absolutely freeze a big lathe chuck that was turning at over 2,000 r.p.m. Use strip lights by all means, but when machinery is being used always supplement them with spotlights containing conventional bulbs.

Heating

Coal, paraffin, and gas are all hydrocarbon fuels. When they burn, their hydrogen content combines with the oxygen in the air to form H_2O – plain, common water. This is expelled into the atmosphere in the form of steam, which condenses on cold metal surfaces. Added to this, workshops usually contain cans of inflammable liquids and cylinders of gas, and naked flames are not exactly safe. Electricity, although expensive, is the best way of heating a workshop unless you can run a spur off the house central heating system. Electricity provides a dry heat, which is kindest to your tools and work. In winter my workshop takes about thirty minutes to come up to an acceptable temperature with a 1·5kw convector heater.

Incidentally, never be frightened of letting tools and work get very cold indeed. One winter the temperature in my shed went down to minus 17 degrees Centigrade, and soluble oil froze into a solid block, staying that way for a week. When the thaw came there was not a single speck of rust on anything. Danger times are cold days that are quickly followed by mild, damp weather, because under these conditions large lumps of metal retain the cold and attract condensation. Once, when these conditions reached an extreme, I mopped over half a pint of water out of my lathe chip tray. So watch the weather, and be ready with absorbent rag and that can of WD40.

Bench and Vice

However ambitious you are, these are the essential items with which you will begin. Even if accommodation or circumstances mean that you can do none of the things I have mentioned so far, you will not be able to do anything without these two items. True, your 'bench' may be nothing more than a piece of stout board placed on the kitchen table or a worktop, and your vice may be a little one that clamps to the table edge, but let us begin by assuming that you have been able to find yourself a workroom of some sort.

No metalworking bench has ever been too strong or too heavy. I have a personal preference for metal-topped benches for several reasons: all wood absorbs spilled liquids, and all woods burn if you put bits of red-hot metal down on them. All woods splinter and chip if you hit them hard enough, and you cannot expect to go through your metalworking life without the occasional mishap. Plastics burn and splinter and are not always as resistant as you might think to chemical attack. Metal stands up well on all but the last point.

There's little point in making a bench wider than about 2ft (61cm) unless you have arms that prove Darwin's Theory, but length is an obvious advantage. My bench is 8ft (2·4m) long, but I have worked on benches as small as 2ft (61cm) square without problems. Working

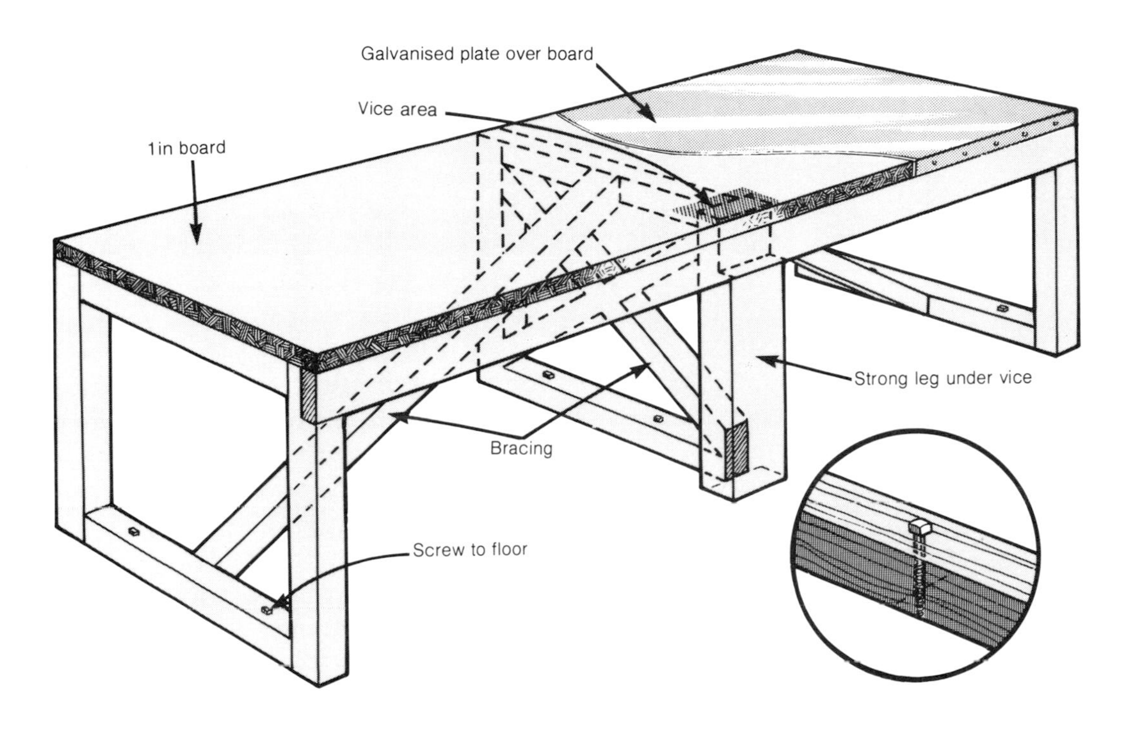

This has proved to be a sound design for a workbench. Extra rigidity is provided by screwing it to the floor and, in my case, to the back wall as well.

height is a matter of personal choice, and the height that suits me is 3ft 2in (96·5cm). The frame of my bench is of 2in (50mm) square timber, but it has the advantage that the back edge is strongly supported by the comparatively massive timber structure of the building, and the frames are also screwed to the floor. If you are building a free-standing bench, use 3in (76mm) square timber as a minimum, and incorporate plenty of cross-bracing.

As for the bench top, if you are to cover it finally with sheet steel, you can use 1in thick (25mm) chipboard. Do not use chipboard for an uncovered bench because water and most liquids dissolve it and you will end up with a horrible, mushy mess instead of a clean working surface. Steel facing need not be thick – mine is 0·7mm galvanised plate. If you do not want to use steel to face your workbench, make the top from timber at least an inch thick.

All this assumes, of course, that your bench is to be used only for hand-tool work and that any machine tools you may acquire will be mounted elsewhere. If you want to stand a machine on a bench it may have to be much more massive than described here, but that will be discussed in a later chapter.

Now for the vice: like the bench, it cannot be too big or strong, but obviously you are limited to what you can sensibly afford and what your bench will bear. A good size for most general work is the old 4in (102mm) jaw Record, which has a maximum gape of 4·75in (120mm). Secure it to the bench with the biggest bolts that will fit through the mounting

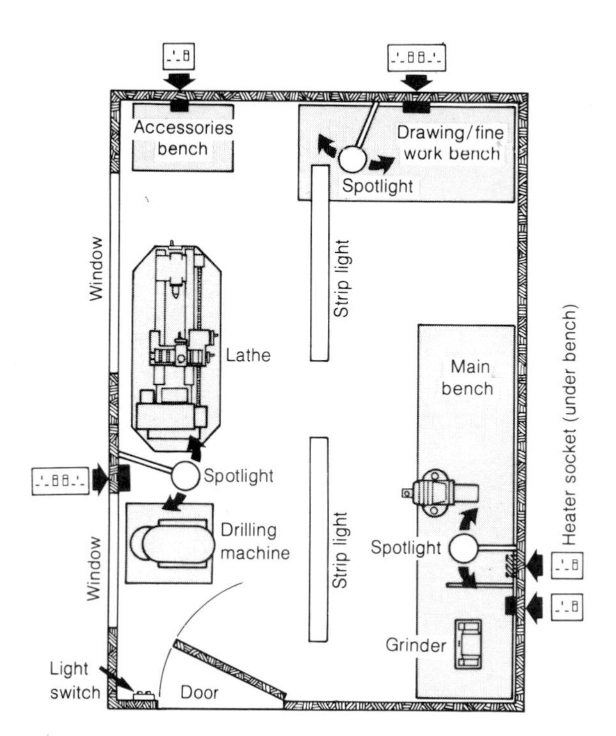

This is the electrical layout of my workshop. Spotlights are positioned so that they are shared by lathe and drilling machine, and main bench and grinder, while a third illuminates a drawing/fine work bench. In practice you cannot have too many plug points, providing there is no danger of overloading the circuit.

holes, and tighten the nuts down against the largest diameter washers you can find.

You should also ensure that your bench has a support leg directly under the vice. If you cannot mount the vice over a convenient existing leg, build in a special leg just to support the vice. With a chipboard bench top it will also pay you to add some further reinforcement under the bench, and provide some cross-bracing for the support leg. This rigid mounting is very important, because in an amateur workshop the vice gets misused as both an anvil and a press, and you may also want to use it for cold-bending some quite substantial lumps of steel. There is nothing worse than a vice that decides to move when you put some pressure on it.

Design of the vice itself is not important as long as it is made of rigid lumps of cast iron, and the jaws, closed by a thread of adequate dimensions, shut with reasonable accuracy. For a first vice, avoid those with special features like swivelling bases unless you want to concentrate on very fine modelling work, and go for mass and strength. Fancy vices can be acquired later if the need arises – and they can also be made when you have mastered your tools.

Almost every vice you buy will come fitted with the standard, serrated jaws, and the first thing you will find is that these serrations leave ugly criss-cross marks all over your work. The standard way around this problem is to cut a pair of 'L'-section jaw covers out of soft copper sheet. They save your work from being marked, but you will also spend much of your working time picking the things up off the floor. In recent years I have discovered a much better system:

When you buy the vice, buy a spare pair of jaws as well. As supplied these jaws will be quite hard, so heat them to red heat, hold them red for a few minutes, then let them cool very slowly. You can do this with a gas blowlamp, or in a solid-fuel fire. After this treatment they will be soft enough to work, so you either take them to a friend who has a milling machine or settle down to a careful session with a file. One way or another, remove those serrations and leave a smooth, flat surface. If you are fussy you can reharden the jaws but this is not really necessary. In fact, if you do not want to buy spare jaws, you can make a pair out of bright

The old Record No.3, with a four-inch jaw width, is an ideal bench vice for a small workshop.

These smooth jaws may be scarred with use, but they are superior to knurled jaws for most jobs.

A lump of flat-faced scrap steel, like this disc, makes an ideal small anvil for hammering jobs if you do not have a proper workshop.

mild steel strip and they will work just as well.

These smooth jaws will not damage your work, and they rid you of the need for jaw covers. The number of times you need serrated jaws are so few and far between that I cannot think why vices are not supplied with smooth jaws as standard, and serrated as an option. That is a point for the tool industry to ponder.

Finally on vices, here is a tip for very delicate work: if you cover your smooth jaws with a single strip of masking tape, you can grip polished surfaces on soft metal with confidence.

SMALL PREMISES

Most of what has gone before has assumed that you have been able to find some sort of permanent working space, either in a room in your house or in an outbuilding. What if you live in a small apartment, for example, where every single inch of space is in use?

Take heart, because even if you pursue the metalworking hobby to its ultimate, you will find that you can buy miniature machine tools that can be stored in a box and used on the table top. They obviously do not have the capacity for big work that permanently mounted tools have, but they will produce small work very accurately indeed.

That, however, is to jump ahead,

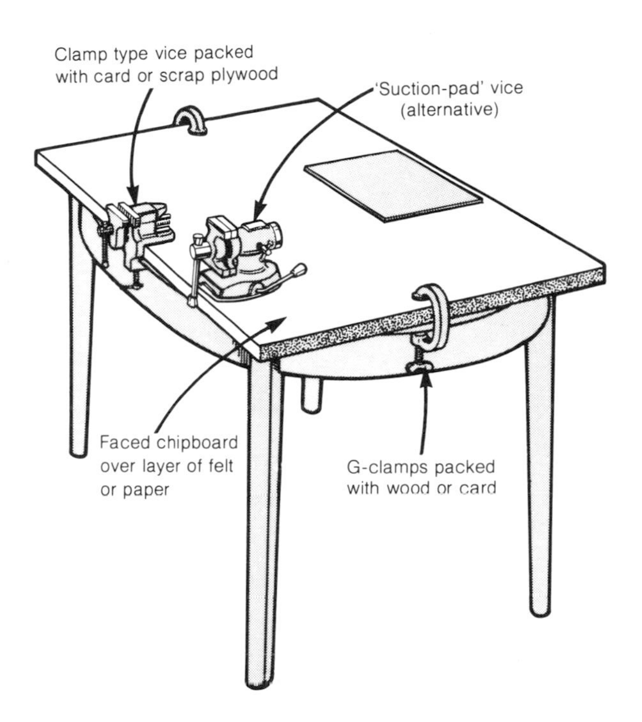

In small premises you can use a domestic table as a bench, covering it with a hefty sheet of plastic-faced chipboard.

because all you may need at an early stage is a bench and a vice. You will, of course, be limited to comparatively light work, but your 'bench' can be a piece of plastic-faced chipboard secured to a table or a kitchen worktop with a couple of 'G' clamps. The clamps can be packed with cardboard or plywood scrap to prevent them from marking the furniture.

You can also buy a small vice of the clamp type, or bolt a very small vice of conventional design to your chipboard sheet. Alternatively, buy a vice that will stick to a smooth surface with a lever-operated sucker pad.

With such a set up, any hammering can be done on a big lump of flat-faced scrap metal laid on the floor or on the concrete doorstep. A domestic gas cooker can be your heat treatment plant, and pieces of hot metal can be placed on the oven shelves while they cool.

In some ways you have an advantage over those of us with outdoor workshops. Your tools, kept in a box in a dry cupboard away from kitchen and bathroom steam, are unlikely to go rusty during long periods of idleness, and your working environment will usually be pleasantly warm.

EVENING CLASSES

If you have nowhere to work, or plan a project that goes beyond the scope of your tools and machinery, or simply want to learn more about metalworking techniques, evening classes will give you all the opportunities. Most secondary schools with a metalworking department run evening classes during the winter, and they generally represent excellent value for money. You usually pay a few pounds to enrol, and buy the items you have made at somewhere near scrap-metal prices.

You will not gain a formal qualification unless you enrol for a long course that has a qualification as a specific objective. After a couple of terms, however, you should be able to make a toolroom lathe perform as it should, and you will probably end up with a good mastery of hand tools and simple welding too. You will be taught and supervised by a professional, on safe machinery, and you will gain something that no book can ever give you – practical experience.

2 The Craftsman's Metals

The main problem facing small-time engineers like you and me is not what to make things out of, but how to obtain it in suitably-sized pieces. You can buy a couple of tons of steel on a phone call to a steel stockholder, but the same man generally does not want to know you if you want a piece that weighs half a pound. The same applies to other metals.

Fortunately there are around the country model engineers' suppliers that deal in small quantities – generally bar and strip materials by the foot, and even small off-cuts and bits of bar end that can be very useful for small components. Prices reflect the difficulty of holding big stocks of odds and ends, but quality is usually good. Locate such businesses through the Yellow Pages, or through the advertisements in magazines like *Model Engineer*.

One problem is you may find yourself living many miles from such an establishment. You can buy by mail, but postage charges on heavy lumps of metal are high, and it is not always convenient or economic to make the journey to collect personally.

Salvation lies just around the corner – often literally. In scrap-yards there are heaps of metal that can usually be bought for a few pence a pound. You do not always get exactly what you want, and you sometimes have to buy a very large piece and cut the best out of it, but the price is usually more than reasonable. The metal is often very dirty, and guarded by a sabre-toothed Alsatian, but it is convenient and available.

Engineering shops often have their own scrap-heaps too, the contents being picked up by contractors when the size of the heap becomes unmanageable. Keep an eye out for such places, because a word in the right ear will often get you permission to sort through the heap. There are some great finds to be made around your local industrial estate – but do always ask permission first.

A final word about scrap-heap materials: you do not always know what you are picking up. That nice bit of half-inch steel bar might be soft and cracked, or it might be too hard to cut. One promising looking piece of stainless plate I found took the teeth off a hacksaw blade and was eventually discovered to be a bit of a military rocket. Expect the occasional disappointment.

Now let's look at some of the engineer's metals in more detail.

STEEL

Whole books can be written about steel composition, but the thing that is often of most importance at our end of the engineering scale is whether or not we can cut and work it easily. As a very rough and ready practical guide, simple steels are a mixture of iron and carbon, the carbon being present in a chemically-combined form. The more carbon there is present, the harder the steel can become when given suitable heat treatment.

For most of our work we will be able to use low and medium carbon steels which are generally accepted as those having a

Mild steel stock in round bar and angle form.

Steel stock in round bar, angle and flat strip form. Most of the steel is high-carbon silver steel, ideal for making small tools. A greasy appearance is desirable - it helps prevent rust.

carbon content from 0·05 to 0·5 per cent. That is a pretty wide specification, which includes some steels capable of becoming very hard when heat-treated. At the lower end, you will find the familiar 'bright mild' bar, which is what you usually get if you just ask for 'a piece of steel.'

You will find that most of the steels in this class are quite free-cutting with either hand or light machine tools. If they are not, heating them to red heat and allowing them to cool slowly will usually do the trick. If you are in doubt about the composition of a piece of iron or steel, there is a simple test that you can try: touch it on a rotating emery wheel and watch the sparks. Cast iron gives a small stream of dull, red sparks with an occasional bright burst, while low-carbon mild steel gives a long stream of bright white sparks. As the carbon content increases the spark stream becomes more 'bushy'. You are unlikely to come across wrought iron these days, most 'wrought iron' work now being done in mild steel. If you do find a piece, it makes sparks a little brighter than cast iron but not as bright as mild steel. The 'high speed' alloy steel, used for cutting blades and lathe tools, makes orange sparks.

All that is fine if you have an emery wheel; if you have not, try a file. If the metal is removed easily, the chances are that you will be able to work it with your other tools. If you remove a little metal and get a bright, shiny glazed finish, it is probably too hard. Do not persevere with metals like this – you will simply ruin your file.

Of course many steels contain alloying elements other than carbon. All are put there to give the metal some specific quality. They may make it free-machining, harder or stronger, or maybe resistant to atmospheric or chemical attack. When you are starting out, concentrate mainly on soft steels that you can work easily, and if you want to go more deeply into the subject go to the local library and find something like *Chapman's Workshop Technology* (Edward Arnold, London).

Silver Steel

This is an 'over the counter' high-carbon crucible steel suitable for making small tools like screwdrivers, chisels and punches. It is reasonably easy to work in its 'as supplied' state, and it can be hardened and tempered with nothing more sophisticated than a blowlamp and a bucket of water. A lot of tool shops that do not normally sell steel stock do carry it on their shelves in 13in (330mm) lengths, and in its most common round-bar form it is usually well finished and dimensionally accurate.

Stainless Steel

There is no one substance called 'stainless steel'. Rather, it is a big family of alloy steels, generally compounded for varying degrees of corrosion resistance. Any steel containing over 11 per cent chromium can be described as 'stainless', but nickel is usually introduced as well, to further enhance corrosion resistance. Some stainless steels are quite soft and workable, while others will take the teeth off a good hacksaw blade in about two strokes. If you are ordering from a metal supplier, be sure to get free-cutting stainless, and do not expect it to be totally resistant to things like salt water or acids. Carefully test pieces found in scrap-yards.

Home heat treatment usually has no

This angle plate is a typical cast iron component. Such plates, useful for many lathe and milling machine set ups, are available in rough-cast form for finishing in home workshops.

effect whatsoever on hard samples of stainless.

CAST IRON

Compared to most steels this is a brittle material and its main strength is in compression. You will not use it much unless you buy castings to make a specific object, like a model steam-engine. It varies quite a lot in hardness, and the easiest to work is called soft grey iron which is used for things like chuck backplates and machine tool cross-slides. Most castings straight out of the mould have a very hard crust which you may have to remove with a large rough file or even a grinding wheel. Under the crust the metal is usually softer and more workable.

ALUMINIUM

This is one of my favourite materials, because it is generally easy to work and it takes a high standard of polished finish. Pure aluminium is soft – so soft that it causes tools to clog and snatch unless adequate precautions are taken. More common are aluminium alloys, where the presence of small amounts of other metals makes it stronger, slightly harder and easier to work in most cases.

In your workshop, beware of a piece of alloy which is very light indeed for its size. It could be a high-magnesium alloy, and if it is the shavings and swarf can catch fire very easily. The heat of a cigarette end can be more than enough to set it off, and in rare cases the heat generated by the tool has been enough. Magnesium burns with a blinding white light and intense heat, and the finer the shavings are, the greater the danger.

Some of the bits of scrap-yard aluminium you will find will have a bright, hard surface finish which can be either clear or any colour you like to name, although greens and blues seem to be most common. This is anodising, put there by an electro-chemical process, and it creates a very hard skin. This skin is usually so thin that it does no harm to good, sharp tools, but in the form of filings or turnings it can be very abrasive, so keep it off precision surfaces like lathe beds. Anodising also usually cracks if you bend the metal, so you may wish to take it off with an old file first, then repolish the surface.

Remember with aluminium and its alloys that the softening process is the opposite to that of steel. Heat it and quench it in water to soften.

BRASS

Brass is an alloy of copper and zinc, and other metals may be present in very small quantities too. Basic quality brass is about 63 per cent copper and 37 per cent zinc, while 'cartridge brass', with a 70/30 ratio, is more ductile. This detail should not worry you too much for most of the things you want to make in brass, but there is a point to beware of with scrap brass. If it is in the form of pipe it may have been thrown out because it has gone brittle and porous, while old brass plumbing fittings may be poorly cast in inferior metal. Having said that, I did once find some very fine brass rod in the ballcock arms of a demolished Victorian 'Gents'. 'Shanks's Improved Niagara' lives on as pins inside one of my fishing reels.

Another 'brass' you may come across in sheet form is gilding metal, a very ductile high-copper mix which is nice for beaten work like brass bowls and ashtrays. It is not very strong in engineering terms, but very good where looks and ease of work are the primary factors.

Brass is hardened by cold-working and drawing – processes used to manufacture many of the brass sections and components we buy. Like aluminium, it can be softened by heating and quenching in cold water, but it can be worked with most tools even when it is fully hardened. Usually only bending operations require that the metal should first be softened or 'annealed'.

Brass can be very snatchy to work with machine tools, but this problem can be overcome by grinding tool tips to

A typical short end of brass stock, such as you might find in a scrapyard – if you are lucky.

different angles to those used on steel. The swarf comes off it in a fine spray of splinters, making eye protection an absolute necessity. These splinters, even those produced by some filing and sawing operations, are very tiny and very sharp. They worm their way into your skin and are extremely painful, requiring instant removal with fine tweezers and a magnifying glass. The moral is never to handle brass swarf or filings unless you have to.

COPPER

This can be a pleasant material to work in sheet form, but sawing, filing, turning and milling can be very difficult. It clogs the teeth on saws and files, and unless you are careful, machining operations can leave a very rough and ragged finish. Tools must be very sharp.

Finished work looks good, and copper is essential for model locomotive and steam-engine boilers. It has excellent heat conductivity, but as a general engineering metal it has a very severe drawback. Vibration reduces it to a crystalline and fragile form very quickly, and copper components subjected to these kinds of stresses can, in extreme cases, simply fall apart with little warning.

To work copper, ordinary lubricating oil may help stop the clogging of saw teeth and make life easier for lathe tools, drills and milling cutters. Files do not clog so easily when first dusted with talcum powder or chalk.

Copper is softened by heating and quenching, and this annealing process may have to be repeated several times if complicated shapes are being beaten out.

BRONZE

There are many different bronzes, all having a base of copper and tin plus other metals to give desired qualities. Phosphor bronze, which contains a little phosphorus, is hard, with excellent wearing qualities, and is often used for bearings on machinery built in home workshops. Oil-retaining, porous 'Oilite' bronze bearings and bushes can be bought. As a general rule, work bronze like copper.

PLASTICS

There is a world of difference between cheap nasty plastic used in cheap toys and some of the high-duty engineering plastics available today. Often you will find that metal stockists also sell nylon and Tufnol in bar form, and you can also get PTFE from some sources. PTFE is easy to machine and it is a good bearing material for small machinery. Do not smoke when you are working with it, because when heated it gives off an extremely poisonous gas. More than one engineer has come to grief by getting a bit of PTFE swarf on his cigarette end.

CUTTING LUBRICANTS

Most metals can be worked quite satisfactorily dry, with hand tools like saws and files. Drilling and turning operations are often eased with the use of a cutting lubricant, and a plentiful supply of lubricant keeps turned work and tool tips cool. Listed below are the best practical cutting lubricants for the common metals.

Aluminium components such as these can be machined to a fine finish if white spirit is used as a cutting lubricant.

Steel

Generally saw and file dry, although a little light lubricating oil may save a saw blade binding in a very tough job. For turning, milling and deep drilling there are many sophisticated lubricants available to industry, but soluble oil (the familiar 'white water' in engineering shops) remains one of the best for amateur use. A 1lb jam-jar full of neat oil, scrounged from an engineering shop or bought from someone prepared to deal in small quantities, dilutes with plain water to make about 10 pints. The oil usually contains a small amount of disinfectant to save problems with minor cuts and scratches. If you cannot get soluble oil, use light machine oil. A lick of paraffin or white spirit tends to stop files clogging.

Aluminium

Use white spirit or natural turpentine for all operations. Aluminium worked dry with machine tools produces a build-up of metal on the leading edges of tool tips. The aforementioned lubricants stop this problem. In a situation where spirit or turpentine could be considered a fire risk, use soluble oil.

Brass

All machining and hand tool operations on brass are performed dry.

Copper

Light machine oil for deep drilling and turning. White spirit or talc helps to stop files clogging. Treat bronze the same as copper.

Plastics

If you have difficulty in working plastics dry, try plain water as a lubricant. Dry metal surfaces and tools carefully after use.

3 Everyday Hand Tools

Every household can muster up a few tools, even if no one present has the slightest interest in practical metalwork. Now might be a good time to have a hunt around to see what you can find that will be suitable for your new-found interest.

SAWS

The engineer's primary means of cutting metal is the hacksaw, and I would bet that almost every home has one of those little 'junior' saws that takes a 6in (15cm) blade with very fine teeth - 36 to the inch, if you care to count. Some of these saws have a simple frame bent from steel rod, while more sophisticated versions have a cast metal grip and a screw for tensioning the blade.

Whichever type you have, do not dismiss it as a toy. They are very good for fine cuts in non-ferrous metals and soft steel, but the teeth do tend to wilt when confronted with high-carbon steels. For most of your general metal-cutting you will need a man-sized saw.

When buying, get a good, strong frame that takes a 12in (30cm) blade. The most rigid type has a frame back made from oval section tube, and it is a good idea to make sure that the blade can be rotated through 90 degrees for those awkward cuts. When fitting blades to this type of saw, fit the blade over the pins with the teeth pointing forwards and turn the screw far enough to take up the slack, then tension the blade further with three more full turns.

Do not waste your money on cheap carbon steel blades for this type of saw - get the high-speed variety. They come in two types (stiff and flexible) and the more common flexible type is best until you are a little more experienced. Flexible blades will accept an amount of steering by the operator, while stiff blades break very easily unless used for carefully aimed straight cuts. Treat stiff blades as tools for the experts only.

Hacksaw blades are available with a wide variety of different tooth pitches, but I would recommend just two different blades for a start. Get a coarse blade with 18 teeth to the inch, and a finer one with 28 teeth to the inch. The coarse blade can be used for general rough cuts in all metals, and it will be particularly useful for cutting soft metals which clog easily, like almost-pure aluminium, in which the build-up of sticky metal particles between fine teeth causes quite a problem. You will find the fine blade best on brass; brass is one metal for which the blade must be very sharp and generally in top condition.

Hacksawing Tips

Make long, clean strokes and use all of the blade. This sounds obvious, but it is surprising how many people try to make long cuts through tough metal with just the middle two inches of blade. Using all of the teeth makes the blade last longer, and saves your own energy too.

Saw cuts are usually made along the waste side of a scribed line, with the metal

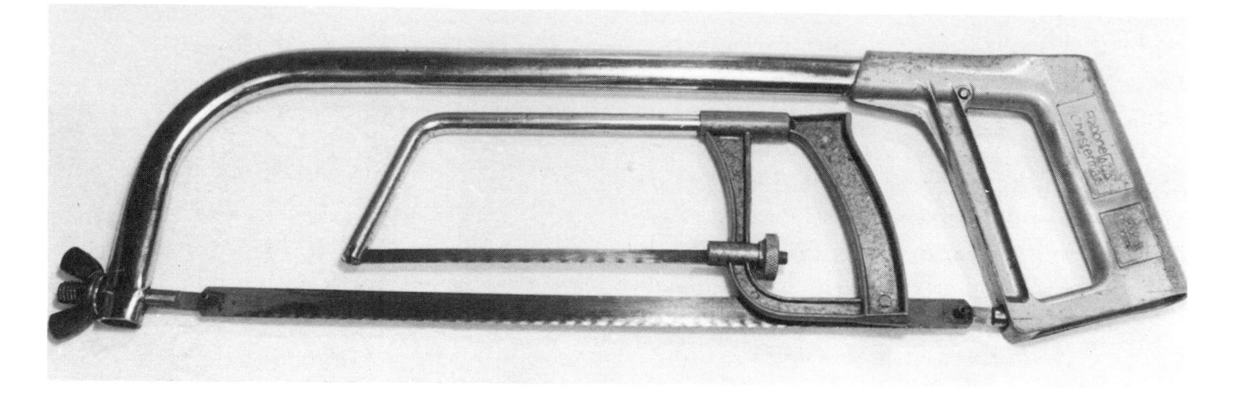

This pair of hacksaws will cope with most of the workshop's metal cutting requirements.

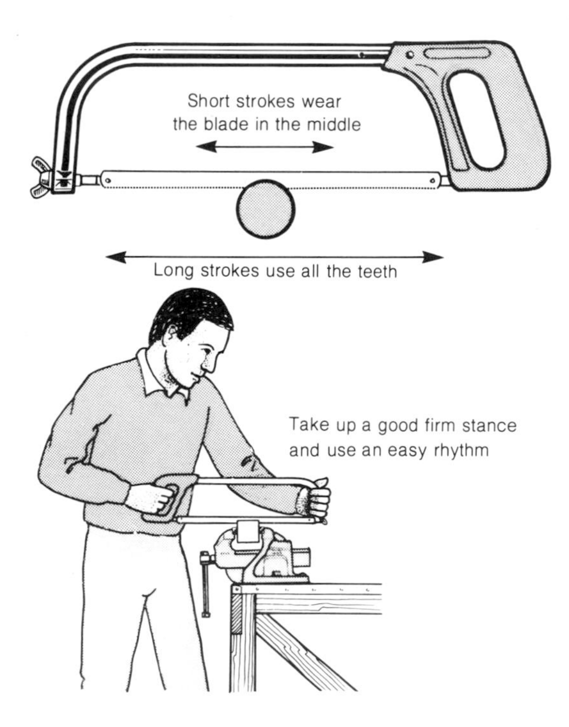

When hacksawing, use all of the blade rather than just the bit in the middle, and take a firm, comfortable stance.

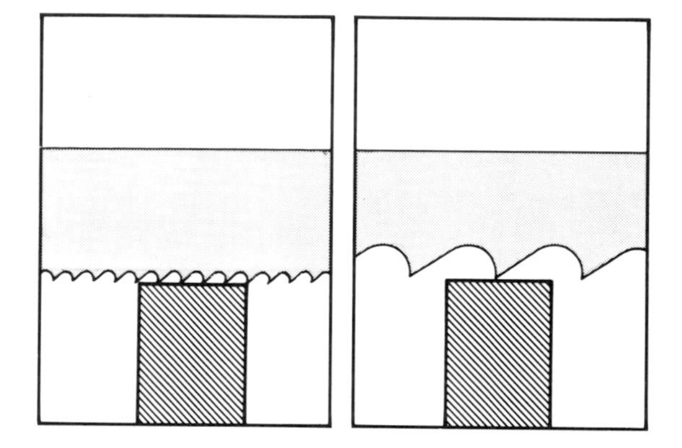

Use fine teeth on thin sections of metal, so that there are as many teeth as possible in contact with the job. Coarse teeth will be hard to use, and give an inferior finish.

to be cut securely held in a vice. Awkward pieces of sheet metal can be clamped to the bench with 'G' clamps. Assuming you are right handed, start all cuts with a few gentle strokes, guiding the edge of the blade with the left thumb. Once the cut is started, transfer the left hand to the front end of the saw and get into an easy rhythm of strokes. The weight of the saw and your arms will usually be enough – there is no need to press down hard as you saw.

For cutting round bar or tube material, rotate the work about an eighth of a turn every dozen or so strokes so that the cut does not wander off straight, as this will waste material. Waste on an inch round bar should be no more than a tenth of an inch, and a good operator with a saw will waste less than that. The same applies to square and rectangular material except flat strip – mark and saw from all sides, so that the cuts meet in the middle. Tackle strip from one wide side only.

When cutting thin plate, do not saw at too steep an angle. Use a shallow angle so that more than one or two teeth are cutting at a time. When only a few teeth are cutting at a time the saw binds and the cut becomes ragged.

FILES

If the hacksaw is the home engineer's rough-cutting tool, then the file is the fine-finishing device. Even amateur engineers these days tend to be obsessed with the capabilities of machine tools to the point that they forget the file, which in a craftsman's hands can be used to produce very accurate work.

This book could easily be filled with file specifications, but fortunately that is not necessary. A hand file is flat on both sides with a squared-off end, and other useful sections are triangular, half round (which is less than a half circle and pointed at the end), square, round and knife section. Eventually you will collect several of each, but the hand file and the round are the most useful for a start.

In addition to different sections, there are different lengths, cuts, and standards of 'roughness' too:

Length

Measurement is made from the shoulder to the tip (excluding the tang) and, unless you want to concentrate on miniature work, 8in (203mm) is a good starting point. An eight-inch (203mm) file is big enough to get hold of properly, but not frighteningly large for a newcomer.

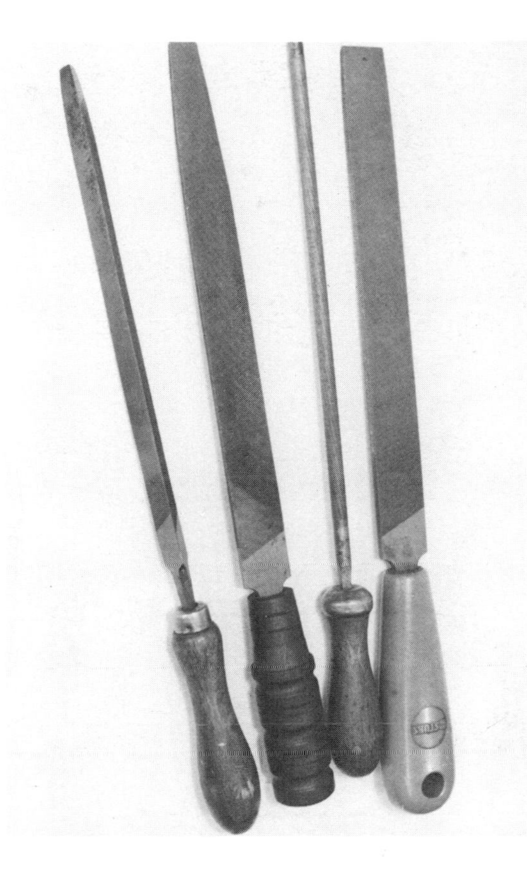

Files in this selection include flat, round and triangular. Half-round is another useful type to have.

Cut

This refers to the pattern of teeth on the file. In a single-cut file the pattern of teeth appears as a series of diagonal lines across the surface, while a double-cut file has teeth that appear in a diamond pattern. Double-cut files are in general use, presumably because they remove more metal per stroke, but I have a preference for the single-cut. They seem less likely to clog, easier to clean, and – for me at any

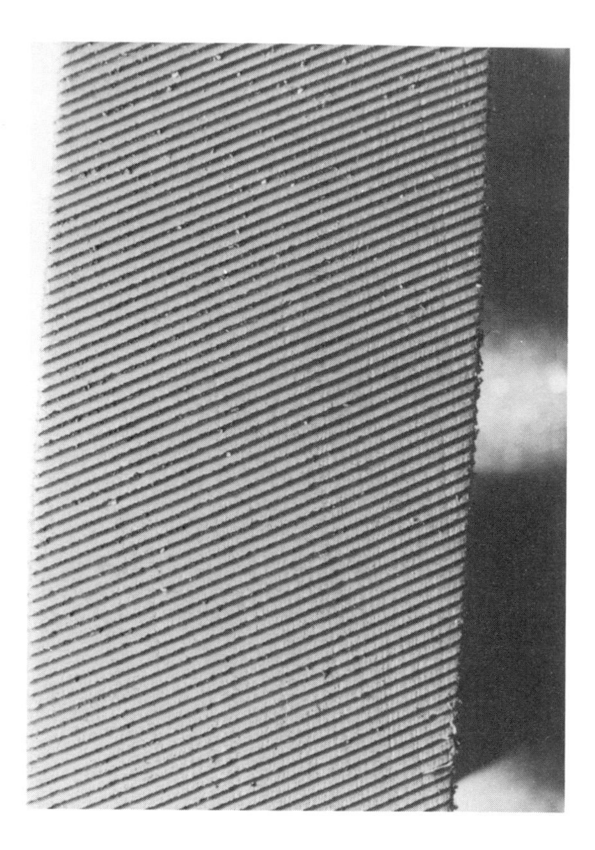

Simple, diagonal lines indicate a single-cut file. Files of this pattern are usually less likely to clog and easier to clean than the double-cut type.

Cross-hatched tooth pattern indicates a double-cut file. This is the most common pattern found in tool shops.

rate – produce a better standard of finish. The choice is up to you.

Roughness

Just to confuse things, this is also known as 'cut' in most engineering books. For general work, forget rough files. A file known as a bastard has relatively coarse teeth for rapid metal removal and a fairly rough finish. Unless you have a lot of heavy filing to do, do not bother with one of these for a start; a second-cut is better, which has finer teeth and leaves a reasonable surface. A smooth file is just what its name suggests: it is for fine finishing.

Now let me preach a bit and hammer home an important safety point. *Never* use a file without a handle. A file with no handle only needs to baulk in the work once, and the tang is driven straight into the palm of your hand. The operator gets a very severe injury, for the want of a wooden or plastic handle costing a few pence.

Cleaning Files

A lot of people have trouble achieving a smooth surface with a file and that is usually because, as they work, the file gets tiny particles of metal embedded between the teeth. These particles form deep scratches in the metal being worked.

Prevention is better than cure, and a suitable lubricant on the file helps in most cases. A little paraffin or white spirit helps stop a build-up with soft metals,

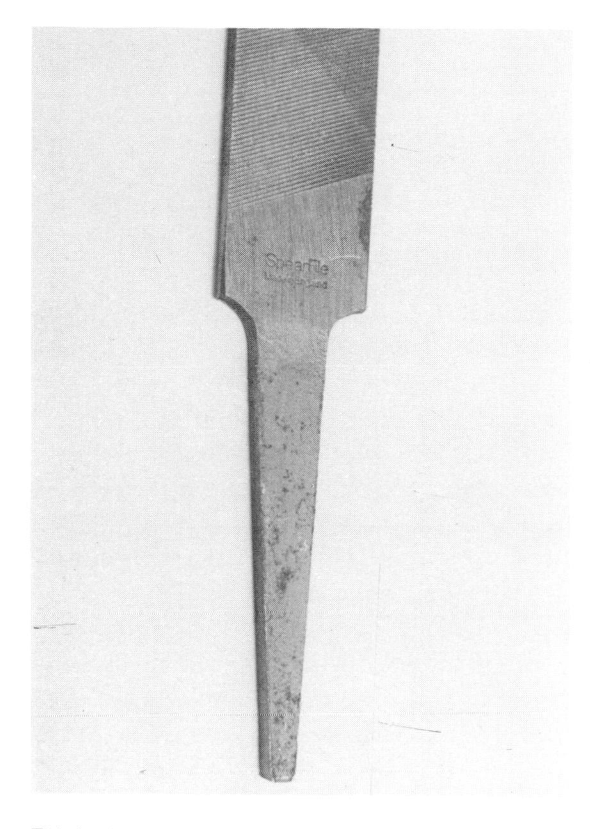

This is the tang end of a file, as supplied. It must be fitted with a handle.

while powdered chalk or talc is often helpful, too. However, even lubricants do not solve all your problems, and when seeking a fine finish always stop to examine the surface of the file after every few strokes. If metal particles are building up, most will come out when brushed with an old toothbrush.

Any tool shop will sell you a file-cleaning scratch pad, which is like a large, flat, flexible wire brush with millions of wire bristles. You can use one of these, or a wire brush, on obstinate particles, but I suspect that a lot of wire brushing dulls file teeth quite quickly. My favourite file-cleaning tool is nothing more than a flat piece of hard wood, about the same section as the file itself and one end cut to a chisel edge. Push this edge across the teeth, maintaining firm pressure, and you will be surprised how much dirt comes out of even a 'clean' file. If you find an obstinate chip of metal bedded in,

This is why a file must be fitted with a handle: if the teeth baulk on the work, the tang will be driven into the palm of the hand.

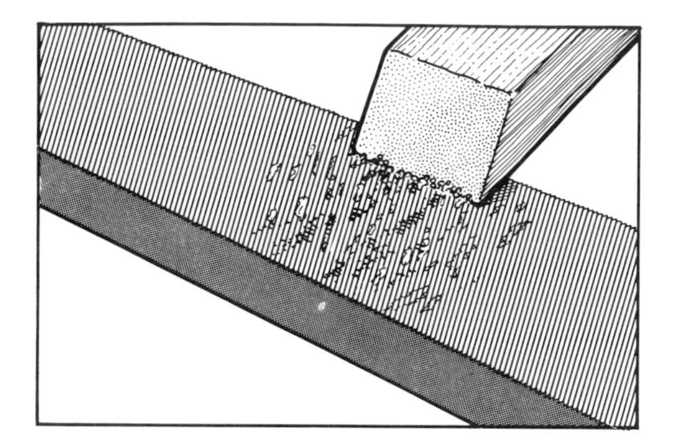

Files can be cleaned by pushing a piece of hard wood along the line of the teeth. The same technique with a bit of soft steel bar will remove really obstinate fouling.

perform the same operation with a bit of soft steel bar.

Use of Files

As with the hacksaw, if you have an eight-inch file use most of it, not just the small section in the middle. When filing material held in a vice, the most difficult fault you will have to combat is removing metal with a rocking motion, which produces a convex surface. Concentrate and work slowly, checking every few strokes until you have the knack of producing flat surfaces.

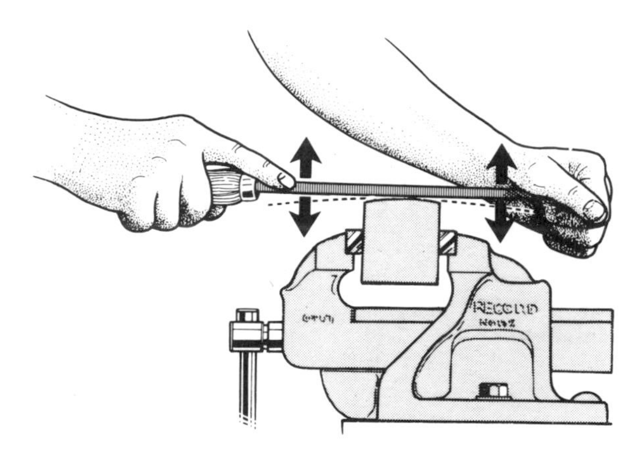

When filing, an unintended 'rocking' movement produces convex work. You can improvise guides but, generally, practice makes perfect.

Safe Edges

Some flat hand files have teeth along both edges, some have teeth on just one edge, and some have no edge teeth at all. These bald edges are called safe edges, and a file with one safe edge is preferable. Unwanted edge teeth are no problem if you have a grinding wheel, but remember that while they are easy to grind off, you cannot put them back again.

Even some supposed 'safe' edges warrant a little attention either with a grinding wheel or a small hand stone. The machinery that makes files sometimes seems to make these edges slightly

These small files, sometimes known as 'Swiss' files, come in the usual variety of sections - flat, round and triangular are shown here.

concave, with the result that the file will still cut sideways when you do not want it to. It is only the work of a few minutes to produce a flat, polished edge that will work cleanly up to a corner.

Small Files

As well as your large files, you will need some smaller ones if you plan to do fine work. It often pays to buy these as a complete set in a plastic wallet. A lot of these little files have knurled, parallel shanks to afford a hand grip. Personally I find these thin shanks very difficult to hold with any degree of accuracy, and I suspect there is still some danger of the tang injuring the palm. For these files, I make up little handles from hardwood dowell.

Storing Files

Files are best hung up, because if they clatter together in a drawer or box the teeth will soon be dulled. If you want to do things the hard way, you can drill through the handles and hang the files on nails. Better, and easier, is to mount a rail on your workshop wall and put a lot of your hand tools, files included, behind it.

HAMMERS

The familiar claw-hammer is a carpenter's tool. An engineer's hammer is what is known as a ball-pein hammer, because the reverse-end of the head has a ball-shaped knob for knocking down rivet heads. The most used hard hammer in my

Files are best hung up for storage. A single rail is enough, but do be careful not to grate the teeth together when withdrawing them.

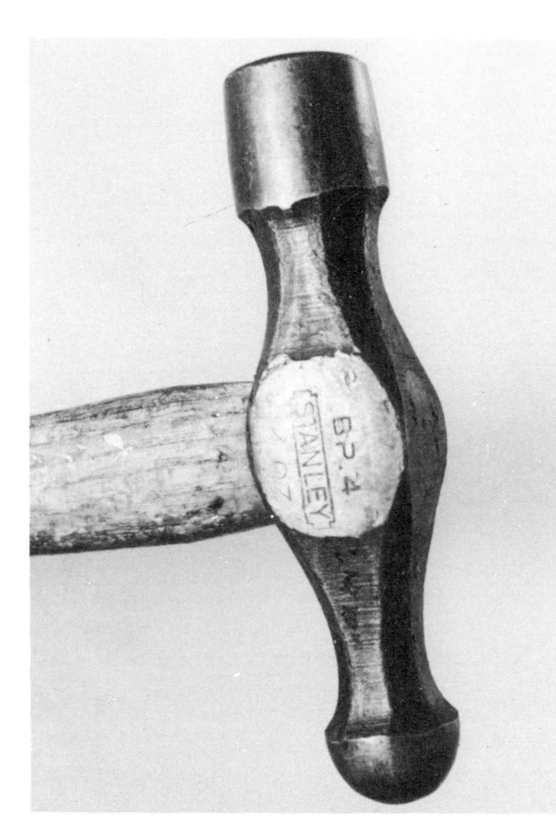

The engineer's hammer has one flat face and one ball-shaped face. The ball end, or 'pein', is traditionally used for knocking down rivets.

This soft hammer has one face in copper and the other in rawhide. Modern plastic faces are less prone to damage.

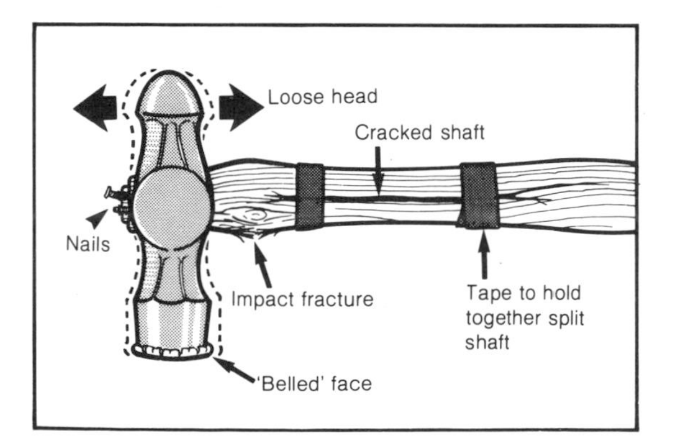

This illustrates just about everything that can be wrong with a workshop hammer - any of the faults shown render it dangerous.

workshop has a 4oz (112g) head, which is more than heavy enough for most of the punching and tapping that goes on. There is also a thumper with a 1lb 12oz (793g) head that is used more in the garden than in the workshop.

One point to watch on a well-used hammer is that the striking surface does not start to go bell-shaped. It should not if it is made of good steel, but if it does then take it to someone who has a grinding wheel and restore its original slightly coned shape. This will prevent steel splinters from flying off during a heavy hitting job.

Overall, soft hammers are used more

than hard hammers in my workshop. They are safer, and they do not mark your work. The traditional soft hammer has one copper face and one face made from a coil of rawhide, but a wide variety of plastic faces are now available.

A useful weight for a big soft hammer is about 1lb 4oz (567g) and a further refinement might be a large soft rubber ferrule fitted to the bottom end of the handle. This ferrule can deliver a very soft bump indeed, which is useful when polished work has to be tapped into position.

If you have the use of a lathe, a good first exercise is to make yourself a tiny 3oz (85g) hammer with one face in copper and the other in lead or very soft plastic. This is not so much for striking things as for aligning work on milling and drilling tables. Some suggestions on how to make one appear in Chapter 13. It is capable of moving lightly-clamped components about one thousandth of an inch at a time.

PLIERS

Surprisingly, conventional pliers are a thing that a mechanical workshop can almost do without. There is always a temptation to use them for undoing nuts – which they invariably ruin – and their only real use is for holding things that are otherwise too hot to handle. For this latter job, an old pair of pliers, with the handles extended by tubes brazed or welded on, is quite useful.

Other useful pliers are round nosed (for wire bending), and a pair of Mole grips which form a useful 'third hand' clamp when soldering, brazing, or assembling difficult bits of machinery.

SPANNERS

If you have an adjustable spanner, do yourself a favour and hide it where it is difficult to find. With a bit of luck you might even forget where it is, because all of them tend to take the corners off nuts and spoil your work as well as skinning your knuckles.

Probably the best spanners of all are ring-spanners, but there are some awkward nuts they will not get hold of, when you will have to resort to a conventional open-ended spanner. A full socket spanner set, with all of the attachments, is a useful thing to own but very expensive if you insist on quality tools like Britool and Snap-On, which last a lifetime.

For items that you make yourself and wish to assemble with screw-threaded

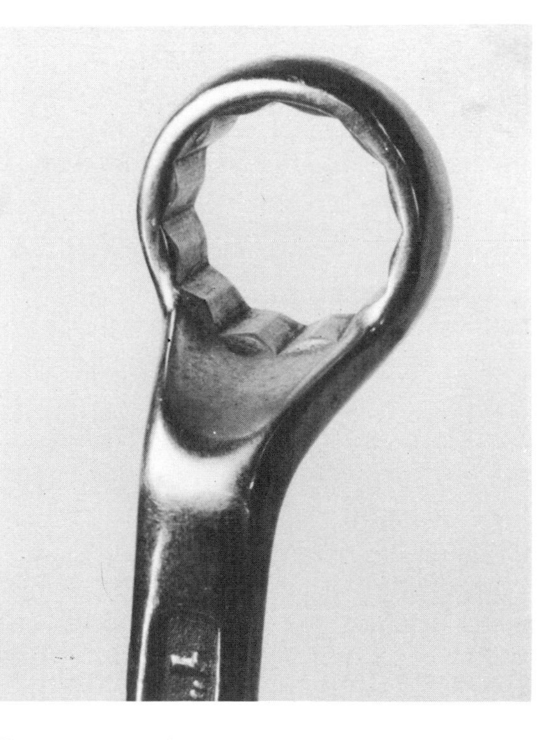

This ring spanner is the finest nut-turning tool made. Adjustable spanners knock the corners off nuts, and the skin off your knuckles.

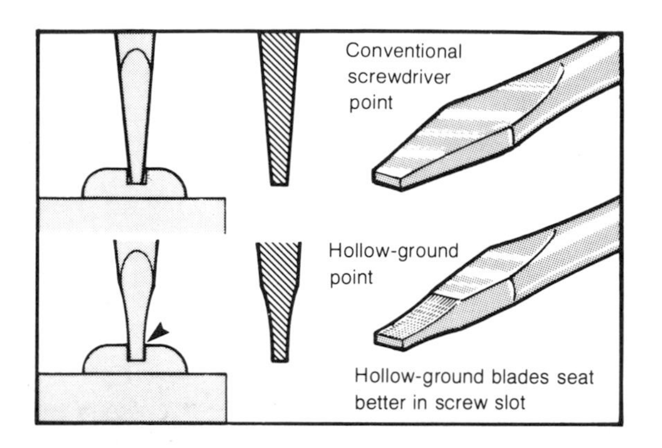

Beautiful work is often spoiled by chipped and burred screw heads. If you are fussy on this point, take your screwdriver to the grinding wheel and give it a hollow-ground point which exactly fits the slot.

fastenings, a useful and very neat looking alternative to conventional screws and bolts are socket-head Allen screws. These screws are available in cap, countersunk and grub forms in all common imperial and metric threads, and the advantage with them is that the keys to drive them are about one tenth of the price of good spanners.

SCREWDRIVERS

Nothing looks worse than a well-finished engineering job marred by screws with chipped and burred heads. The fact is that every different size of screw head ideally requires a different screwdriver to turn it. Obviously there has to be sensible compromise or you would not be able to move through the workshop door for screwdrivers, but I know that I have over twenty. These range from tiny jewellers' screwdrivers with blades down to about a millimetre across, to a heavy-duty model with a 0.625in (16mm) tip.

Even if you have a lot of screwdrivers, never hesitate to take one to a grinding wheel to make its profile ideal for the screw you are about to drive. This is particularly important if you are fussy about the appearance of screws made of soft metals like brass or aluminium.

The ideal blade form for a screwdriver is hollow-ground, not the chisel-like profile on those that you so often buy. Hollow-ground blades do not jump out of the slots in screw heads as easily as those ground like chisels.

DRILLS

A hand brace that takes drill bits up to about 5/16in (8mm) in diameter is ideal for a start, although in metal you will have difficulties when drilling holes much bigger than 0.25in (6mm). For bigger hand-drilled holes you can get a heavier version with a ½in (12mm) chuck.

All hand-held drills, including electric drills, must be used very carefully in order to produce holes that have parallel sides, are round, and somewhere near the diameter of the drill bit. If you have an electric drill, a vertical stand for it will be a great benefit. In fact, an electric drill on a vertical stand is about the best hole-boring arrangement you can have, short of a proper drilling machine. Most electric drills turn too fast for precision work, and the quality of some of the stands reflects the price you pay for them, but for beginners they are very good – particularly if you already have the drill. There are a few things you can do to improve some vertical stands (*see* Chapter 7 for details).

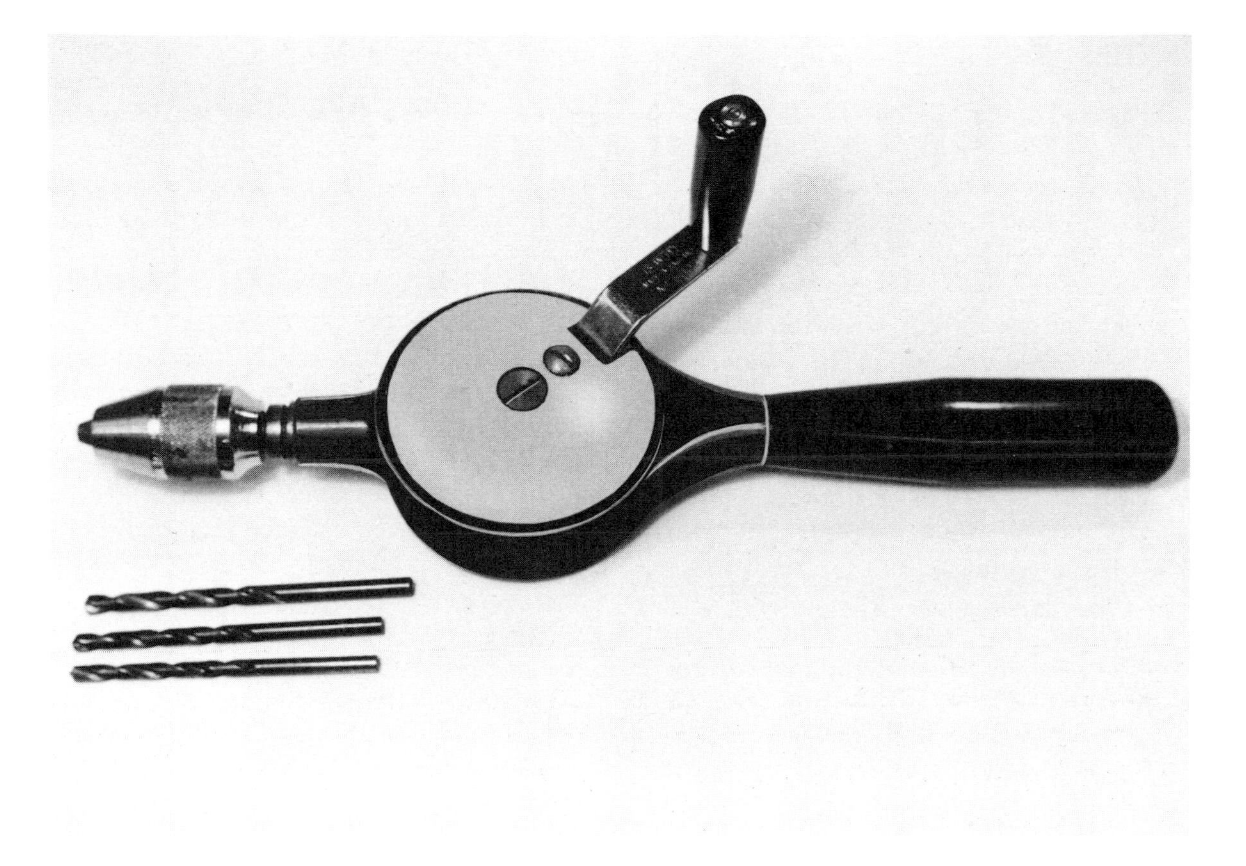

A hand-held drill is fine for odd jobs, but do not expect it to produce a hole that is straight, round and parallel sided.

Drill Bits

At an early stage it may be a mistake to buy big boxed sets, because you will be paying for a lot of drills that you may never use. The sizes you buy will also depend on whether you wish to operate on an imperial or a metric standard. If you are over the age of twenty-five you may find the imperial standards more familiar and easier to visualise, while younger people will be happier with the system they were taught at school. If you plan to do some of your projects in evening classes, go for metric because most teaching is now on the metric standard.

Further advice on this subject is difficult because so much depends on the items you wish to make. The main point is to buy good, high-speed steel drills in the sizes you need, and to keep them sharp and clean.

4 Measurement and Marking Out

To be able to work well in metal you will have to be capable of measuring in much smaller increments than are used by craftsmen in most other media. For instance, you can produce some very good carpentry if you can work within a tolerance of a millimetre, or a thirty-second of an inch, but many metalworking jobs will call for you to work to accuracies of less than one hundredth of a millimetre, and less than one thousandth of an inch.

Do not worry – you are not expected to work to those tolerances with a ruler and a pair of calipers, although for rough everyday measurement a ruler will obviously be the first thing you buy. The engineer's more common measuring tools are discussed below in the order in which you may want to buy them.

THE ENGINEER'S RULER

This item must be made of steel, because you will be marking along its edge with steel instruments and these would soon ruin the edge of a wood or plastic ruler. 12in or 300mm is quite long enough, and it is best to get one marked in both inches and millimetres. You will find a ruler with a matt chromium face easiest to read in all light conditions, resistant to rust, and easy to clean with a bit of soft rag.

THE VERNIER GAUGE

This is another dual-marked instrument, and one of average size allows you to make measurements up to 5in or 125mm. It will measure to 0.001in or 0.01mm and it can be used in a wide variety of different modes. With the same instrument you can measure internal and external diameters, the height of steps, and the depth of holes.Some people say they find vernier gauges hard to read. The actual mechanics of reading the gauge are simple (*see* panel). The vital requirement is good light, and a small magnifying glass if your eyesight is less than perfect.

Overall, the vernier is the most adaptable of the engineer's measuring instruments. Nothing else that a home workshop enthusiast might buy is dual-marked, nothing else can be used in more than one mode, and a 5in range of measurement is quite remarkable.

THE MICROMETER

You can buy micrometers for all sorts of different jobs, but the common instrument is for checking external dimensions. No mechanical micrometer is dual-marked – you have to make the choice between inches or millimetres when you buy – and a usual first purchase is an instrument calibrated from 0 to 1in, or 0 to 25mm. If you want to make bigger measurements accurately, you have to

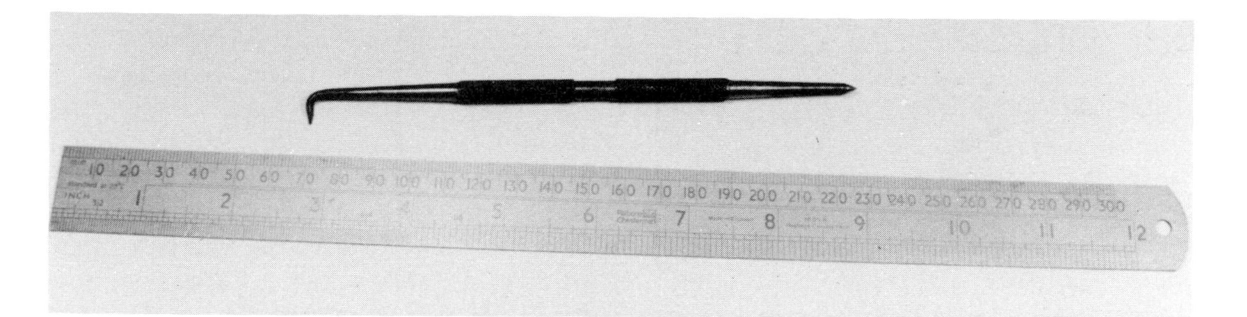

The engineer's ruler is the primary measurement and marking-out tool in the workshop. This satin-chromed example is easy to read in most light conditions. A scriber is shown alongside.

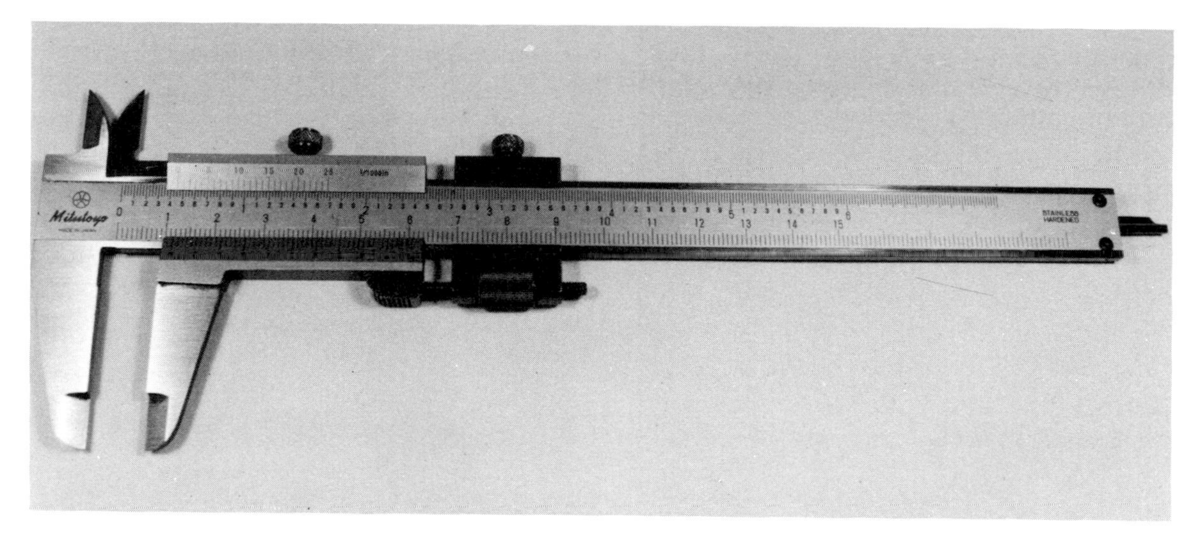

This Mitutoyo instrument is a good example of a medium-priced vernier gauge. Such a gauge will measure diameters (both inside and outside), hole depths and step heights.

buy another micrometer – either 1 to 2in, or 25 to 50mm. You can get instruments with adjustment pieces that allow a bigger measurement spread, but to maintain accuracy they have to be very well made, and are therefore very expensive.

The 0 to 1in micrometer is calibrated in thousandths of an inch, but it is easily possible to read it down to about 0.0002in, by 'reading between the lines'. Alternatively, the instrument may have an additional vernier scale marked on the barrel to account for the ten-thousandths.

The metric micrometer will be calibrated in hundredths of millimetres, and again you can get down into the thousandths by using the same methods as with the imperial instrument. However, there are practical limits to which you can measure in a home workshop. To explain why, it is necessary to refer to industrial practice.

A good industrial standards room will

measure down to millionths of inches or hundred-thousandths of millimetres with very sophisticated instruments. One of the keys to this incredible precision is accurate temperature control, so that both instrument and work are at exactly the same temperature. They do not use conventional micrometers; however you can see that if a job was slightly warmer than the standard temperature, it would be in an expanded form, while if it was cold it would be contracted.

In a home workshop, even given new and very accurate instruments, you cannot control the temperature of both micrometer and work well enough for absolute precision. In addition, remember that even the tiniest grain of dust or the thinnest lick of oil or moisture actually has a thickness, which is another factor working against you, even if the article to be measured has something approaching a precision exterior finish. Then there is the degree to which you tighten the micrometer: the thimble screw, which should always be used for final tightening, might have an almost unnoticeable stiff segment; there might be a tiny speck of dirt on the anvil face, or a microscopic grain of grit in the screw . . .

Overall, with a good, clean micrometer that is more or less the same temperature as a good, clean job, you can measure within a practical tolerance of plus or minus 0·0002in or 0·004mm. I would not rely on reading smaller increments than those. For details of how to read the metric and imperial micrometers, *see* panel on page 43.

A selection of micrometers. The instrument on the left has metric calibrations, 0 to 25mm, while the larger instrument in the centre is an imperial 1-2in micrometer. The 0-1in version is on the right.

HOW TO READ A VERNIER GAUGE

Imperial Measurements

The main inches scale on the vernier is divided into segments of 0·025 inches, so every fourth division line represents 0·1in. These fourth division lines are numbered.

Now refer to the picture. The initial reading is taken against the 0 (zero) on the top scale, and you will see that this zero mark is showing 0·9in, plus an unknown fraction. Write 0·9 down on a piece of paper.

The next stage is to add up the 0·025 sections that are also showing to the left of the zero, and in this case you will see that it is two and a bit. Two segments equal 2 × 0·025, which is 0·050, so write that down too. At this stage you will have a bit of simple arithmetic, which is written down as 0·9 + 0·050 = 0·950.

Our measurement, however, is obviously more than 0·950, but how much more? To determine this last little bit, look along the top scale to the right of the zero, and find a line which coincides exactly with a line on the bottom scale. In this case that point of coincidence is opposite the line numbered 15 on the top scale. These top scale segments represent 0·001in, so write down 0·015.

The rest is simple addition. Add 0·015 to 0·950 and you get 0·965. Congratulations: you have just measured to a thousandth of an inch.

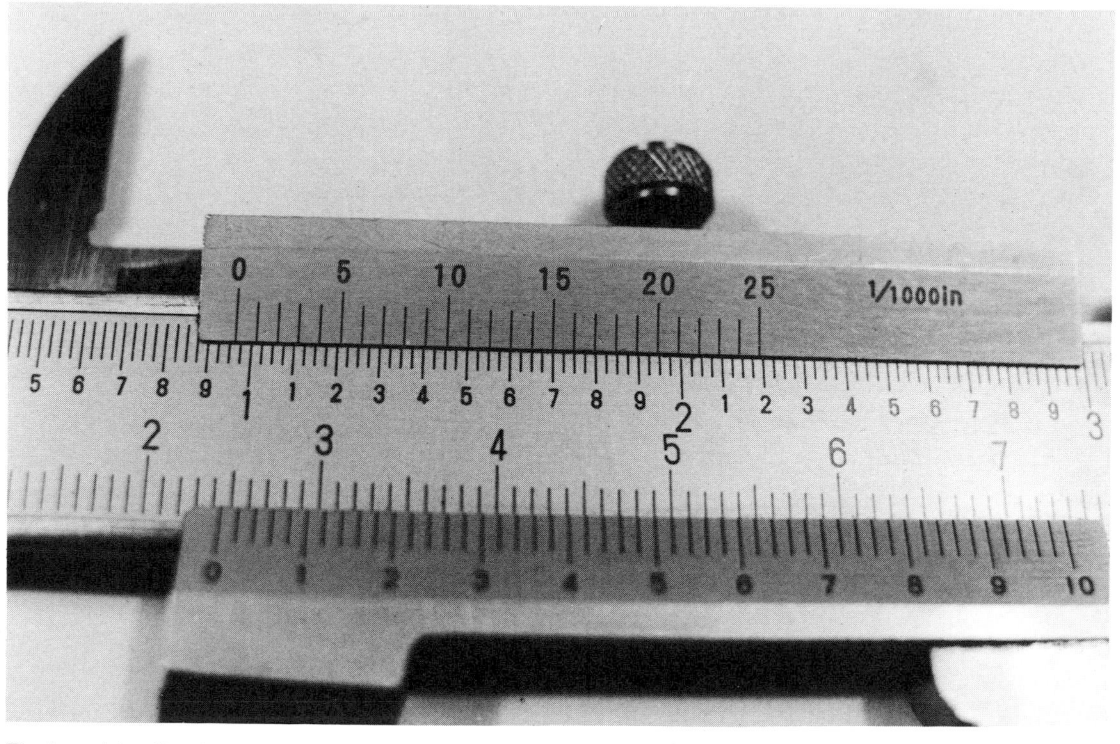

The imperial calibrations on the vernier gauge are set at 0•965in (*See* text for details).

The metric side of the vernier gauge is set at 24·52mm (*See* text for details).

Metric Measurements

The same principles that you used for your imperial measurement apply, but the addition is simpler. The main scale is calibrated in millimetres, so look to the immediate left of the zero on the bottom line, and write down 24.

The bottom metric scale is calibrated in divisions of 0·02mm, and again we are looking for two lines that coincide. This point of coincidence is just past the 5 – in fact, on 0·52. Adding 0·52 to 24 gives an answer of 24·52.

Error

Those of you who are clever at maths will notice that there is an error between the imperial and metric measurements quoted above of approximately 0·00039in or 0·009mm. That would obviously be unacceptable in some industrial situations, but in a home workshop it can be classified as an acceptable error.

Now try it!

Now you can try this test to see if you have mastered the vernier. Read both the imperial and metric scales shown below using the principles outlined above. The answer is given at the end of the chapter.

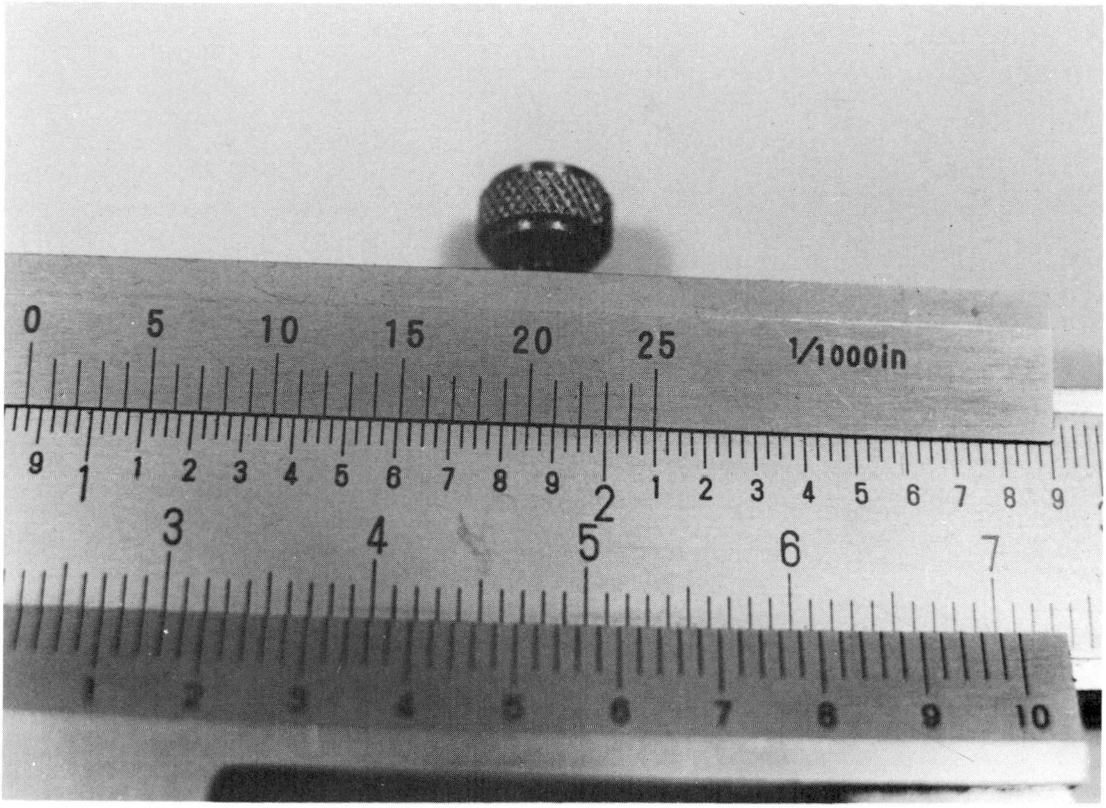

Now try it for yourself. You are trying to read the imperial side of the gauge. The answer is on page 48.

THE DIAL GAUGE

You will not need one of these unless you do a lot of precision lathe work and need to set jobs in independent-jawed chucks. Dial gauges are rarely used for straight measurement, their most frequent use being to measure the eccentricity of rotating work. They are available with both metric and imperial calibrations. They are usually used in conjunction with a stand and magnetic base, and if ever you set up a lathe in a workshop you will need to borrow one to check the alignment of the bed. (For more details, *see* Chapter 8).

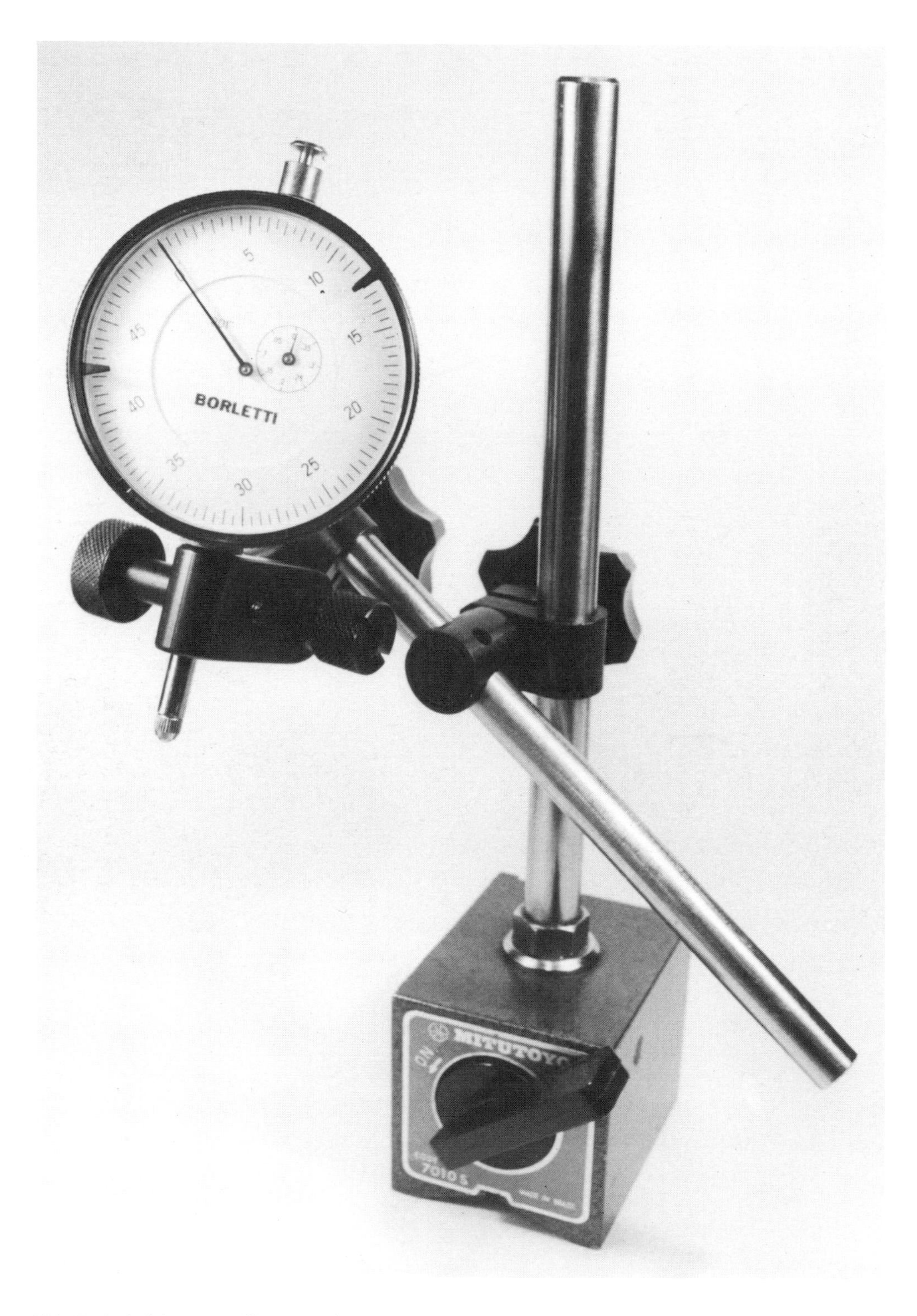

This Borletti dial guage will accurately measure a movement of 0•4in in segments of 0•0005in. A magnetic base allows it to be clamped to machine tables.

HOW TO READ A MICROMETER

Imperial Measurements

The barrel of the imperial micrometer is divided into segments of 0·025in. To take a measurement, be sure that the instrument and the work are clean, then tighten the micrometer using a ratchet only.

The main figures on the barrel are tenths of inches, so look at the picture and you will see that the measurement shown is 0·4in plus a small amount. One additional marked segment is showing, so add 0·025 to 0·4 and you get 0·425.

Now, to get the 'thousandths' figure, look at the figures on the thimble. The figure showing against the datum line is 6, so the final sum of the measurement is: 0·4 + 0·025 + 0·006 = 0·431. Easy, isn't it?

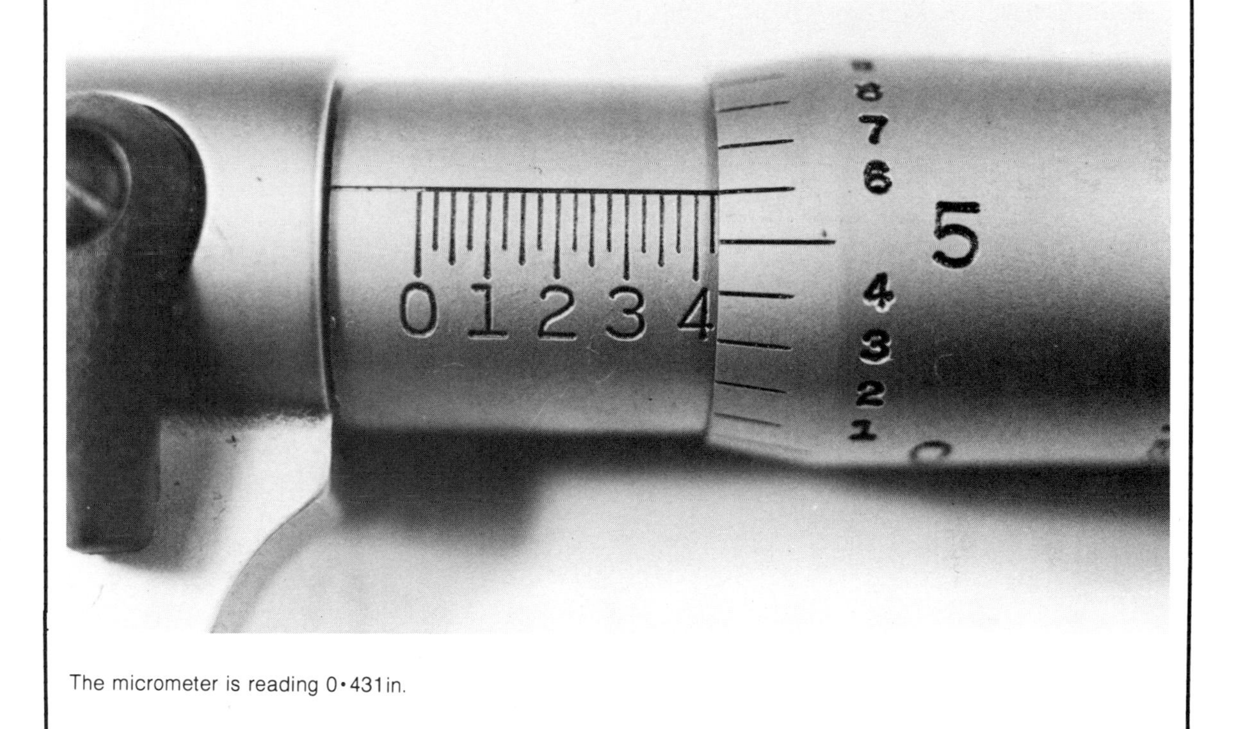

The micrometer is reading 0·431in.

Metric Measurements

Again, nothing more than simple addition is called for. The barrel is calibrated in segments of 0·5mm, while hundredths of millimetres appear on the thimble. The micrometer in the picture is showing 10 + 0·5 + 0·07mm = 10·57mm.

The metric micrometer reads 10•57mm.

MARKING OUT INSTRUMENTS

The Scriber

The scriber is what its name suggests – a little, pointed hard-steel spike used to produce a scratch mark on a smooth metal surface. In engineering it is the equivalent of the carpenter's pencil, although a soft pencil can be used for rough marking and a coloured or white wax pencil may be used for the coarse marking of very uneven surfaces.

The scriber must be kept sharp, and the hardened steel from which it is made will be much too hard to sharpen with a file. You must use either a rotary grindstone or a little hand stone. If you do not have a rotary grindstone, do not let the scriber get too blunt, because restoring the point by hand will take a long time. Whatever

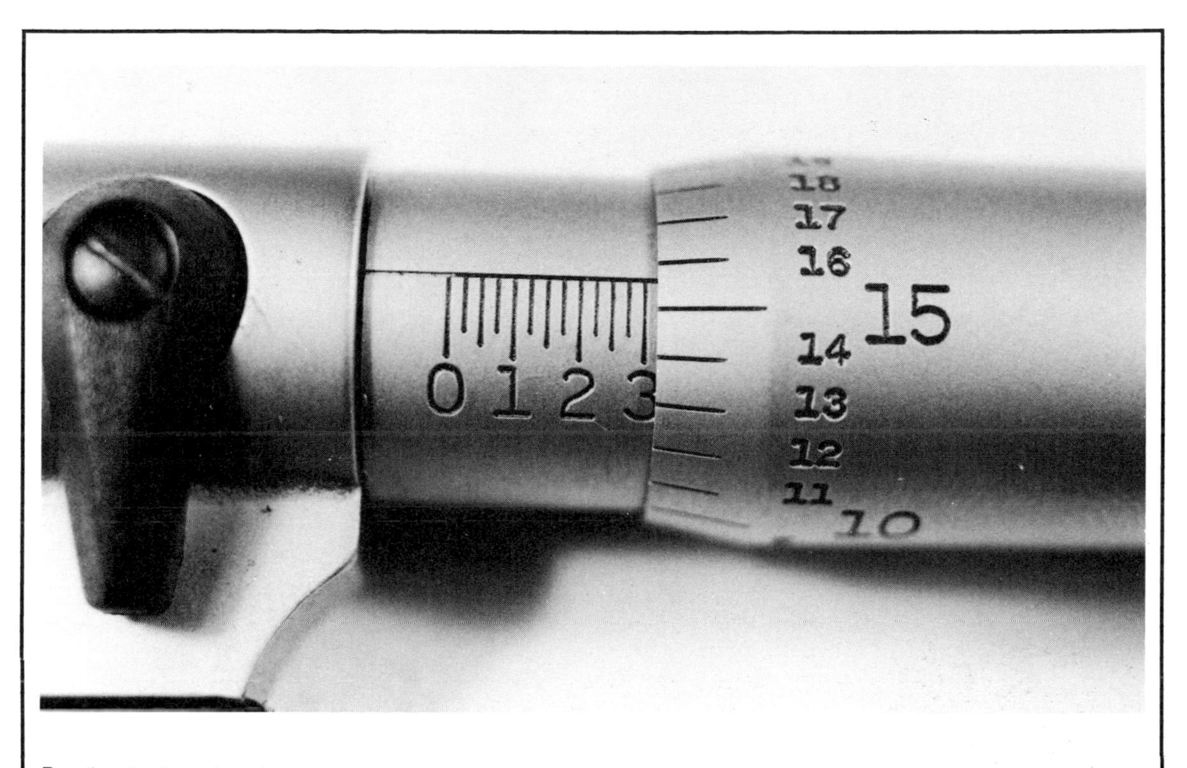

Reading the imperial micrometer 'between the lines'. The measurement falls between 0·315 and 0·316in. An intelligent 'guess' is 0·3157in.

'Reading Between the Lines'

The picture above shows a micrometer where the measurement has fallen between 0·315 and 0·316in. In fact, it is nearer 0·316 than it is to 0·315. If you mentally divide the thousandths segment into 10, a good guess at the measurement would be 0·3157in. You can use the same principle to get into thousandths of millimetres with the metric micrometer. Some micrometers have a separate vernier scale to help you get down among the ten-thousandths of inches or thousandths of millimetres.

you do, do not overheat the scriber on a rotary stone.

Use the scriber along the edge of a ruler, and construct right angles with an engineer's set square, which is like the familiar carpenter's set square but usually smaller and of all-metal construction.

Sometimes scribed lines can be very hard to see on shiny metal surfaces, and you will need some sort of aid to make them clearer. The traditional industrial solution to this problem was to darken steel first, by the application of copper sulphate solution, while sometimes whitening or blue compounds are used. None of this is very practical in a home workshop, but there is a simple answer if you have a spray can for touching up your car. If you first spray the metal with a *very* light coat of almost any colour you will knock the shine off just enough for the scribed line to stand out. If the paint has been applied to a slightly greasy surface it will usually rub off when no longer needed, while Brasso will take a very thin layer off polished surfaces. On coarse work, use emery paper or wet-and-dry.

A scriber line shows up more clearly on the surface that has been slightly darkened. A light spray with cellulose from an aerosol can is as good as anything in an amateur workshop. The line on the bright surface in this picture is twice the depth of the other line.

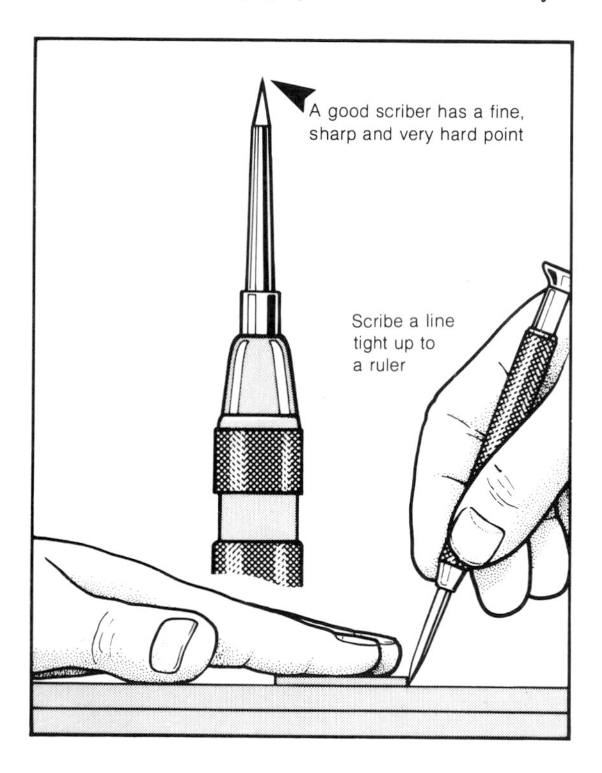

The scriber is the engineer's equivalent of the carpenter's pencil. It is used against a steel rule, and it must be kept sharp.

OTHER MARKING OUT TOOLS

A proper engineer's marking out area will have a large variety of specialist instruments. There will be a surface plate, which is an accurate flat area to use as a datum; right angle and 'V' blocks for constructing vertical lines and marking round work; compasses and trammels for marking circles of various sizes; scribing blocks for supporting scribers at known heights; and parallel strips for supporting work on the table.

In workshops like yours and mine such things would be a luxury, but most of the time we simply have to improvise.

For example, for marking circles the scriber can be put in conventional drawing compasses with a little wood or metal packing, while geometry aids like plastic protractors can be used in place of the proper engineer's items.

The trick to a lot of improvised marking out, particularly on plate work, is to mark and cut the longest line on the job, and to use the edge so produced as a datum to mark out the rest of the job. This can be particularly important when you are utilising scrap materials on which the edges, when you start, may be very rough and ragged.

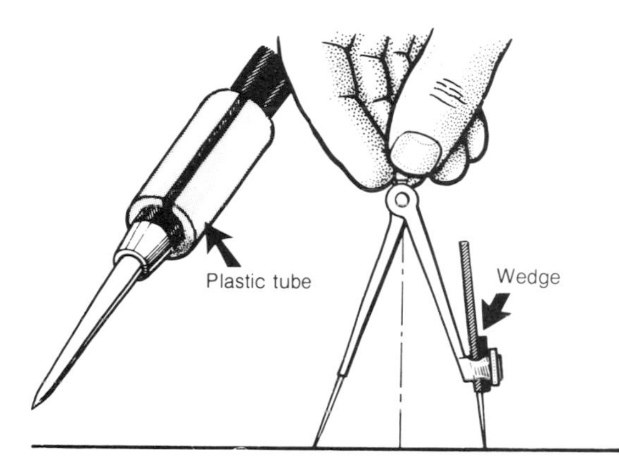

For scribing circles conventional drawing compasses can be used, with the point located in a light punch dot. The scriber can be secured by one of the two methods shown.

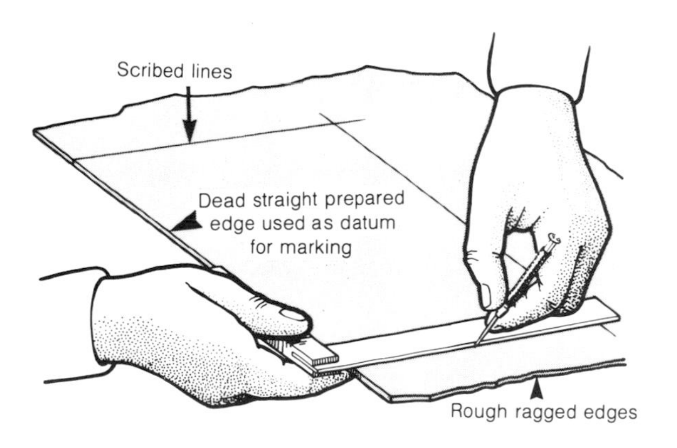

When marking work on scrap plate, first prepare a perfectly straight edge to use as a datum.

The Centre Punch

Ideally you should have two of these – one with a 90-degree point for marking the centres of holes to be drilled, and one with a much finer, shaved point (somewhere nearer 60 degrees) for providing a location for the points of dividers and compasses. The drill will pick up a 90-degree punch dot cleanly, while the divider point will locate better in the narrower-mouthed dot. Whatever you do, do not use the scriber as a punch, because you will almost certainly chip the end off.

If you look up 'marking out' in some engineering textbooks, you will find it recommended that all scribed lines

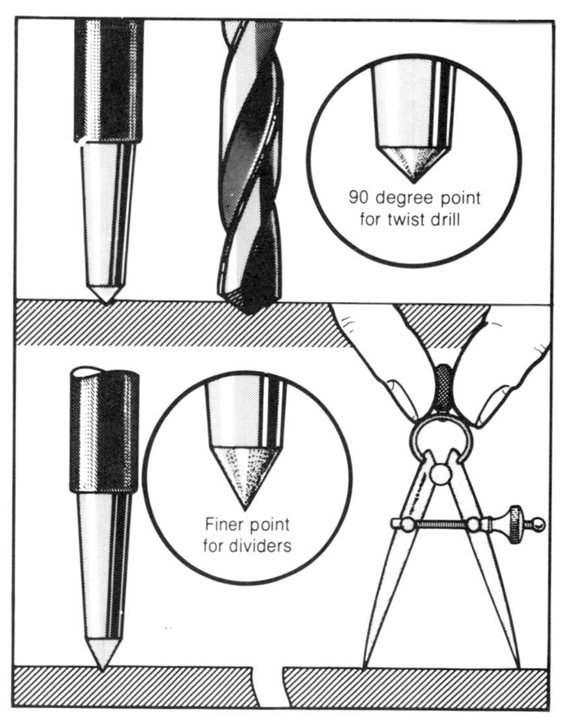

It pays to have two centre-punches in the workshop – one with a 90-degree point for marking holes to be drilled, and one with a finer point for locating the points of compasses and dividers.

should be punch-dotted at intervals along their length. This was done in engineering shops for a simple reason: when you have cut metal right up to a scribed line, you cannot see the line any more. If the boss examined the job and saw a neat row of half punch dots along the cut edges, he knew that the worker had done his job properly. No half dots, and there was a good chance that the job was under size. In your own shop, you are the boss, so there is no need for the dots.

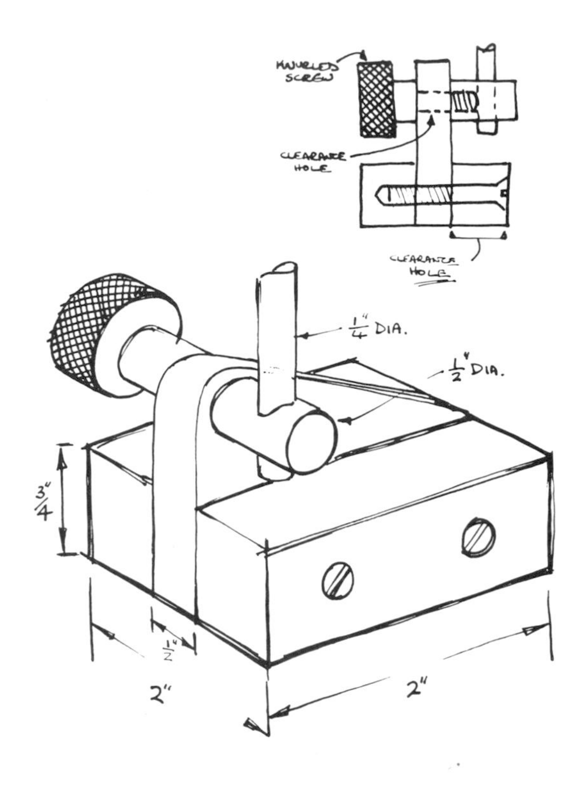

Even if your drawing is not very good, a sketch like this can save you a lot of time and precious metal.

DRAWINGS

Engineering drawing is really a subject on its own, and it is outside the scope of this book. Much simple amateur engineering work does not require drawings of any great quality, although it always pays to draw any component before you begin to cut the metal. Such a drawing need be no more than a sketch on a beer mat or a bit of scrap paper, but even a crude doodle may save you a lot of time and precious material. Even if you are good at visualising objects in three dimensions, you can suffer the occasional lapse.

Only very rarely is it necessary to produce full-scale plan and elevation drawings. In fact, a three-dimensional sketch is often best and easier to follow if you are unused to reading plans. If it is any comfort, one of my engineering heroes, Ettore Bugatti (the classic racing car designer) always drew his plans in three-dimensional perspective, like an artist, rather than as conventional engineering drawings. I often wonder if he doodled on beer mats, too!

Finally, when precision is important, only treat scribed lines as a rough working guide. A scribed line can be up to 0·010in (0·25mm) wide, so always check with a micrometer, vernier gauge, or some other precision measuring instrument, before taking a final cut. Eventually you will have a wide variety of cutting tools in your workshop, but nobody has yet invented a tool which puts metal back, for engineers who forget to measure and slice off too much!

ANSWER TO VERNIER GAUGE PUZZLE

See panel on page 41: the gauge is reading 0·873in (0·8 + 0·050 + 0·023), or 22·17mm.

5 Screw Threads

The screw thread is the most common form of fastening used in engineering. Used properly, screw threads are a strong and practical means of holding the different elements of an item together and in their simplest form – nuts and bolts – they can be used without the necessity for any specialised tools. All you need are suitable drill bits to bore clearance holes for the bolts.

However, simple nuts and bolts are not always the best way of achieving a firm assembly. The arrangement may look fine in theory, but final assembly may be so awkward that you cannot get at the nuts to turn them. Even if you can, the nuts may stick out and get in the way of some other component, or they may simply look ugly.

Providing that one of the components to be joined is as thick or thicker than the average nut in the thread diameter you plan to use, there is a lot to be said for tapping threads in the component. You are going to get a neater, cleaner-looking job, and if the component to be tapped is very thick you can get a good, deep tapped hole that will take full advantage of the strength of the bolt. Instead of a bolt you can use a stud and a nut, an arrangement that will give you very accurate relocation if whatever you are making has to be stripped and reassembled at any time. The chances are that your car cylinder head is fitted on with this sort of arrangement.

Some of the same principles can be applied to threads in general, whatever their type.

COARSE OR FINE?

A coarse-threaded bolt is not as strong as a fine-threaded bolt of the same diameter because its core diameter (in other words, the inner part of the bolt which is not penetrated by the thread) is smaller. However, a fine-threaded bolt needs a longer nut or a deeper-threaded hole so that it can be tightened fully without fear of the thread stripping. Coarse threads are generally used for tapped holes in soft metals like aluminium, where the risk of thread stripping, either on tightening or when bearing working stresses, is greatest. Only use fine threads in soft metals either where stresses are light or the tapped hole is good and deep – about three times the bolt diameter.

TYPES OF THREADS

Threads fall into two main families – those based on measurements in inches, and those based on measurements in millimetres. While engineering is, in some cases, still being slow to change to a metric standard, metric bolts and screws seem to have almost taken over in industry, and a lot of the old inch-based threads are becoming hard to find. However, there are still a lot of inch-based taps and dies about, and many of the imperial threads still have a place in the home workshop.

The whole scene with inch-based threads is very confusing. In the old days almost every engineer must have

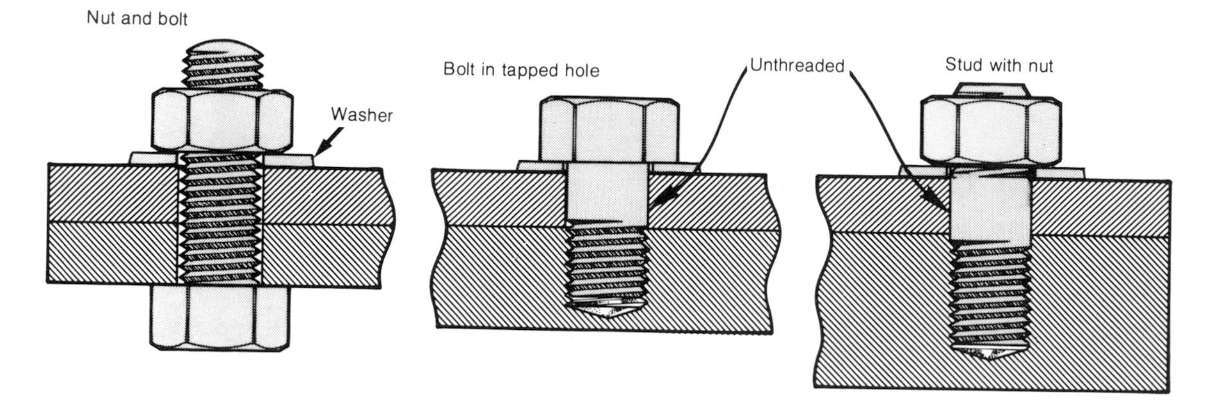

Three ways of using screw threads to join components. The nut and bolt (left) is satisfactory for thin plate, but the alternatives are better with thicker material.

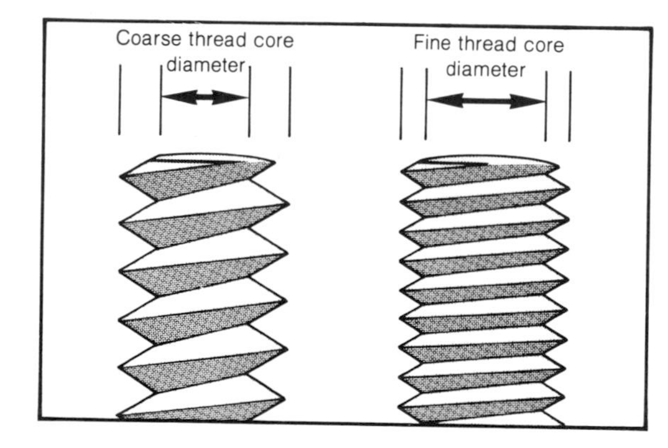

A bolt with a fine thread is stronger than one with a coarse thread, because it has a bigger core diameter. However, coarse threads must be used in soft metal so that there is no danger of the thread 'stripping' when the bolt is tightened.

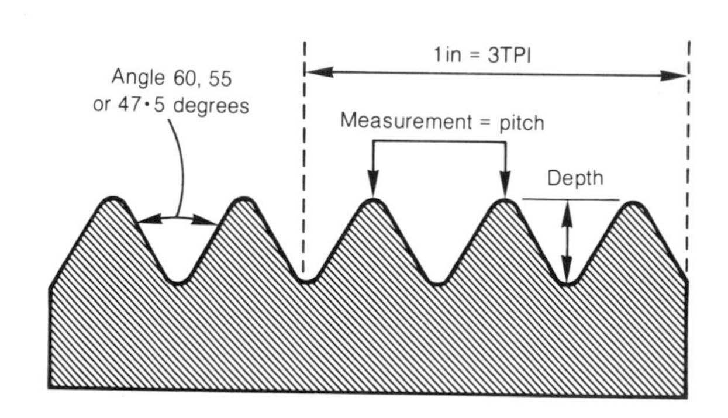

These are the points by which threads are identified.

invented a thread of his own, and many trades developed threads that were peculiar to that trade alone. Cycle thread and gas thread are examples.

However, an imperial-based home workshop need bother with only three threads. BSF (British Standard Fine) and BSW (British Standard Whitworth, usually known as 'Whitworth') are both good threads from 0·25in up. Smaller diameters are well catered for in the BA (British Association) range, which, if you have the eyesight for it, go right down to 16BA; this has a screw just 0.027in (0.68mm.) across. More useful sizes are 2BA (about 0·187in or 4·76mm), 4BA (just over 0·125in or 3·2mm) and 6BA (about 0·109in or 2·67mm).

The metric-based workshop need bother with only two types of threads – ISO Metric Coarse and ISO Metric Fine. In fact, the Metric Coarse is quite adequate for all but the most delicate home workshop applications, and Fine is not used much at all.

Now let's have a look at these threads in a little more detail:

BSF Threads

These threads have a 55-degree form, and generally an easily-remembered number of threads per inch. Those you will use most will be $^{1}/_{4}$ (26 threads per inch), $^{5}/_{16}$ (22 threads per inch), $^{3}/_{8}$ (20 threads per inch), and $^{1}/_{2}$ (16 threads per inch). The most used tap and die set in my workshop is $^{1}/_{4}$ BSF.

Whitworth Threads

These also have a 55-degree form and easily-remembered pitches in the more common sizes in home workshops. $^{1}/_{4}$ Whit. (20 threads per inch), $^{5}/_{16}$ (18 threads per inch), $^{3}/_{8}$ (16 threads per inch) and $^{1}/_{2}$ (12 threads per inch) are the common ones. Even in a metric workshop you will need $^{1}/_{4}$ Whit. if you plan to do any work on camera equipment. Even modern Japanese cameras have $^{1}/_{4}$ Whit. threaded holes to fix them to tripods and other accessories.

BA Threads

These have a much 'sharper' form – 47·5 degrees – although the 'peaks and troughs' are much more rounded than in either BSF or Whit. Diameters and pitches are usually quoted in metric terms; for example, 6BA is 2.8mm diameter with a 0.53mm pitch.

ISO Metric Coarse

This is the 'everyday' metric thread, with bolts and screws in common use ranging from 1.6mm diameter in a series of logical steps right up to 68mm. Thread form is 60 degrees.

ISO Metric Fine

This is a good thread if you need a big, fine-thread bolt. In a range from 8 to 64mm there are only six different pitches, which also makes it handy if you need to resort to screw-cutting in the lathe and only have a limited number of change-wheels.

Other Threads

If you take plumbing fittings to bits you will find British Standard Pipe Threads, while before the motor trade accepted the metric standard, British cars used to contain a lot of UNF and UNC threads. There are many more.

'Bastard' Threads

Now and again you will come across a thread that totally defies identification, even with a full set of screw thread tables. It will be one that some manufacturer had made because there was not a standard thread to suit a particular purpose. You will not find many nuts and bolts like this, but you may find things like screw-threaded collars that retain components on shafts. In a home workshop the only practical way to duplicate threads like this is to set up a lathe for screw-cutting. (*see* Chapter 12.)

THREAD-CUTTING TOOLS

Taps

These are the tools for cutting internal threads. Think of a tap as being like a bolt, made of very hard steel and with cutting edges ground into it. The slots, called flutes, which form the cutting edges, also allow for the clearance of swarf.

Taps usually come in sets of three for each thread diameter and pitch. There is a taper or 'first' tap which, as its names suggest, is tapered so that it enters the hole in almost perfect alignment. It also enables the tap to start cutting the thread gradually. The second tap has a very small taper on the end, and its use is usually sufficient to produce a finished thread unless it is necessary to thread a blind hole right down to the bottom.

If this is the case you need a 'plug' or bottoming tap, which is fully threaded and should have a squared-off end. Why the tool industry supplies so many plug taps with an unwanted point on the end is a mystery; you usually have to grind the point off before you use the tool.

Tapping holes

The first stage is to drill a hole of suitable diameter. There is no magic formula for arriving at this diameter – you will have to buy a set of thread tables and get the diameter from that. About the best set of tables is the *Zeus Precision* booklet, which is printed on plastic-coated paper, so it can be put down in oily places and handled with wet and oily fingers without fear of damage.

With a hole of the correct diameter, put the taper tap in a tap wrench and coat it with a suitable cutting lubricant. You will find the lubricants for various metals on page 24.

Now hold the job firmly in a vice, unless it is heavy enough to remain steady under its own weight on the floor or bench. A little lubricant down the hole does no harm at this stage.

Insert the tap, but before you start to

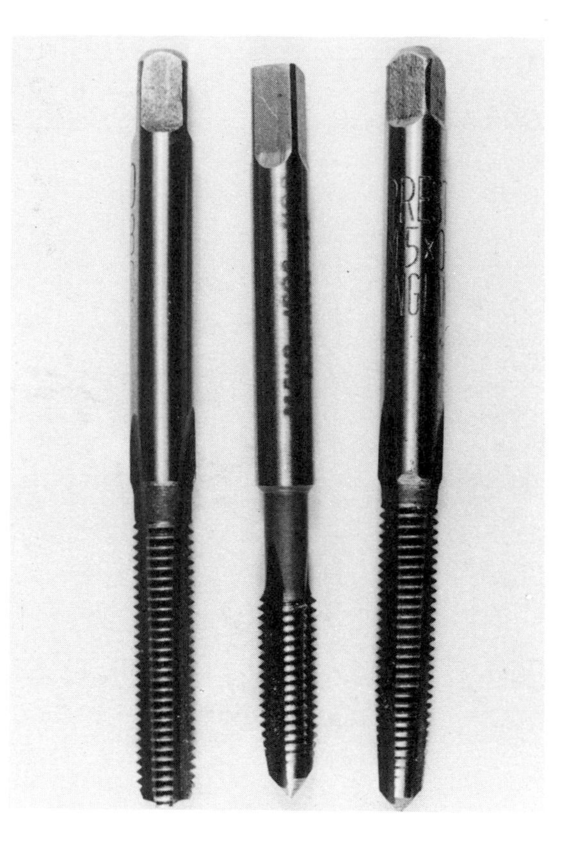

A set of three taps – these are for the metric 5 × 0•8mm thread. Note that the 'plug' tap has had its tip ground off, so that it will cut a thread almost to the bottom of a hole.

turn it, be sure that it is in as near vertical a position as possible. Taper taps are, to a degree, self-aligning, but a thread started off crooked cannot be restored to truth. If you persevere in driving the tap when it has been entered crooked, there is a fair chance that you will snap it off in the job. With a few years' experience behind you, you will know that extracting broken taps is one of the most difficult jobs in the workshop.

Start to turn the tap slowly. Unless the metal is very hard, go for one full turn, then turn the tap about half a turn backwards before you proceed. The tap will gradually get stiffer to turn as more

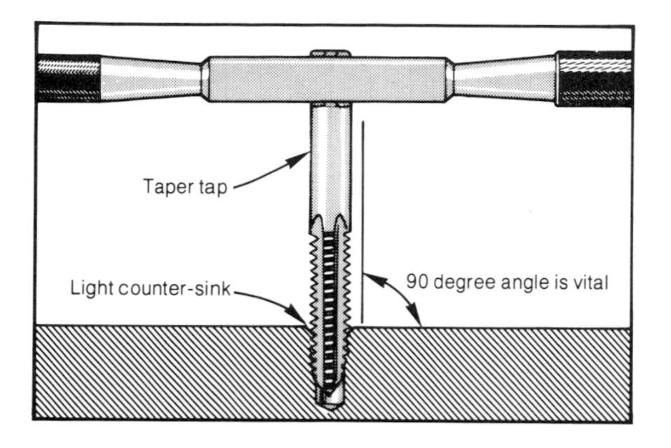

Before entering a tap, lightly countersink the hole. Be sure to start the tap at exactly 90 degrees to the work face.

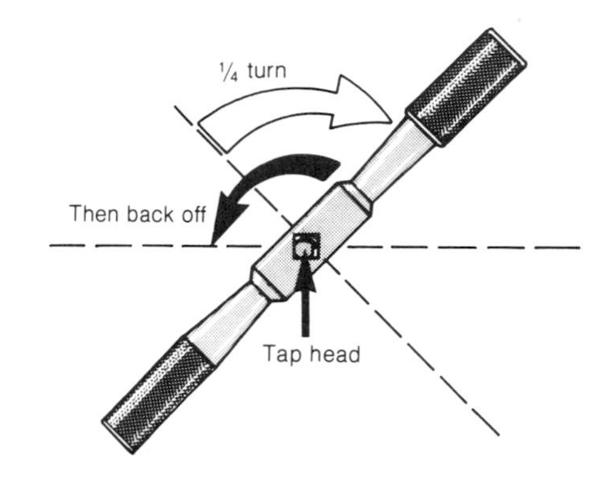

Do not try to cut a thread at one go, especially in hard metal. Back off frequently.

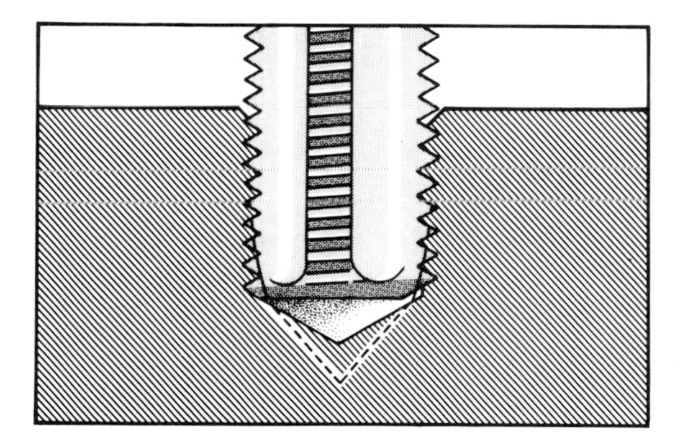

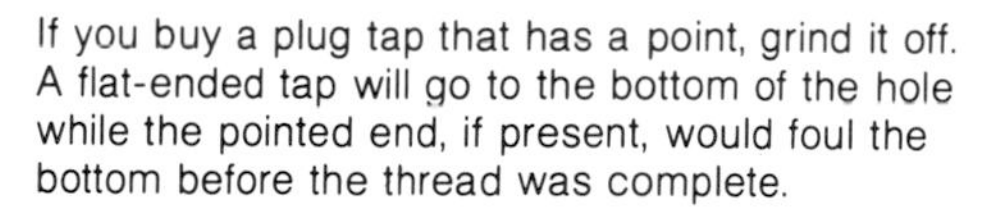

If you buy a plug tap that has a point, grind it off. A flat-ended tap will go to the bottom of the hole while the pointed end, if present, would foul the bottom before the thread was complete.

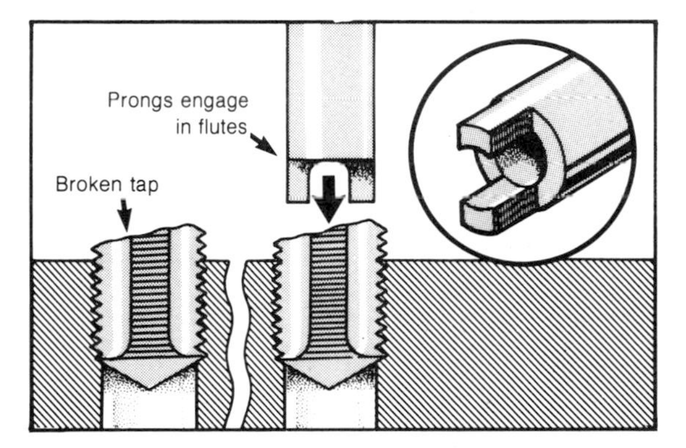

Extracting broken taps is one of the nastiest jobs in the workshop. A little tool like this will sometimes get them out.

cutting edges start to engage with the metal, so when you proceed again, stop and back off after about half a turn. After that, stop and back off every quarter turn.

This backing off has two functions: it allows the swarf to clear from the cutting edges, and as the swarf clears it allows lubricant to flow in. As you proceed, a slight change in resistance may tell you that the tap has run dry, so stop and squirt some more lubricant down the flutes. A 'crunchy' feel as you turn indicates that the flutes in the tap are full of swarf. If this happens, screw the tap right out and clean it. If it is a blind hole you may have to clean the hole too, and the best way to do this is to invert the component and shake the swarf out. Blowing it out, either by mouth or airline is the quickest way known of getting it in your eyes.

Once the first tap is at the bottom of the hole, withdraw it and go in with the second tap. This will spin in easily for a turn or two, and will gradually get stiffer to turn as it cuts out the metal left by the taper on the first tap. Observe the same sequence of turning and backing off until you reach the bottom of the hole. If it is a blind hole and you need it threaded right to the bottom, observe the same sequence with the plug tap.

Do observe this backing off sequence carefully. With hard metals you may have to cut your advance to an eighth of a turn at a time. Whatever you do, do not force the pace, or you may be left with a broken tap.

Extracting Broken Taps

Do not try to drill out a broken tap, because it will be just as hard as the drill bit. If there is a little bit sticking up out of the hole, try gently turning it anticlockwise with pliers. If it refuses to budge, give it a very gentle tap with a hammer and try again. If it still does not move and the component will stand heating, heat it up and try again.

By now you are running out of options. You can try a long-term soak in penetrating oil, or even Coca Cola (yes, honestly), or risk breaking off your only hope of salvation by giving a really hard heave on the pliers.

If the tap breaks off below the level of the top of the hole, get a bit of hard steel strip that will just go down the hole, and grind or file a two-pronged fork shape in the end. Enter these points down the flutes, and try to turn the tap in that way.

You can try hitting the remains of the tap very hard with a soft steel drift, but the blow is just as likely to bang it in tighter as it is to free it or shatter it. Your final option is to take the job into an engineering shop that has an ultrasonic means of extracting stuck components.

Dies

If a tap is like a precision bolt with cutting edges, a die is like a precision nut with the same facility. Dies in the threads you will probably be using come in three common outer diameters: $^{13}\!/_{16}$in (21mm), 1in (25·4mm), and $1^{5}\!/_{16}$in (33·3mm). Each size of die requires a separate die holder.

You will find that your die holder has three screws that go through its circumference. The two outer screws are to compress the die and secure it in the holder, while the centre screw has a hardened, coned end which engages in the split in the die. This enables the die to be forced slightly open for a first cut.

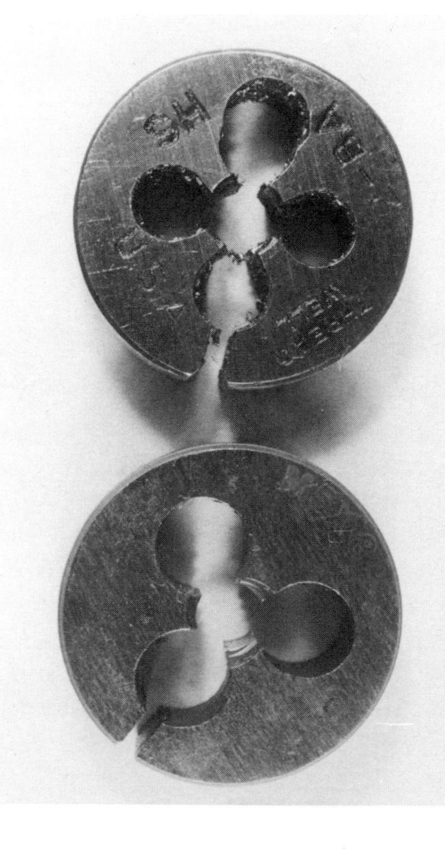

Two dies, one for a BA thread and the other metric. Both are of $^{13}\!/_{16}$in outside diameter.

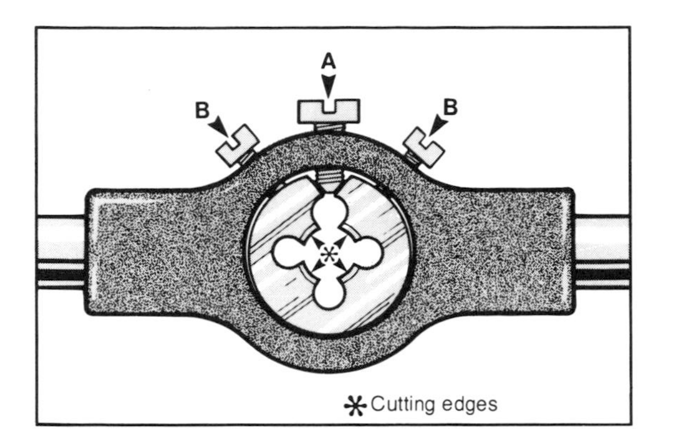

Loosening screws B and tightening screw A spreads the die. Loosening screw A and tightening screws B closes the die.

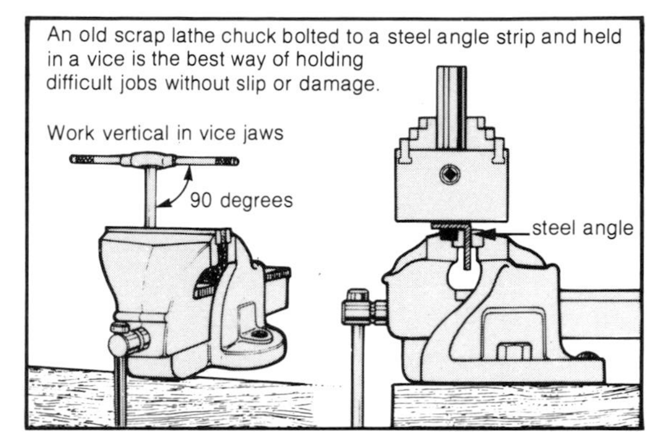

Work to be threaded with dies can be held in a conventional vice, but an old scrap lathe chuck bolted to a length of steel angle makes the ideal work-holding device.

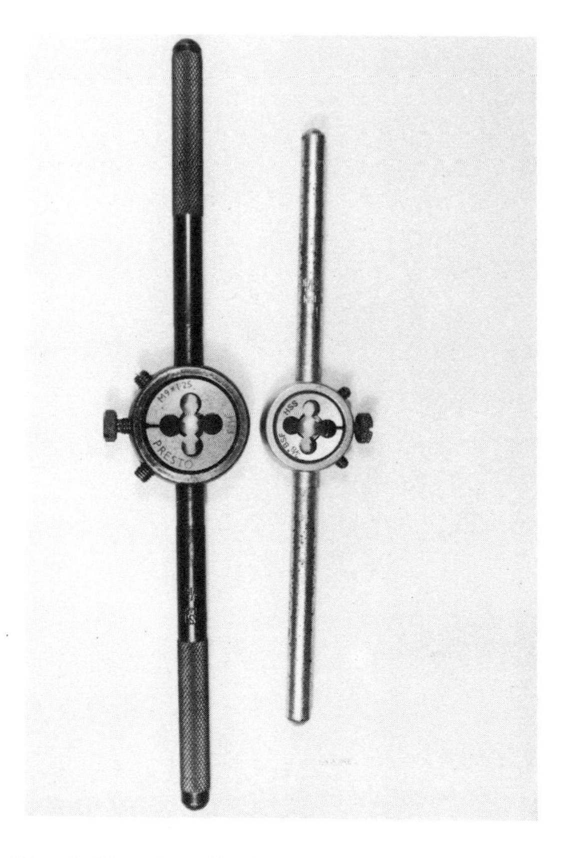

Dies of different outside diameters need different die holders. The smaller of this pair is 1 in, and the larger 1 5/16 in. This larger size is as big as you will generally need to go in a small workshop.

Forming Threads with Dies

First, use the micrometer or vernier gauge to check that the rod is of the required diameter. It does not matter if it is a bit undersize unless you are seeking the ultimate precision, but it must not be oversize.

Now loosen all the screws in the die holder, and insert the die with its bell-shaped entrance facing outwards. Tighten the centre screw until the die spreads to fill the holder, then tighten the two outer screws.

Starting the die cutting straight is essential, and it often helps to file or turn a slight taper on the end of the rod. In fact, if you have a lathe and plenty of material you can turn about a quarter of an inch on the end of the bar down to the core diameter of the thread, and cut this 'guide piece' off once the thread has been formed. Screw thread tables will give you the core diameter.

Hold the rod to be threaded in a vice, coat it with a suitable lubricant, and put a little lubricant on the cutting area of the die. Being careful to start straight, give the die about one full turn, and then proceed with the same 'turn and back off' technique as described in tapping. In fact, this backing off is not quite so important in die work as it is in tapping, as liberated swarf usually just falls out of the die (often into your socks), but it still pays not to go at it like a bull at a gate.

Once you have threaded as far along the bar as you wish to go, wind off the die and try the thread with a known accurate nut. If you have not got one, try it in the tapped hole that has been prepared for it. If it fits without binding then the job is done, but if it is tight you will need to take a second cut.

To make this cut, loosen the centre screw in the die for no more than about a third of a turn, tighten the outer screws to compensate, and run the die along the thread again. If the thread still does not fit, back the centre screw off another third of a turn and try again. Keep at it until the thread passes your test.

IDENTIFYING SCREW THREADS

To identify a screw thread, first measure the diameter. If you work in inches and you come up with an unfamiliar fraction, try a metric measurement. Write down whichever measurement seems most logical.

Now you need to count the number of threads in a known measurement to determine what is known as the pitch. Inch-based threads are based on threads per inch so, with the aid of a magnifying glass if necessary, you can count the threads against a ruler. You make life easier if you buy a pitch gauge (*see* below).

Metric pitches are usually listed as the measurement, in millimetres, between two adjacent 'peaks', and if you have not got a metric pitch gauge this may involve you in some mathematics. For instance, if you count 12½ threads in a centimetre, divide 10mm by 12·5 and you get a figure of 0·8. This will be the pitch figure you

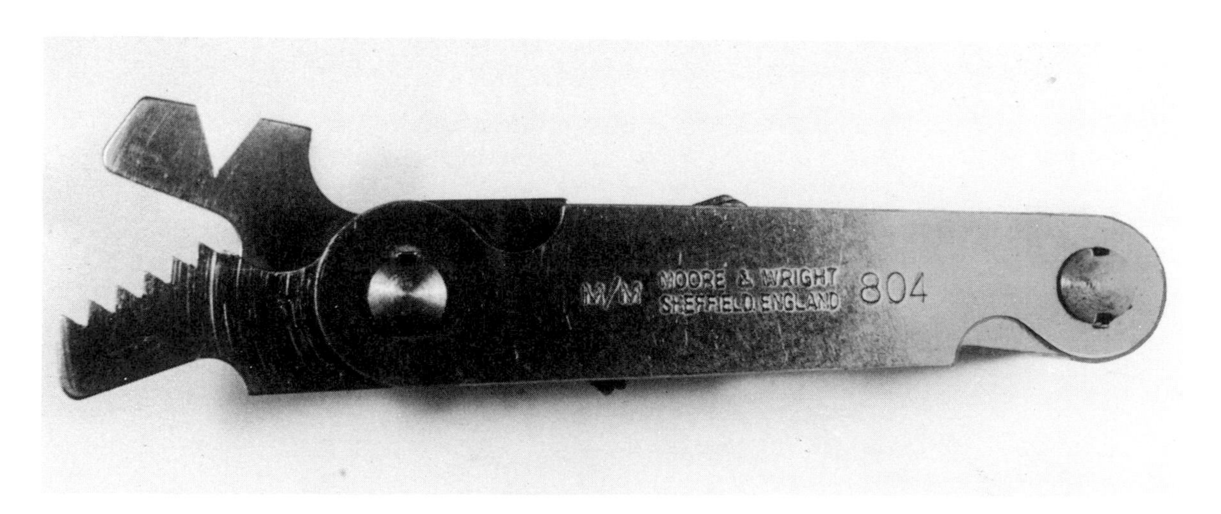

Threads can be identified by comparing them with a pitch gauge. This is a metric set, and the large 'V' is a 60 degree tool-grinding guide.

are looking for in the tables.

Taking this metric thread as our first example, if the pitch is 0·8 and the diameter is 5mm, a good first bet is metric coarse. A glance at the tables will confirm it. In fact, do not be alarmed if the measured diameter is a fraction less than 5mm – production bolts are frequently a bit undersize.

Inch-based threads can be harder to identify. Assuming that you have found a 3/8 bolt with 16 threads to the inch, it looks coarse, so a good first try is Whitworth. 3/8 Whitworth certainly has 16 threads to the inch, but so has 3/8 UNC. The only way to sort out one from the other is to look very carefully at the angular form of the thread, unless the bolt is head-stamped with the information. Whitworth is 55 degrees and UNC is 60 degrees, which in small diameters can be difficult to spot against a pitch gauge, even with a magnifying glass.

If the threads are cut with precision, a 1/4 UNF bolt will not enter a Whitworth nut because the core diameters are slightly different, but with many production nuts and bolts the threads seem to be completely intechangeable. In a lot of everyday, low-stress situations it does not matter if you do get them mixed, but it is important to keep them separate if you want to get the ultimate tensile strength out of the fastening. In these situations good, full-depth thread contact is important.

In fact, Whitworth and UNC are identical in pitch throughout most of the diameter range.

CLEARANCE DRILLS

Many screw thread tables list clearance drills for the various diameters. These clearances are good for most everyday engineering jobs in that they are generous enough to allow for rapid assembly and they also compensate for minor errors in hole placement. However, when precision location of a component is required it is often possible to tighten up these quoted clearances, by as much as 0·1mm in some cases.

6 Soldering and Brazing

The ability to form a strong joint between one piece of metal and another is one of the most useful skills. Welding in one form or another is the accepted way of forming most high-tensile joints between similar or compatible metals, but it is not always a possibility in a home workshop.

The main problem is the expense of the equipment, plus the fact that gas and electric welding are skills that take some time to acquire. Initially, it is better to concentrate on methods that can be performed with a good soldering iron, or a gas blow torch costing a few pounds.

WORKING AREA

Even an electric soldering iron generates enough heat to ignite timber, while a gas torch can start a very serious fire in a few seconds. That is one reason why steel-topped workbenches are preferable, although a thin layer of steel over wood or chipboard can be considered as *some* protection against accidents. You cannot do serious soldering or brazing directly on the bench top, and it is best to produce a portable heat-proof surface on which to operate.

While you are doing this, you may as well make something on which you can braze as well as solder, and my brazing area is shown opposite. It is a tray made from 1·2mm stainless steel (although any grade of steel will do), standing on legs about 2in (50mm) high. Dimensions of the tray are approximately 9in × 2ft × 1½in (230mm × 610mm × 38mm), although these are not critical. A big tray provides plenty of room to put down pots of flux, brazing rods, clamps and other things that need to be kept together. The legs are important, because they stop heat being conducted through the base and into the thin metal skin on the bench.

Fire-bricks are an important part of this set up, because not only do they shield the tray and the bench from heat, they reflect a tremendous amount of heat back into the job. This saves you a lot of gas, and it also enables you to tackle jobs that are beyond the capacity of the torch on its own.

A good tool shop may be able to sell you fire-bricks, but there is an easier way. Go to a builders' supplier and get a couple of the bricks that are used to contain ordinary domestic coal fires. These bricks are 7·5in × 8·75in × 1·25in (190mm × 222mm × 32mm). One makes a good base, while the other can be cracked in half with a big chisel to form two walls. These walls help to contain the flame, and give you a corner for heating small components to high temperatures.

For difficult jobs, when you are trying to pour a lot of heat into an object, it also pays to have some smaller pieces of fire-brick to pack around the area to be heated and create a maximum amount of reflection. Small pieces of very highly reflective fire-brick are found in the reflective surfaces of old gas fires, and ten minutes spent on a rubbish tip with a hammer and chisel may liberate all you need.

As a final note on the working area, before you light even a small gas torch, do

Brazing operations in my workshop, and a lot of soft soldering and heat treatment operations too, are performed on this heavy steel tray in the area shielded by fire-bricks. If you have a pair of tatty old pliers and some bits of steel tube you can make yourself long-handled tongs for handling hot objects.

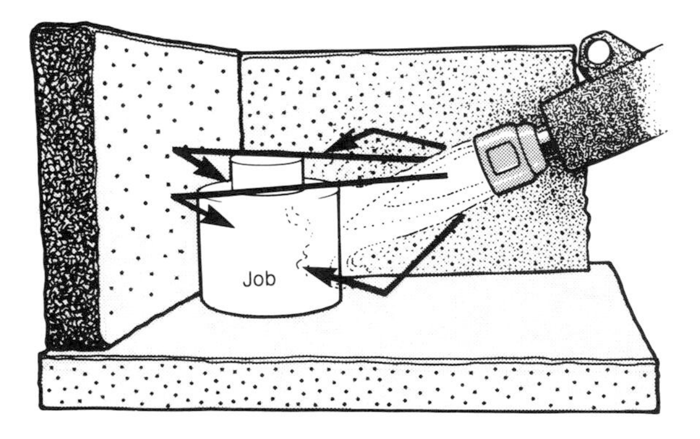

Fire-bricks are an essential brazing aid, particularly when big jobs have to be tackled with a small torch. Heat that would otherwise be wasted is reflected into the work, and gas is saved.

clear all inflammable articles from your bench top. On my bench top there are usually plastic containers of oil, paint-brushes in jars of thinner, aerosol cans, spare gas cylinders, and other potentially dangerous items. *All must be moved to a safe area before a brazing job commences.*

CLOTHING

Even when using a small gas torch there can be accidental splashes of hot, liquid solder, or a lump of hot metal can fall and hit you. Thick clothing and ordinary leather shoes offer reasonable protection, but it is unwise to operate in shirtsleeves and sandals. Nylon material is terrible stuff for burns – it disappears in a flash when exposed to flame and leaves an incredibly hot, sticky residue on your skin. Natural materials like cotton, on the other hand, smoulder before they catch fire, and a thick cotton boiler suit with long sleeves is a good investment. If you feel you need further protection, get a good leather apron.

Eye protection is a thing I tend to forget about because I wear safety-glass prescription spectacles all the time; however, if you do not wear spectacles, or your everyday spectacles have ordinary glass lenses, it is wise to wear proper eye protection for many workshop operations, not just those involving heat. Some protective spectacles you can buy are big enough to fit over an ordinary pair of glasses. Brazing operations with the sort of gas torches I shall be talking about do not require dark lenses unless you have very sensitive eyes, but suitable dark lenses must be worn for all gas and electric welding jobs.

SOFT SOLDERING

Soft solder is the solder used with the familiar soldering iron, so a word or two about that implement is not out of place. The little electric irons you can buy for making electrical contacts will usually also handle very thin plate, although you will be working very much on the limit. An iron of 140 watts should handle most solderable metals up to about half a millimetre thick, although some constructions in some metals will conduct heat away from the joint too fast.

Also, you should be aware that some electric irons you buy are not rated for continuous production work. For light jobs of a short duration they are fine, but they are not meant to be left switched on all day, and after a long period of use their handles become uncomfortably hot. If you want to do a lot of soldering-iron work, seek the advice of a good tool shop.

Solder Composition

Soft solders are alloys of lead and tin. Flux-cored solders sold for electrical contact work are formulated to have a low melting point and are quite soft when cold. For industrial applications many solder formulas are available, each suited to a particular task, but not all are commonly available. However, you should be able to get plumbers' solder, which has a slightly higher melting point and is a bit harder than electricians'.

Metals Suitable for Soft Soldering

Copper, brass and tin-plated steel solder very well, although no soft-soldering operation in any metal produces a really high-tensile joint. Bare mild steel is a little more difficult, and stainless steel requires a special formula. All of these metals can be joined to each other.

Special soft solders and fluxes are available for joining aluminium and high-aluminium alloys, but they are not in general use in amateur workshops.

Fluxes

Fluxes for soft soldering take two forms. Some just form a passive film on the work to keep it clean and prevent it from oxidising while you work. Some paste fluxes like the commonly available Fluxite are examples. Other fluxes are chemical compositions that take an active part in cleaning the metal as well as protecting it, and Baker's Soldering Fluid is an everyday example. This latter class of fluxes is corrosive, so they must be carefully cleaned off after the joint is complete.

Forming a Joint

The golden rule of all soldering is that the surfaces to be joined must be spotlessly clean and free from grease. When joining plate material, do not try to solder it edge to edge, but make a small overlap. If joining blocks of metal, do not press them tightly together but leave a tiny gap so that the solder can run in. Thinly coat the surfaces to be joined with flux.

If you are using an iron, clean any old flux or dirt off the tip with a wire brush or scratch pad, bring the iron up to temperature, lightly flux the tip, and 'tin' it all over with a thin layer of solder. If you are using a big copper iron of the type that is heated in a fire or flame, the old instruction used to be to heat it until the flame turned green. *See* the diagram on page 62 for how to feed solder into the joint.

If the job is beyond the capacity of an iron you can use a blow-torch flame. The

Various soft solders and a tin of flux. The flat coil of solder contains its own flux in the core and is generally for electrical work, while the tall coil and the bar are formulated for plumbing work.

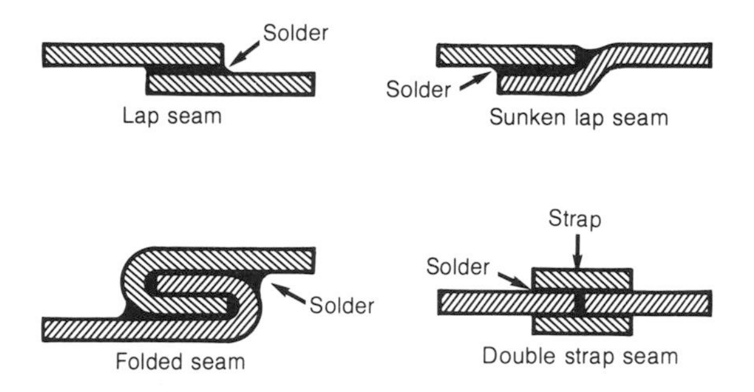

Types of joint suitable for soldering and brazing structures from plate. The simple lap seam is the weakest of the lot, while the sunken lap is a fraction stronger and much neater. Folded seam is strong in very thin material, while the double strap is strongest in thick material.

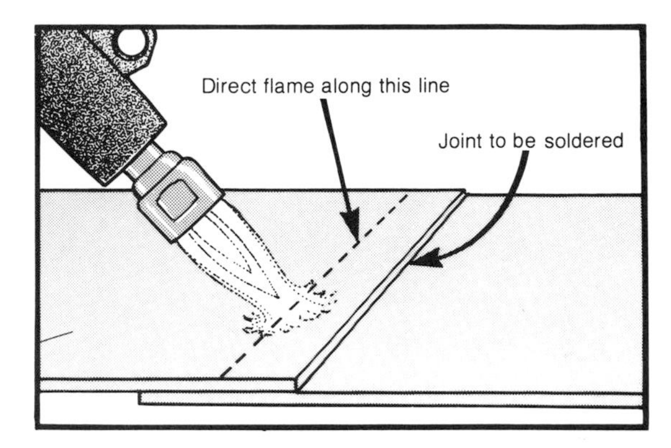

If you have to resort to a flame to form a soft soldered joint, lightly flux the joining faces and apply the flame as shown. Heat will be conducted into the joint, and you will not set fire to the flux.

danger with the flame is that you may overheat and burn the flux, forming a surface on which the solder will not flow. To avoid this situation, keep the flame turned down as low as is consistent with providing enough heat, and do not point it directly at the joint. Instead, heat the metal close to the joint, and allow the metal to conduct the heat to the joint faces.

HARD SOLDERING

The most common hard solder is known as silver solder, some samples of which contain over 60 per cent silver. This makes it quite expensive, but you need very little and it does produce some very strong joints in a wide variety of metals. Its melting point is usually in the region of 700 degrees centigrade, or more, more than twice that of most soft solders, so it is always applied with the aid of a torch.

Compositions vary according to melting point, and on complicated jobs where several joints have to be made, one after the other, it is possible to take advantage of this range of melting points by making the first joint with the highest melting point you can get, and using a lower melting point on a subsequent joint. That way, if you are careful, you can make the second joint without the first falling apart.

The solder is usually supplied in the form of wire 1·5mm thick, and it requires a special flux which is bought in powder form. Easiflo is the best-known example.

In recent years there have been fears about the cadmium content in many silver solder mixes, as there is a health hazard in inhaling the fumes of heated cadmium. Using silver solder in a home workshop is not the same as using it in industry, where operators may be exposed to the fumes for all of the working day. In our situation the solder is usually only in molten form for a few seconds, so the exposure is very small indeed. Nevertheless, it is still wise to use solders that contain cadmium in a well-ventilated area, where the air current takes any fumes away from you, and to avoid bending over the job while you work. Alternatively, you can now buy cadmium-free solders.

Metals Suitable for Hard Soldering

Suitable metals include brass and copper, all steels in common use including high-speed tool steel and stainless, nickel, and cast iron. Silver soldering is particularly recommended for zinc-plated (galvanised) steel because the temperature involved is not high enough to burn off the zinc or form the brittle zinc/iron alloy which is often the result of conventional welding.

Forming the Joint

Surfaces to be joined must be spotlessly clean and free from grease. The flux can be sprinkled into the joint dry, but in this form it can be blown away by the approaching torch flame and distributed on parts of the work where you do not want it. It is better to mix the flux to a thin paste with a little clean water, and apply it with a small brush. Do avoid getting it into any cuts – it is extremely painful.

Heat the area to be joined with the torch and observe the flux. First the water will boil off, then not much seems to happen for a while as the temperature rises. However, as the temperature at which the solder will melt approaches the flux vitrifies and runs over the surface like a clear liquid. With steel this temperature is usually just a little short of red hot, although further heating to dull red does no harm.

A thin flux coating on the end of the rod of silver solder can be beneficial, and always melt the solder against the job rather than directly in the heat of the flame. Good silver solder runs like melted butter into a well-prepared joint. If you melt the rod in the flame before the job is up to temperature it lands as a little molten blob which is very difficult to dissipate. Molten silver solder usually flows evenly over fluxed surfaces, so it is important that flux should only be present where you want solder to flow.

When the joint is complete, let it cool naturally because dunking it in cold water to promote rapid cooling weakens the joint. After cooling remove all the flux because it is slightly corrosive. It can be chipped off with something like an old scriber point when cold, but wire brushing usually does no more than polish it. However, it is soluble in water and a soak in a very mild acid solution is best of all.

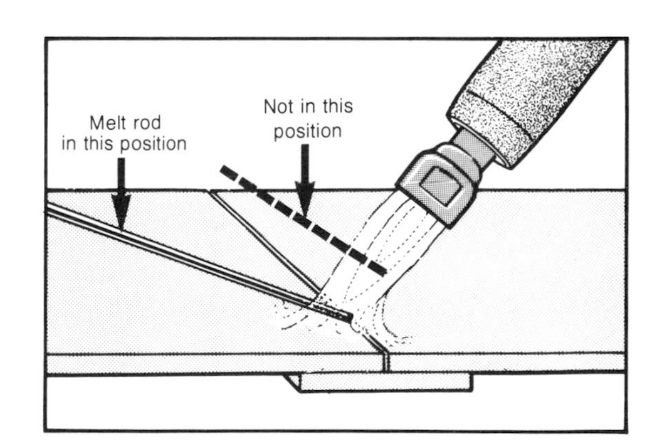

Melt hard solders against the job, not in the flame above it. Melted just in the flame, the solder will run in ugly blobs all over the work.

BRAZING

Brazing is similar to silver soldering, but the jointing medium is brass rather than silver alloy. Brazing spelter, as the brass rod is called, has a higher melting point (900 degrees Centigrade, or more) so it may be beyond the range of some small gas torches. In a home workshop brazing is usually used for joining steel. A brass job may melt at the same temperature as the spelter.

You can braze using silver-soldering flux, but you will probably be taking it a bit beyond its intended temperature range. Brazing flux can be bought in powder form, but unless you mean to do a lot of brazing it may be cheaper to buy flux-coated rods from shops specialising in car bodywork repair accessories.

Brazing spelter does not flow as easily as silver solder, but the rules for its application are pretty much the same. Steel will be red hot before you reach the rod's melting point.

GAS TORCHES

These fall, broadly, into two types: those fed by a big cylinder via a pressure regulator and hose; and those with a small, self-contained cylinder.

The former type is a luxury in a workshop. They are expensive, but well worth the money if you have a lot of silver soldering and brazing to do. Most of these big torches can be bought with several different burners that give you anything from a pencil-point flame to a great roaring blaze a couple of inches across. Seivert is the good name to watch for when buying.

However, most of us have to make do with cheaper torches with self-contained cylinders, and over the years I have owned most of the popular types. I now have two, and the most-used is a Taymar 3000, which is fed by screw-on propane cartridges. This torch produces a flame about 0·9in (23mm) across at its base and, with the aid of fire-bricks, produces quite enough heat for most silver soldering and very light brazing. It also has the advantage that it can be turned down very low for soft soldering jobs that are beyond the range of the iron.

My second torch is the American-made

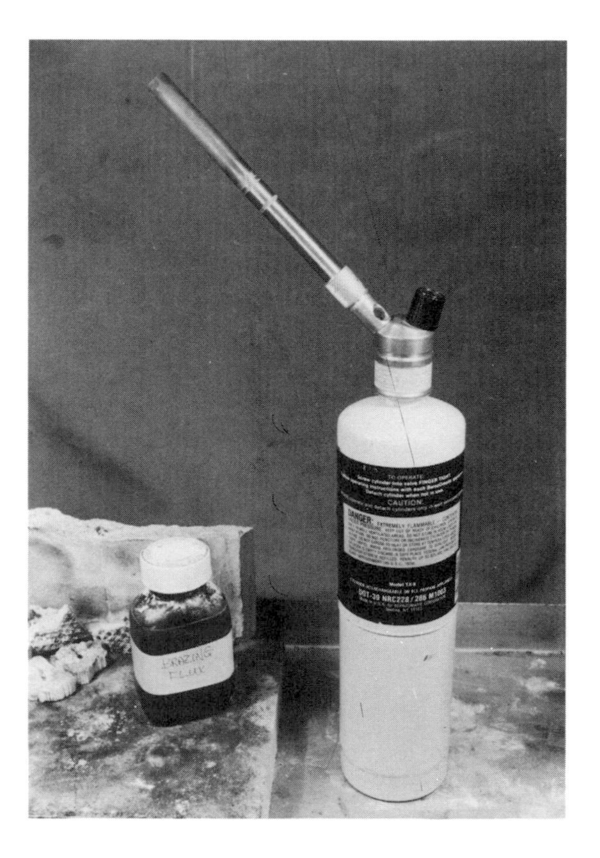

This American-made Spitfire torch is the most powerful heat source in my workshop. It is powerful enough to handle most hard soldering and brazing and, with the aid of fire-bricks, small sections of high-speed tool steel can be brought to a temperature at which they can be bent.

Spitfire VTK (300 series) which produces a very hot flame from the Bernz-O-Matic screw-on propane cylinder. I use this torch when I need a lot of heat for brazing. It is efficient but very noisy, and the flame cannot be turned down low or the torch overheats.

All of these little torches use either propane or butane fuel, which is heavier than air. Both of the cylinders mentioned are self-sealing, and I always make a habit of removing the burners from the cylinders after use. A torch is easily left with the valve very slightly open, and leaking gas collects near the floor where it constitutes an explosion hazard. The risk is done away with if you remove the head.

HEATING THE JOB

It has been mentioned before that a careful arrangement of fire-bricks helps to concentrate heat into the area where it is required. Also remember that the flame is not of uniform heat all along its length. Close to the nozzle it will be comparatively cool, with much unburnt gas present, increasing in temperature to a maximum at the tip of the easily visible blue cone. Beyond this area it starts to cool again. Therefore, to apply maximum heat point the tip of the cone at the spot where the most heat is needed.

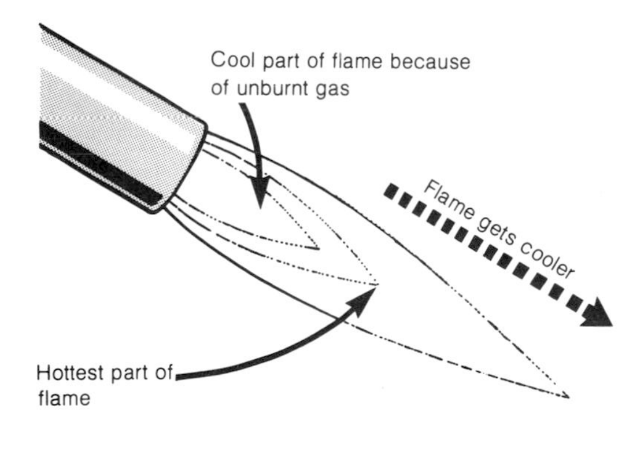

A gas torch flame is not of uniform heat all along its length.

ALUMINIUM

Neither hard soldering nor brazing is possible on aluminium or alloys containing large proportions of that metal. For these metals you need aluminium alloy filler rods which, in turn, require special fluxes.

The general rules of silver soldering apply, although the jointing medium is more reluctant to flow. The big risk is that the melting point of the jointing medium is usually very close to that of the job, and many a carefully-machined aluminium component has finished up as a puddle on the fire-brick. Great care is needed because aluminium gives no visual clue that it is about to melt. There is no colour change – it simply suddenly goes droopy and falls to bits.

For this reason, it is wise to have a practice on a bit of aluminium of similar composition before you do the real job. And remember – thin sections heat up and melt more quickly than thick ones.

7 Drilling

Ordinary hand drills and hand-held electric drills like the familiar Black and Decker are fine for doing their usual household jobs: everyday carpentry, rough metalwork, and chores like drilling holes in brick walls. However, if precision is required they have some quite severe limitations. In brief, they tend to make holes that are neither straight nor truly round, cone-shaped rather than parallel-sided, oversized, and often in the wrong place.

Most electric drills in this hand-held category also turn too fast for precision work. Even a model with a two-speed gearbox may give the choice of, for example, 900 or 2000 r.p.m., while what we are looking for to do most of our work is 300 r.p.m. or less. With an expensive hand-held drill we may also be paying for features we do not want, like 'hammer' features that belt hard-tipped drills through reinforced concrete, or the ability to drive jig-saws, hedge trimmers, or even small wood-turning lathes.

However, when you first begin to work seriously with metal the only drill you may have at your disposal is more likely to be the ordinary household electric variety than anything else, and the first thing you can do to improve its accuracy is to buy a vertical stand. Most of these stands are somewhat flimsy and lightweight when compared to a proper vertical drilling machine, but they do allow you to place holes more accurately and drill them straight. They also introduce you to another vital aspect in both accuracy and your own safety – the ability to clamp work firmly to the baseplate.

A lot of these lightweight vertical stands can be improved by taking up any slack movement, which is usually present in the horizontal plane more than anywhere else. On some models the vertical movement of the drill is controlled by a tongue running in a groove, and the tongue sometimes fits with a more than generous gap. On one Stanley Bridges model I owned I managed to pack this gap with strips scissored from the walls of a beer can, held in with epoxy resin, and the tool thus modified would drill small holes with near drilling machine accuracy.

Sooner or later, however, you will realise the limitations of a rig like this and want to buy a proper drilling machine.

THE DRILLING MACHINE

If the possible cost of buying a machine frightens you, you can take heart, for there are currently two reasonably priced alternatives available to you: either buy a second-hand machine, perhaps in a factory sale, or buy a new machine of Far Eastern manufacture. Either way, £100 or more is realistic.

Second-hand Machines

If you take the first course there are a few points to watch and the first is size. Even a relatively small (by industrial standards) bench model may weigh the best part of a hundredweight (50 Kg) and a floor-mounted model will be more than

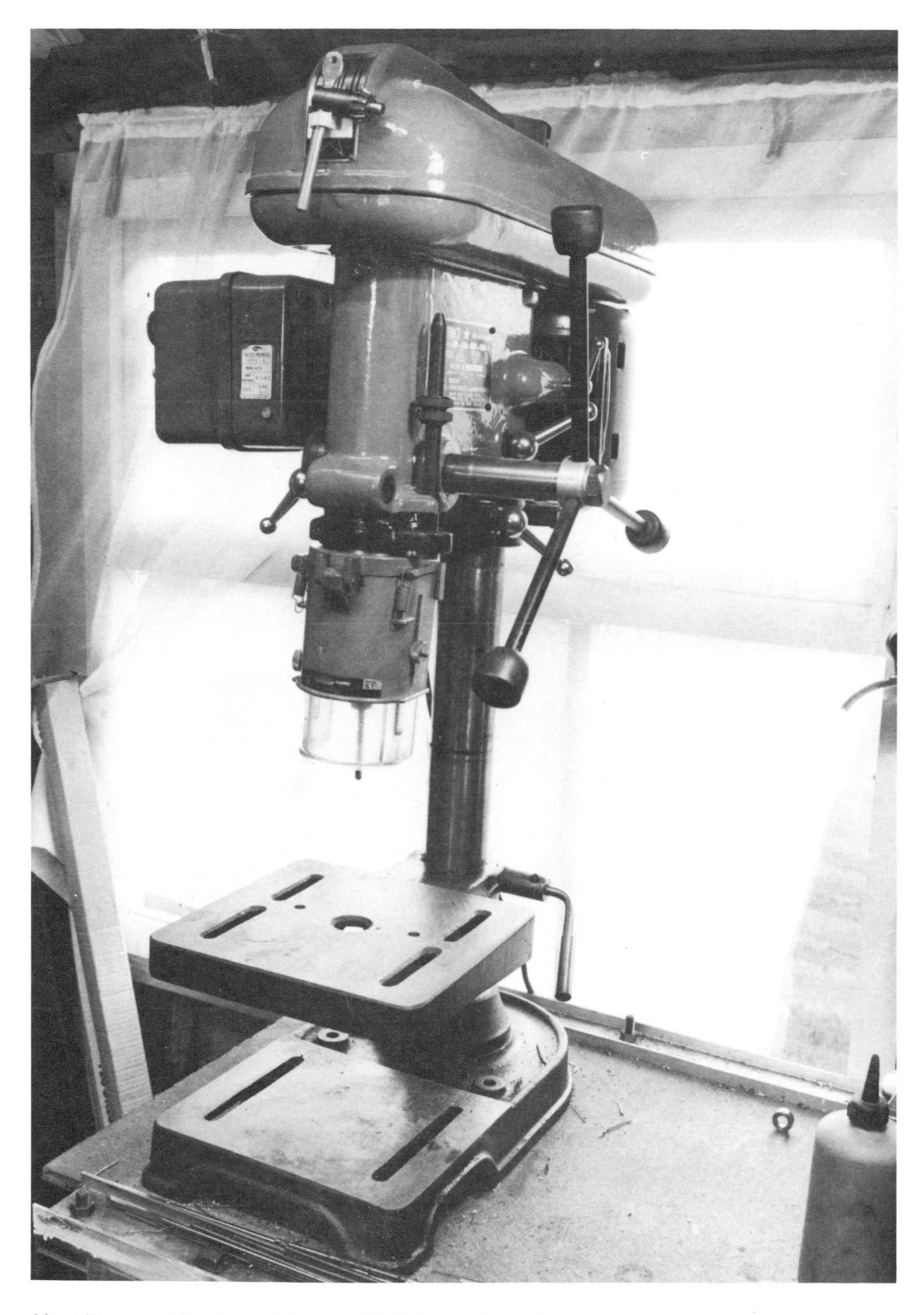

My drilling machine is a slightly modified Fobco Star, with a speed range from 475 to 4360 r.p.m. In all the years it has been in the workshop, it has never been out of bottom gear.

you can lift or carry in the average car boot. Something about the size of my Fobco Star (page 7) is about right for anything but the biggest jobs; it does not take up a ridiculous amount of workshop space, and yet it has sufficient power to cut half-inch holes in relatively hard metal. In addition, there is not too much to wear out on such a simple machine, and when something does go wrong you can usually put it right yourself. For instance, you can change the main bearings for a few pounds and in about an hour's work.

One important point to check when buying second-hand in a factory sale, is that the electrics are single-phase and not three-phase. A single-phase machine works off your normal household power supply, while three-phase needs the industrial 440 volts which would be very costly to instal in a home workshop.

It is true that, in industrial situations, single-phase electrics wear out faster than three-phase, but a machine that is working all day, five days a week in a factory, may be doing no more than about an hour a week in your workshop. I have never suffered a failure with a single-phase industrially-rated motor yet, and even if I do, rewinds and second-hand motors are quite cheap.

With a light industrial machine made out of big lumps of cast iron, worn bearings are not much to worry about. They can be knocked out and replaced for a few pounds, but worn sliding metal surfaces are something to beware of. They cannot be put right, or, at least, not at reasonable cost. The diagram above explains the points to watch: a bit of wear at point A is probably a worn-out bearing; any shake or wobble at B is likely to be a more serious problem.

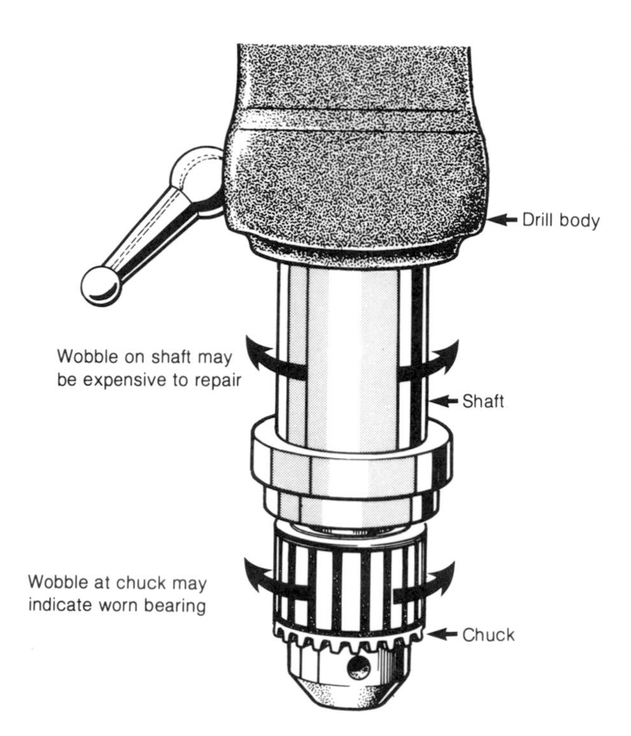

Points to watch when evaluating a second-hand drilling machine. A bearing may be easy and cheap to replace, while wear on the shaft and drill body may be expensive to put right, or even impossible.

Look for a machine with a speed range from around 300 r.p.m. up to about 1200. On machines in the price range we are looking at the speeds will be controlled by 'V' belts and cone pulleys, and you are unlikely to find a range of more than four speeds. If there is a speed lower than 300 then it is useful: if top speed is only about 900 do not worry, because you will use the machine in bottom gear most of the time anyway.

The maximum chuck capacity on such a machine will be about 0.5in (12mm) and the way in which the chuck is attached to the machine is not important unless you anticipate wanting to bore some very big holes. For big-hole drilling, 0·625in

(16mm) or more, it is best if the chuck can be dispensed with and the drill fitted direct into a Morse taper in the drill's quill shaft.

Again there are some points to watch in this department: if there is a Morse taper in the quill, place a wedge in the slot, clout the taper out, and examine the taper's internal bore. A few light marks are nothing to worry about, but deep scores present a problem. The condition of the male taper is immaterial if the price of the machine is right, because a new one costs only a few pounds.

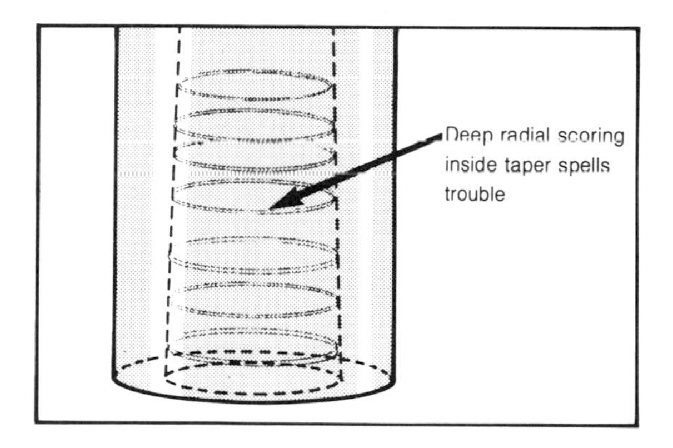

If the second-hand machine has a Morse taper, examine it for deep scoring. It can be remachined - but at a price.

With no Morse taper in the quill you will usually find that attachment is by a male Jacobs taper, ground on the end of the quill shaft itself. With this type, tap wedges under the chuck until it comes off, and examine the male taper carefully. Scoring, or the presence of engineering adhesives like Loctite, are the danger signs. A chuck of acceptable accuracy costs about £10, so take that into account if the chuck itself does not look of good quality.

When considering a *new* machine there is not a lot to say, except that it must be strong and rigid, and turn at the right speeds. For a given price even a Far Eastern machine will be of smaller capacity than a second-hand bargain in an engineering shop sale.

Safety Points

New or second-hand, there are a few safety points to watch. For instance, belts must be covered and if you rig covers yourself remember that they are not simply to keep straying fingers out of the machine: they must be strong enough to keep *you* safe if you fall on the machine.

The Health and Safety at Work regulations have a lot to say about drilling machines, and while the provisions do not apply to you in your amateur status, the machine should be electrically safe and should have a fast-acting stop switch mounted somewhere where you can hit it in a hurry. As a mechanical engineer, you may find it wiser to leave electricity to the experts.

A chuck guard is also worth buying, because those lovely long worms of swarf that come out of big holes are both sharp and hot.

TWIST DRILLS

An understanding of some of the characteristics of the twist drills you may be using will help you to achieve the high standards of accuracy you are looking for.

The drills that we normally buy over the tool shop counter are known as 'jobbers' length' drills. If we need them to be shorter for any reason we can ask for 'stub' drills, and for very deep holes we can ask for 'long series' if ever the need

This is a guaranteed way of hurting yourself with a drilling machine. When the point breaks through the plate, the flutes will snatch, forcing the work to rotate.

This is a much safer way of drilling, with the work firmly clamped to the machine table.

arises. In fact, jobbers' drills can be entered into the work beyond the limit of the flutes, but they have to be withdrawn very frequently to achieve swarf clearance, and great care must be taken to avoid seizure.

Diameters are the cause of a lot of confusion because there are three standards in common usage. Firstly there is the familiar 'fractions' series which is calibrated in fractions of an inch and normally increases in diameter in increments of $\frac{1}{64}$in.

Metric sizes are calibrated in millimetres and normally increase in increments of 0·1mm, although you can get drills in lesser increments if you require them. Then there is the old British number and letter series. Numbers go from 1 (5·79mm) to 80 (0·34mm) in more or less even steps, while letters go from A (5·94mm) to Z (10·49mm).

At first this number and letter series sounds a bit odd, but in fact it contains a lot of very useful tapping and clearance sizes for many of the threads you may be using. Indelibly printed in my mind is the fact that No. 44 is the tapping drill for 6BA, No. 4 is the tapping drill for $\frac{1}{4}$BSF, and Letter P is the tapping drill for $\frac{3}{8}$BSF. However, a complete metric set in

This is the safest way of all. The work is firmly clamped, and a chuck guard is positioned to contain the sharp, hot swarf that will be produced.

increments of 0·1mm takes care of all these tapping and clearance provisions quite adequately.

Forming Holes

Now comes the most important thing to remember in all metal-drilling operations: when pressed straight into metal, *a drill will make a hole bigger than its nominal diameter.* Not sometimes, but always, and on a big hole the error can be several thousandths of an inch. So how do we get round this problem, and get drills to make holes whose dimensions fall within acceptable limits?

First of all, what are the causes of these errors? The first cause, which occurs even with a perfectly-sharpened drill fresh from the factory, is that the pressures of drilling and rotation force the cutting edges of the drill to splay outwards, and the more power we apply to the drilling, the greater this splay will be.

The second cause of oversize holes is poor drill sharpening. If the centre of the drill point is away from the true axis of the drill, the drill will rotate around the point and not around its axis. This kind of error can produce holes that are vastly oversize, and the only cure is to regrind

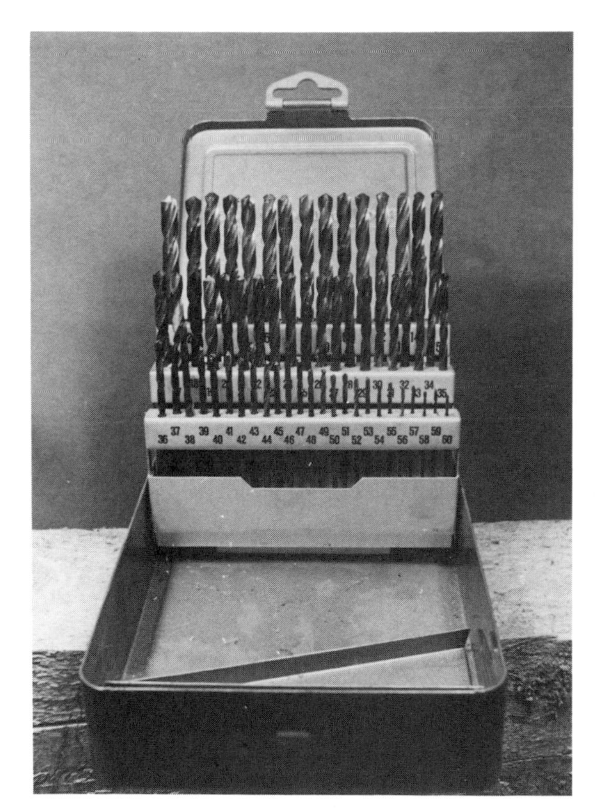

Boxed sets of drills are a good buy if you are likely to need a lot of tapping and clearance sizes. This set of number drills from 1 to 60 covers a range from 5·8mm to 1mm. Unless you do fine model making, drills below 1mm are rarely needed.

the drill tip accurately.

In industry, holes that have to be accurate in diameter are first drilled a tiny fraction undersize, then brought out to their full diameter with a reamer. However, reamers are expensive and there is a way of achieving excellent accuracy with a drilling machine. As an example, assume that we want to drill an accurately-placed half-inch hole through a piece of steel an inch thick. This is the working sequence:

1. Mark the position of the centre of the hole with a punch dot, and roughly position the work on the drilling machine table.
2. Put any very small drill into the chuck (something about 1·5mm is fine) and lower it towards the work. As the point enters the punch dot you will almost certainly see the drill bend very slightly.
3. Manoeuvre the work until the drill point enters the punch dot cleanly without bending. Check the final placement by viewing both from the front and one side.
4. Tighten up whatever clamping arrangement you have on the machine table, and check alignment again by lowering the drill. If all is well, proceed to the next stage; if the job has moved you will have to start again.
5. Prepare a cutting lubricant. Soluble oil, or failing that, any light machine oil, is fine for steel. For aluminium use white spirit or paraffin, and always drill brass dry. Some special tips for drilling brass are included later. A small plastic 'squeezy' bottle, or a little jar with a brush, is fine for cutting lubricants.
6. Select a speed of about 300 r.p.m. if you have a choice, chuck a $\frac{1}{4}$in drill, and start to drill the hole. Try to observe that the point enters the punch dot cleanly and does not wander about as it goes in.
7. As soon as the point has entered the work, squirt on some of your lubricant and continue to drill with firm but gentle pressure. If you slacken the pressure now and again you will break up the swarf, which is a good safety point. Withdraw the drill completely now and again, and squirt in more lubricant. Continue until you have gone right through the work.
8. Now drill through with a $\frac{3}{8}$in drill. When you change drills, remember that

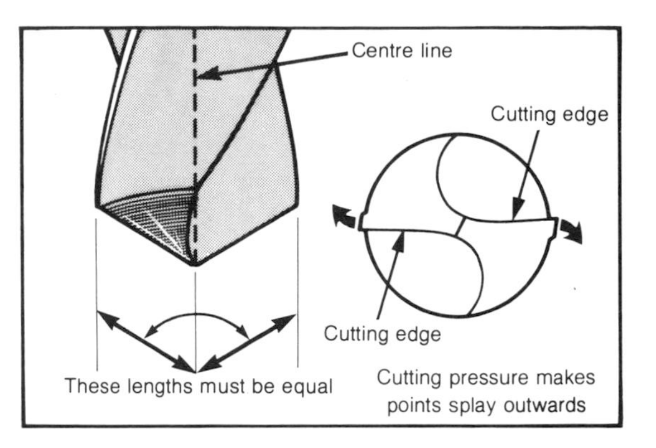

This is how even a well-ground drill will make a hole greater than its nominal diameter. Under pressure, the tips flex outwards.

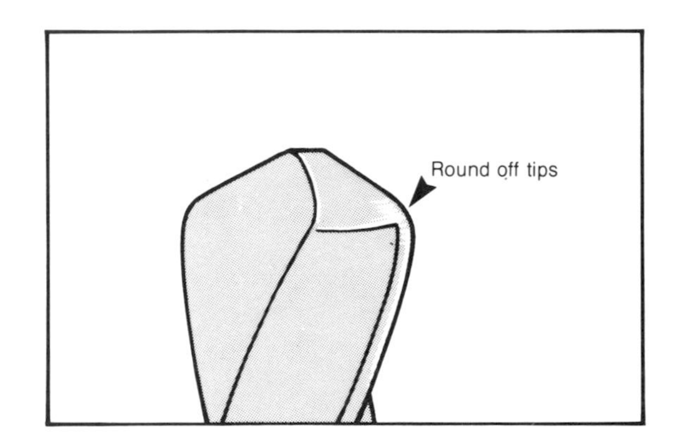

Drills can be made to cut 'tight' holes by grinding a slight radius on the corners of the cutting edges.

the points may be hot. If the larger drill chatters as it goes in, reduce the speed if you can. If you cannot, you will have to go in easier stages – for example, $^{5}/_{16}$in first, then $^{3}/_{8}$in.

9. Using ever bigger drills in easy stages, open the hole out to $^{31}/_{64}$in or 12·4mm, depending on the drills you have in your selection.

10. This last cut is going to be the critical one, so go about it with some care. Always make sure that your final drill (in this case $^{1}/_{2}$in) is properly ground and sharp. If the dimensions of the hole are very critical, take a little hand-held sharpening stone and polish a slight radius on the corners of the drill's cutting edges. Select minimum speed, drown the hole in lubricant, and cut through on a very slow feed.

11. Once through, do not stop the motor. Keep it rolling, pour down more lubricant, and withdraw the drill almost as slowly as it went in.

A hole drilled in this way will be as near perfectly accurate as you can get without reaming. Practice, and a developing 'feel' for both the machine and the material will make perfect. Count yourself amongst the experts when the only way you can get a true half-inch bar to go through your half-inch hole is with a hammer.

DIFFICULT METALS

Some materials are, of course, more difficult to drill than others. Ordinary mild steel is about the easiest and aluminium alloys work nicely, too. Pure aluminium is rather soft and tends to cling, and it requires care and plenty of lubricant, while some stainless steels are so hard that you can hardly penetrate them. With stainless, beware of loud squeaking noises and blue swarf which indicate serious overheating. When working right on the limit with this material, you may find that, once started, you have to drill right through the metal at one go without lifting off. If the drill point skids a turn or two without cutting, it may work-harden the material so much that it is impossible to continue. Fortunately you do not often encounter materials as hard as this in a home workshop, but if you must use them either buy special drills and lubricants, or expect a few breakages.

Brass can be surprisingly difficult to drill, not because of its hardness but due to its rather 'snatchy' quality when cut with drills ground to conventional angles. If you plan a major project with a lot of brass drilling to do, it will pay you to grind some special brass-cutting points on your drills, as shown below. Needless to say, these must be used for brass only until the tips have been reground to conventional profiles.

Big holes (those over $^{5}/_{8}$in or 16mm) are best cut with taper-shank drills that enter, without a chuck, straight into the

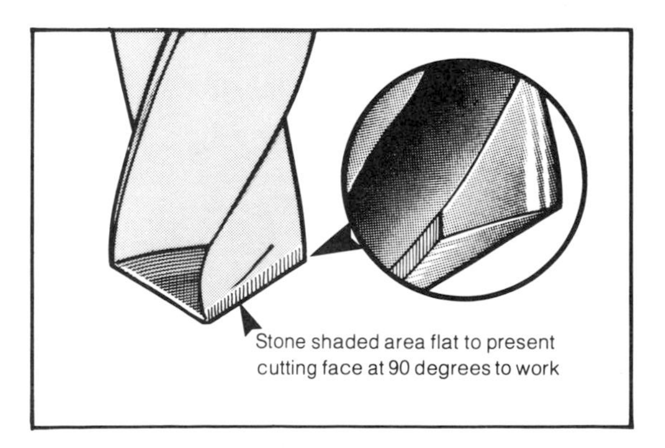

A drill ground like this will not 'snatch' in brass.

female taper on the machine. You can, however, get 'blacksmith drills' in sizes over ½in. These have half-inch parallel shanks and therefore fit conventional chucks. As my drilling machine will not accept taper shanks, I do all my big-hole drilling on the lathe, using the milling attachment. However, as a drilling machine is usually the first machine tool bought when setting up a workshop, you may not have that alternative.

PILOT HOLES

Even when drilling rough clearance holes, do not expect to be able to drill a large hole at one go. The definition of 'large' will vary with the size and power of the machine: a very light machine may not be happy forcing a drill of over ¼in straight into the work, while a bigger machine may be happy with ⅜in or even larger.

The secret is, when in doubt, to drill a pilot hole which can be any diameter that your machine will comfortably handle. As a general rule with my machine I tend to drill a pilot for anything over 5/16in. That is erring on the safe side by a good margin, but the avoidance of high pressures extends the life of the machine and means that even rough holes remain somewhere near their nominal diameter.

CLAMPING

Earlier I touched on safety points and mentioned the desirability of fitting a chuck guard to save you getting cut by flying ends of sharp swarf. The most important safety point on a drilling machine, however, is that the work should always be clamped to the table before drilling commences.

In industry, the drilling machine is about the simplest machine tool in use, and it also has the reputation of causing more accidents than any other machine. The reason is that, because of its simplicity, people treat it with contempt. So, for your own safety, never hold any metal object by hand when you drill it.

Clamping methods vary. Every drilling machine table has slots through which bolts can be passed, and it is a simple matter to make up a variety of clamps from bits of scrap angle iron and strip. Another good acquisition is a machine vice, and the one to go for is the biggest one that will comfortably fit on the table. In all engineering operations, large, rigid lumps of cast iron beat little flimsy bits every time.

The trickiest things to hold on machine tables are big pieces of thin plate, and by the perverse nature of things, thin plate is the most dangerous material to drill because the drill bit invariably snatches as it breaks through. To hold plate, carpenters' G-clamps can be pressed into service, and for a very tricky job do not hesitate to drill and tap a small bolt hole in the machine table itself. It may sound like sacrilege, but by my book tools are meant to be used for solving problems. If you are spending a few pounds on materials to make a component that would cost several hundred pounds to buy, you should not worry about making a couple of ¼in holes in the machine table, particularly as you may be able to use them again for another job some time. However, such action is a last resort, and there are limits: a machine table that ends up looking like a piece of Swiss cheese is one such limit!

8 The Metalworking Lathe

No one knows who invented the lathe, but an Industrial Revolution engineer called Henry Maudslay was the man who made it the highly adaptable machine tool it is today. In an era when steam engine cylinders were bored to the nearest sixteenth of an inch on primitive machinery, dear old Henry laid the foundations that allow even amateurs like you and me to get down among the ten-thousandths of inches - or thousandths of millimetres if you prefer.

In doing this important work he laid down the principles that will serve you well when you choose a modern lathe. He said that no machine could function accurately unless it was of rigid construction, possessed accurate plane surfaces,

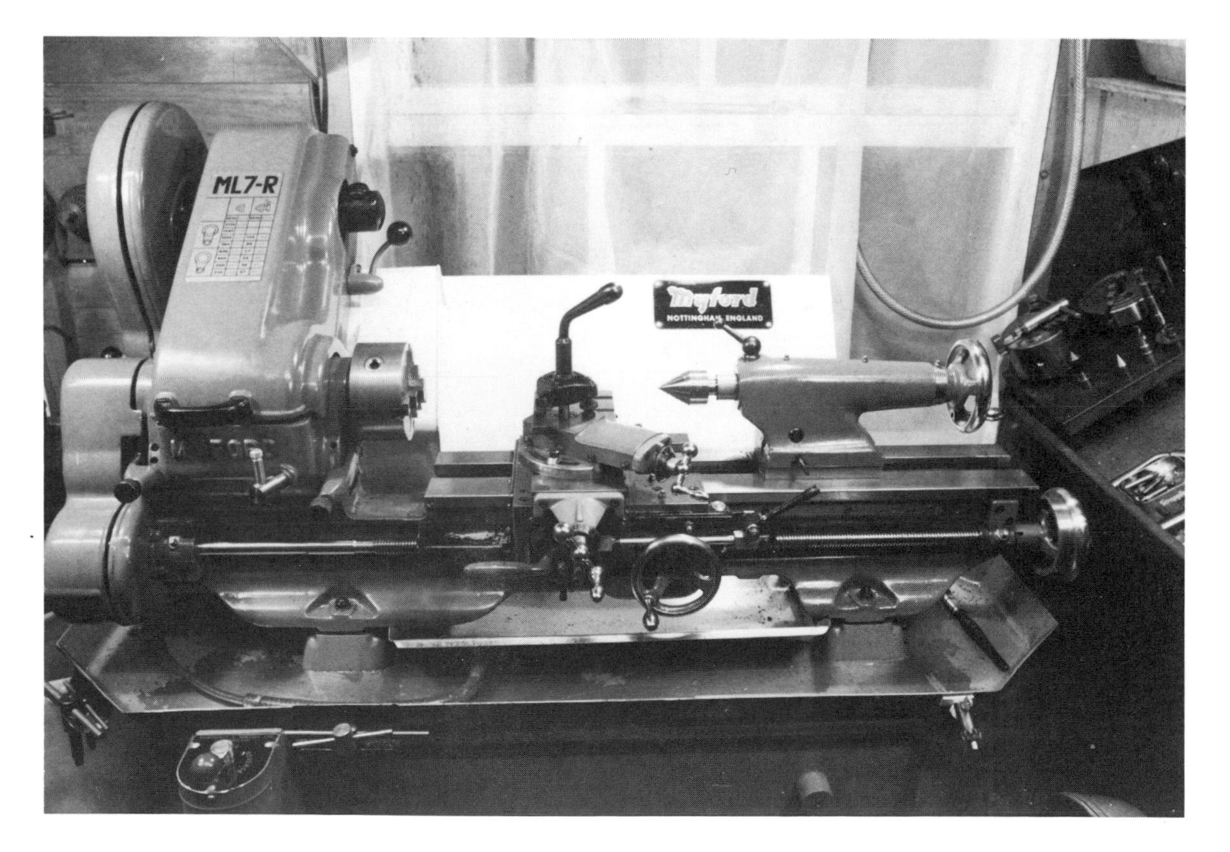

One of my problems is that I cannot let anything alone, and this Myford ML7R shows signs of a few modifications. Nevertheless, it is still typical of the sort of lathe you may consider for your own workshop.

and was regulated by accurate screw threads. Even when choosing a lathe in the 1990s, you cannot expect better than a machine that has those basic qualities, even though there may be some modern refinements that Henry did not get round to developing.

In very simple terms, the lathe is no more than an accurate means of applying a tool to a rotating workpiece, although on occasions in an amateur's workshop the lathe doubles as both milling machine and jig-borer, and applies a rotating tool to a fixed workpiece. This gives the lie to the notion that lathes are for producing items of basically cylindrical form. They are not – lathes will machine forms of almost any section you wish.

LOOKING AT THE LATHE

When you first look at a metalworking lathe you get the impression of a complex machine, bristling with knobs, levers and control wheels. Do not worry – its operation is a lot easier than learning to drive a car.

Look at it this way – when you drive a car you have to master the simultaneous operation of three pedals, a profusion of levers and a steering wheel. While performing this feat of co-ordination you have to navigate through the traffic, know what is going on behind you, keep an eye out for suicidal pedestrians, memorise the Highway Code, and observe the finer points of legislation that runs to thousands of written pages. You can learn the controls on the lathe one at a time, and if something confuses you, simply hit the stop button. No one is going to bother you if it takes half an hour to work out the next move – just try that next time you take the car out in traffic!

The best way to learn the lathe is with the machine in front of you and your hands on the controls.

LEARNING THE FEATURES

Walk up to the machine, and first look for the electrical stop switch. This will be somewhere in the region of your left hand, although on a big machine there may be further remote stop switches placed at strategic points. If your first encounter with the lathe is in a noisy workshop, you may not hear the motor running, so press the stop button just to make sure.

A large machine may be fitted with a clutch, too. If it is, the lever will also be within easy reach of your left hand as you face the machine. Find it, and make sure that it is in the 'disengaged' position.

These two moves are a good safety habit to acquire, rather like always checking that a gun is unloaded when you pick it up. With the switch off and clutch out, you can fiddle with the controls to your heart's content without fear of hurting yourself.

Now you can look at the machine's main features. They are labelled opposite, so spend a few minutes comparing the diagram with what you see before you. Unless you have a lathe identical to the one illustrated, there will be some differences and there may be more or fewer features than are shown here, but the basic principles by which the machine works and is controlled will be pretty much the same as are shown. Now switch on the spotlight, and be prepared to get your hands a little oily.

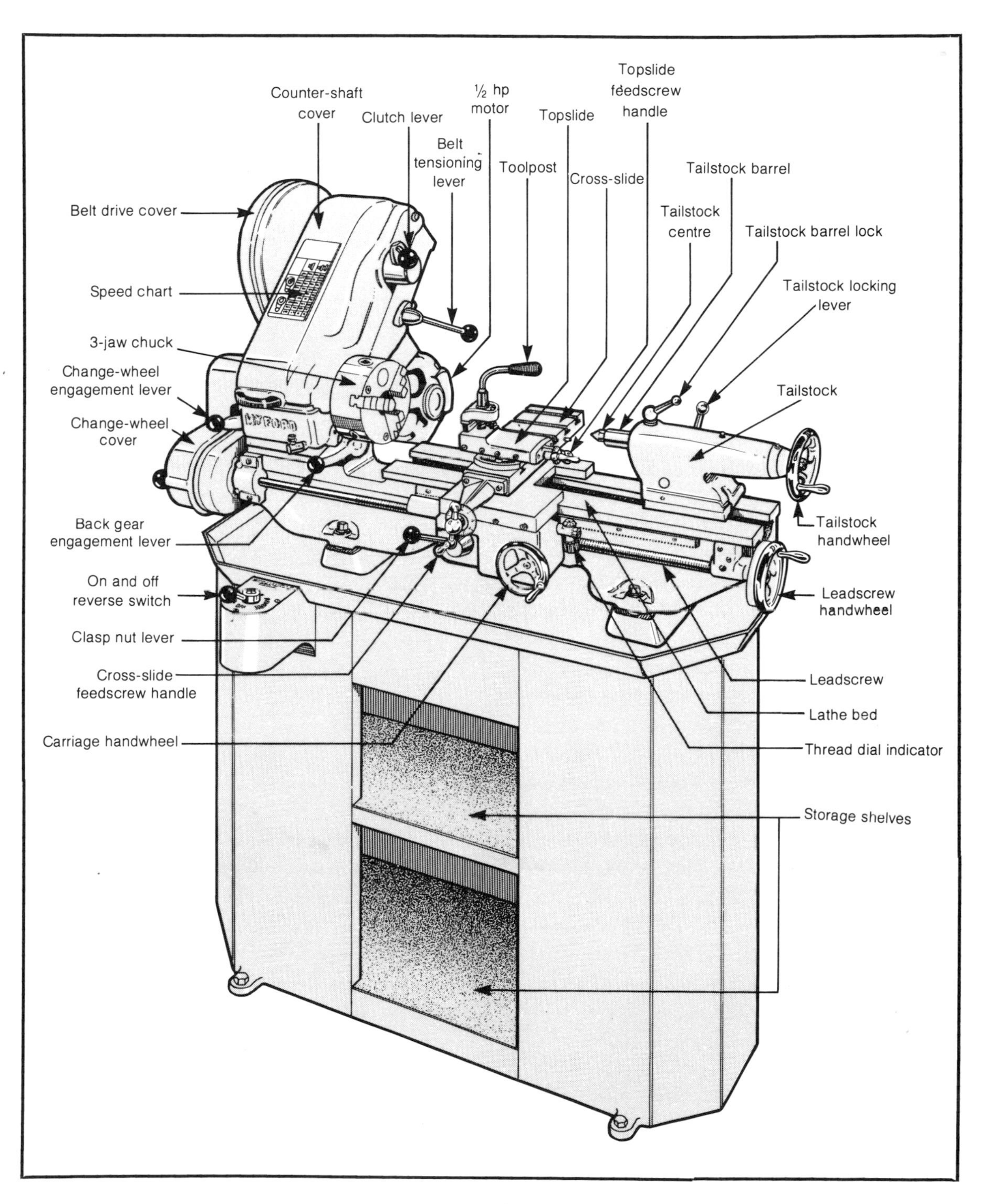

The general features of the metalworking lathe. The diagram is based on my Myford ML7R, although on other machines in this class there are small variations in the way the features are arranged.

Unlock the tailstock, and slide it down to the far right-hand end of the bed, out of the way. Take hold of the apron handwheel, and you will find that if you turn it clockwise, the carriage will travel to the right, while if you turn it anti-clockwise the carriage moves to the left. Practise with this control for a few minutes, and try to make the carriage move as slowly and smoothly as possible, without stops or jerks, for a distance of 3 or 4in (8 or 10cm). To do this you will almost certainly need to have both hands on the wheel. This sort of movement is what is necessary to turn smooth and accurate surfaces when you do not want to engage automatic feed.

Before leaving the subject of the apron handwheel, crank the carriage right up to the left-hand end of the bed and try to stop it as close as possible to the chuck without actually hitting it. When you have done that, rotate the chuck by hand to make sure that there is actual clearance. Try this once or twice and get used to stopping within about 0·25in (6mm) of the chuck jaws. If you actually hit the chuck while the machine is rotating, there will be a big bang and some damage. Make a strong mental note that, when you are working, the safe distance between the carriage and the chuck will vary, depending on the type of tool you are using and the position in which the top and cross slides are set.

Now return the carriage to the centre of the machine, and look at the cross-slide handwheel. It will have a collar graduated in either thousandths of an inch on an imperially calibrated machine, or increments of 0·02mm on a metric machine. Turn the wheel to and fro and get the 'feel' of it. You will notice that when you change direction there is a very small

This is the graduated collar on the cross-slide feedscrew of an imperial lathe. Each segment represents 0·001in.

'dead' segment in which the handwheel moves but the slide does not. This is called 'backlash' – another phrase for your mental notebook. In simple turning it will not have much significance, but you must remember it when you get down to some more advanced work.

Now set yourself a little exercise with the cross-slide. Turn it and stop it at random, then advance it forward exactly 0·01in on an imperial machine, or 0·2mm on a metric machine. Some machines make this sort of exercise easy because the graduated collars can be moved to zero without moving the wheel. Some cannot, so you will have to do a simple sum.

Look at the topslide, and you will see that it works in the same way as the cross-slide but on a different axis. If you look at the base of the topslide, you will find some provision for changing the angle of this axis so that short tapers can be turned. Chances are it will be held at the chosen angle by two nuts, so find a spanner that fits them exactly and experiment with the range of adjustment. Leave the topslide securely locked in position.

Those are the lathe's basic controls. Operating the lathe will be discussed in Chapter 9, but first you should get to know some of the machine's features.

THE HEADSTOCK

The headstock is the big iron casting on the left-hand end of the lathe as you stand in front of it, and it carries the spindle, or mandrel, in strong bearings. The electric motor will be mounted either behind it or underneath it.

There will be provision for driving the spindle through the range of speeds. On a big machine you will find a gearbox built into the headstock, usually with two or more control levers on the top or side. Somewhere you should also find a plate engraved with the speeds obtained by the various lever positions. The actual speeds in terms of revolutions per minute will usually be spread at more or less even intervals from a maximum of about 2,000 to a minimum of about 25 or 30, but for most of your turning you will be using the middle range from about 600 down to 200. With the motor switched off you can safely experiment with the lever positions.

Gearing on the small lathe is achieved by belts. The lathe spindle is at the bottom of the picture, while the countershaft is at the top. There are four speed options here, and another two between the motor and the counter-shaft. Gear cluster at lower right gives a special set of low ratios, giving 16 speeds in all. In practice, only 14 options are used.

On a more simple lathe, the speeds will be controlled by belts. The motor will drive a counter-shaft, and the counter-shaft will drive the spindle. If this is the case, open the covers or doors that give access to the belts, and also look for the belt-tensioning lever which will usually operate on the counter-shaft by a cam arrangement. Push the lever into the 'slack belt' position, and see how the belts are changed from one set of pulley wheels to the next.

Speed Change Potential

Very typical lathes of this type are the Myford 7 series, which have a very well-deserved reputation in amateur workshops as well as training establishments and some light industrial applications. With the exception of a few with lever-operated speed-change mechanisms they work like this:

1. There are two different sized pulleys on the motor shaft, and two on the left-hand end of the counter-shaft. One pair of pulleys gives direct drive so the counter-shaft runs at motor speed, while the other pair gives a reduction of about 3·5 to 1.
2. In the centre of the counter-shaft is a cone of four pulleys, running parallel to a similar, but reversed cone on the spindle. This arrangement provides four alternative speeds.
3. The spindle itself is provided with what is known as 'back gear' mechanism which can be engaged, providing an optional reduction on all ratios of approximately 7·8 to 1.

How many different speeds are there? Think of it as a series of three gearboxes, mounted one behind the other. There are two speeds in the first box (the motor/counter-shaft belt), four in the second box (the counter-shaft/spindle belt), and two in the back gear. Multiply them together to get the number of possible ratios, and the answer is 16. In fact, the two very top ratios on the back gear are virtually duplicates of speeds available without its use, so the number of practical speeds is 14.

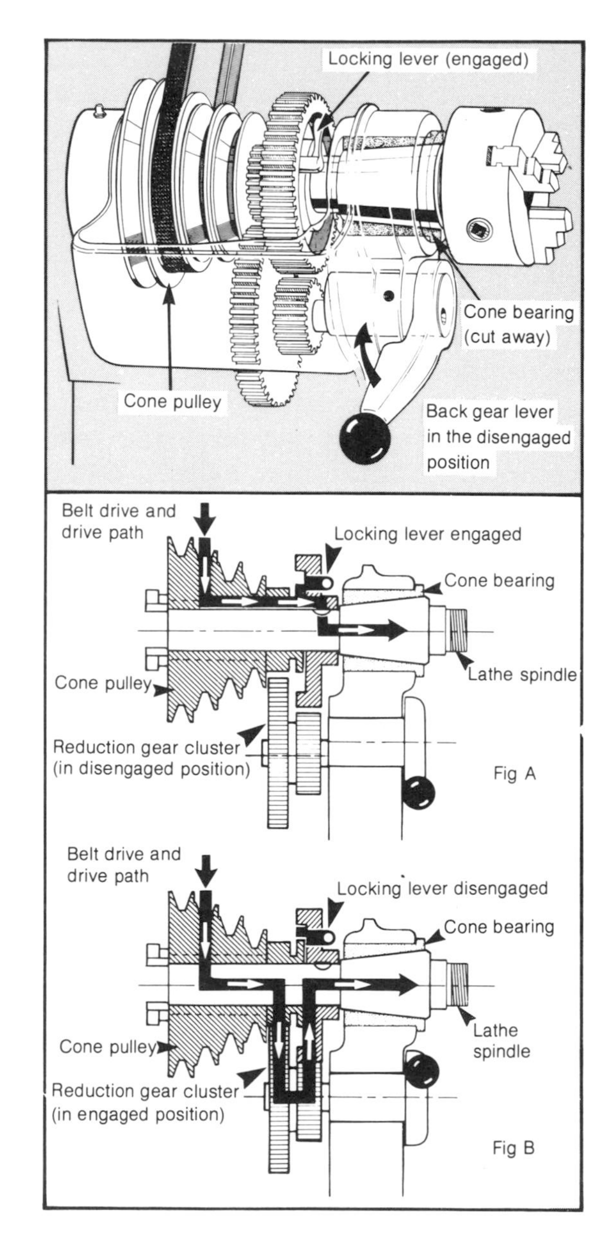

This is how the back gear works. Again the diagram is based on the Myford Series 7 system, but others are similar. In Fig A the drive is taken straight from the cone pulley to the spindle, while in Fig B, with the mechanism engaged, drive goes from the cone pulley, through the back gear, and then to the spindle.

SPINDLE

The spindle has some features that may not be immediately apparent. The best way of examining it is first to remove the chuck, if one is fitted, so if it is not your lathe, get permission from the owner first.

On almost all small and on many medium-sized lathes the chuck is attached by a screw thread to the spindle end. To unscrew this thread you will need to lock the spindle, and some lathes have a bolt that engages in a hole just for this purpose. If there is not one, just put the lathe in the very lowest gear available. Before you go any further, find a piece of scrap wooden board and place it over the bed beneath the chuck, so that if you drop the chuck you will not damage the bed.

It is very unlikely that the chuck will come off with only hand pressure, so you will need a bit of scrap steel bar or rod about 0·5in (13mm) across and up to 24in (60cm) long. Get the chuck key and clamp the bar across the jaws, and use the long end as a lever. If the chuck does not come free with a gentle tug, try banging the end of the bar with the side of your clenched fist. If it is really stuck tight you can tap the bar with a big, soft hammer. Whatever you do, do not lever the chuck off with the key.

Once the chuck is free you can remove the bar and screw it all the way off by hand. Once it comes clear of the spindle nose, do remember that a big chuck will be very heavy.

Now the spindle is bare you will see that it is hollow, with a taper in the front end. Morse-series tapers are used in most British lathes, and many imported ones too, and the Myford 7 has a No 2 Morse taper. This is about 0·625in (a fraction under 16mm) in diameter at its thin end. The higher the Morse number, the bigger the diameter. This taper can be used to hold a centre, or a variety of milling and drilling tools, while the tubular nature of the spindle allows long lengths of bar to pass right through when working with chucks or collets.

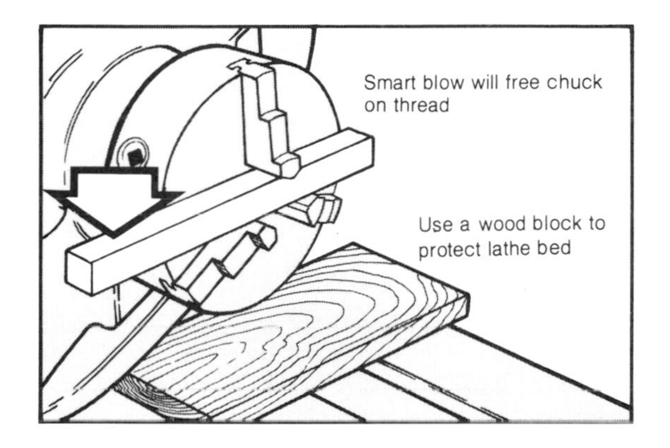

This is the best way of removing a screwed-on chuck. Do not lever it off with the key.

CHANGE WHEELS AND LEADSCREW

The leadscrew is the long threaded rod that runs parallel to the bed, under the apron. On a sophisticated lathe, you will find yet another gearbox at its left-hand end, for the purpose of this screw is to drive the carriage along the ways at a speed directly proportional to the speed of spindle revolutions. In this way the machine can be used to cut accurate screw threads or – when very low ratios are engaged – to achieve high standards of finish. For these very low ratios some lathes have a separate feed rod which runs parallel to the leadscrew and below it, its engagement and speed range being controlled with yet more levers.

However, on a simple lathe there is no feed rod and no front-mounted gearbox. By examining the mechanism, notice how the leadscrew drive is transmitted to the carriage. You will find the engagement lever on the front of the apron, and it controls a hidden mechanism called a clasp nut. This is like a conventional nut cut in half, so that when the lever is in the 'off' position (usually up), the two halves of the nut are held apart, out of engagement with the thread on the leadscrew. Movement of the lever closes the two halves, so that the leadscrew thread engages with the nut and the carriage starts to move.

How is the leadscrew driven? To discover this, you will need to remove the cover from the extreme left-hand end of the machine. Once the cover is off (on many lathes this is simply a matter of opening a door), do not be alarmed by the profusion of gear wheels you may find – just look at the left-hand end of the spindle where it emerges from its rear bearing.

On the end of the spindle you will find a fixed gearwheel, and immediately below it there will be what is known as the tumbler gear. This gear is controlled by a lever, so move the lever and see what

The big screw is the leadscrew, while the lever controls the clasp nut mechanism, which is hidden behind the apron casting.

happens. You should find it has three positions: forward and reverse, and a neutral position in which the tumbler gears are out of mesh with the gearwheel on the spindle.

From the tumbler you can now follow the gear train down, and you may find a profusion of wheels that lead to a gear-wheel on the left-hand end of the lead-screw. Close examination will show that all of these gearwheels can be removed. Somewhere near the machine there should be a load of spare wheels of different sizes, and there should also be a chart that shows you how the wheels are arranged to achieve the full range of feeds for both screw-cutting and fine finishing.

When you have put the cover back, ensure that the tumbler lever is in the neutral position. You are now ready to look at the lathe's last major feature.

THE TAILSTOCK

Right at the beginning of this lathe examination you shunted the tailstock right up to the far end of the bed; now walk up to that end and have a look at it. You already know how its locking lever works, but what about the rest of it?

A variety of tools, or in this case a 'live' centre, can be entered into the tailstock taper.

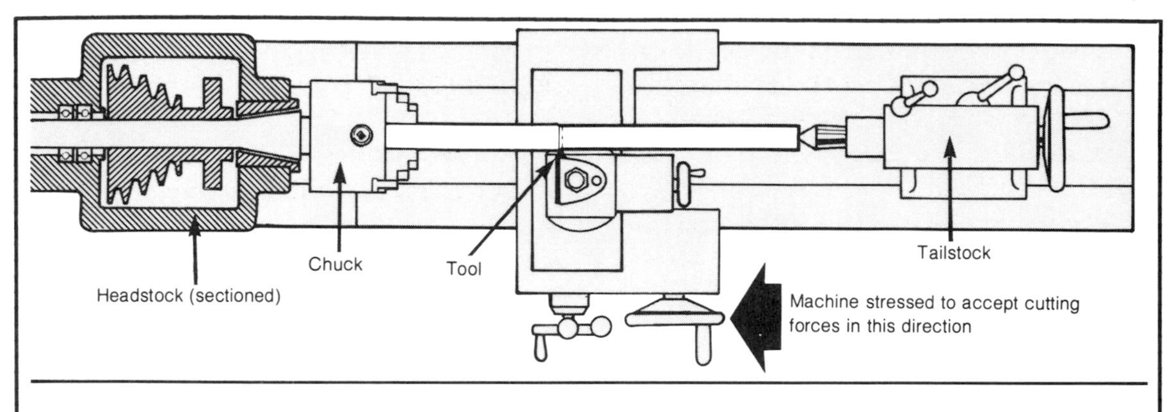

The lathe is stressed to take cuts from right to left. If the nature of the job forces you to turn from left to right, take light cuts.

GENERAL RULES FOR ALL TURNING

1. When possible, always work from the tailstock towards the headstock (in other words from right to left) as the machine is stressed for the forces generated by this direction of cut. When circumstances force you to work in the other direction, take shallow cuts at fine feed rates.

2. Before starting work, always be sure in your own mind of what you want to do and how you are to achieve it. Mistakes frequently cannot be rectified.

3. Always carry out pre-work checks on the machine, and any recommended lubrication schedule, before beginning.

4. Observe basic safety rules at all times. In situations for which there are no rules, apply the best safety rule of all - common sense. If something looks dangerous, the chances are it is.

5. A clean machine and a tidy working environment create an atmosphere conducive to precision work. Heaps of swarf crunching underfoot and general grime and untidiness are recipes for danger and sloppy work.

6. If you work on a technical school or evening institute machine, remember that you are responsible for the safety of everyone present, including yourself. Always report any accident, however slight, and always report any damage to the machine or its tools. The person using the machine after you has the right to expect cleanliness, accuracy, and good tooling.

7. If the machine sounds unhappy, something must be wrong. Stop immediately, check tool sharpness and height, and also that the piece of metal you are trying to work is not too hard for the machine or the tool. Ragged, blue swarf and a squealing noise spell trouble.

8. Do not overload the machine by taking too heavy a cut, or working at too high a speed. Feed rates, speeds, and depths of cut for various metals that you may find written in books or on data charts may be intended for heavy industrial machinery. Home workshop machines and tooling are not always strong enough for these work rates. Your own eyes and ears, plus experience, are the best guides.

Firstly, its purpose is to hold a centre, to support the tail-end of work longer than a few inches. Like the spindle, the barrel is hollow and made to accept a taper, so that it will hold a centre, or a drill chuck, or almost any tool that has a corresponding male taper. The barrel can be moved in and out of the casting by the handwheel at the far right-hand end, and usually whatever tool is held in the taper is ejected just before the barrel reaches its fully retracted position. If there is not an ejector, chucks and centres are removed by poking a bit of soft steel bar through from the back. Finally, you will find that the barrel can be locked in any desired position by means of a lever usually positioned on the top or side of the tailstock casting.

SPECIFICATION AND SAFETY

There is an enormous variety of small- and medium-sized lathes about, and it is not possible to list and describe the features of all of them. Some mechanisms may work on slightly different principles to those listed here, so if there is confusion either consult the machine's instruction book, or ask someone who is familiar with its operation. On commercial premises or in training establishments lathes will also be fitted with some safety features not mentioned here. In evening classes or training rooms it may be against the rules for students to examine or operate machine tools without qualified supervision. The golden rule is always to ask first, and remember that primary rule of lathe safety: *electrical switch to 'off' and clutch (if fitted) disengaged before experimenting with the controls.*

9 Simple Lathe Work

Before operating the lathe, one vital aspect of its workings must be considered: the tool, and the way it is mounted to the topslide.

LATHE TOOLS

Lathe tools are made from a wide variety of substances, ranging from hardened and tempered high-carbon steel to those with mild-steel shanks tipped with tungsten carbide, stellite, or very hard modern ceramic substances. In home workshop situations, however, we can generally ignore these extreme ends of the tool scale and concentrate on those ground from square-section high-speed steel.

Eventually you will need profiles like all of those shown opposite, above, but for a first exercise I suggest one like that shown opposite, below. The form can be ground into the end of any piece of HSS Square bar material down to about 0·25in square, or into a piece of even smaller section to be held in an Armstrong-type toolholder.

Now take the tool to the machine and fit it. The fitting will be made into a component on top of the topslide known as the toolpost, of which there are several different types. The important thing is that the tool must be presented to the work dead on centre height, so let us look at the ways in which this can be achieved.

You may be fortunate enough to have a tool clamp of adjustable height, but the chances are you will not, so some packing material will have to be introduced under the tool. For this you will need some little strips of sheet metal about as wide as the tool and as long as its contact surface with the bottom of the tool clamp. About 0·375 × 2·25in (10 × 55mm) is usually sufficient. Thicknesses in a range of 0·005in up to about 0·125in (0·15 to 3mm) are all useful and they can be made from a variety of materials. If you attack a beer can with a pair of tinsnips you can make a lot that are about 0·006in thick, while paint tins yield thicker ones. Keep an eye out for scrap steel or brass strip or plate for making really thick ones.

A variety of these strips can be packed under the tool to bring it up to height, but how do you know when you have got there? Some turners make themselves centre-height gauges that measure the distance between the tool tip and the face of the cross-slide, but the quick way is to swing the topslide into such a position that tool height can be compared visually with the point of a centre in the spindle or tailstock.

Personal Safety

Before you take your tool to the lathe, or to the grinder if it needs sharpening, it is wise to perform a few personal checks. If you are wearing a tie, take it off. Button up your cuffs if they are loose, and remove or secure anything that could dangle into rotating machinery. If you wear a ring, take that off too – I once saw a man nearly lose a finger because he wore his wedding ring in a machine shop.

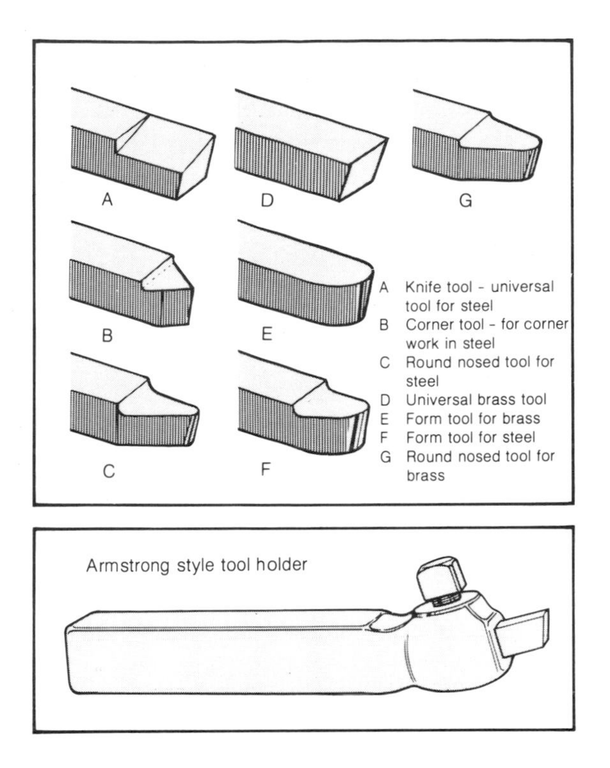

All of the tool forms in the top diagram can be ground from lengths of square-section high-speed steel. The Armstrong-type tool holder (below) allows use to be made of smaller (and cheaper) pieces of tool steel. Brass tools have flat tops while raked profiles for steel generally suit aluminium, too.

Final Preparations

Accepting that the tool is sharp, go to the machine and set the topslide so that it lies parallel to the bed. Clamp the tool so that it too lies parallel to the bed, ensuring that overhang is kept within sensible limits. The shorter the overhang the better your work will be, because the tool will be more resistant to vibration or 'chatter'.

Now's the time to do the pre-work checks on the machine. Remember: *electrical switch off, clutch out*. Make sure the leadscrew and feed rod drives are disconnected, and that a three-jaw self-centring chuck is fitted and screwed up tight to the spindle nose. Next, choose a spindle speed of no more than 400 r.p.m., and go through the machine's pre-work lubrication routine if there is one.

Now put the workpiece in the chuck so that there is about 1in (25mm) protruding from the jaws. Tighten the chuck and *remove the key*. If you start up with the key in, it will fly out and hit you or someone else like a bullet.

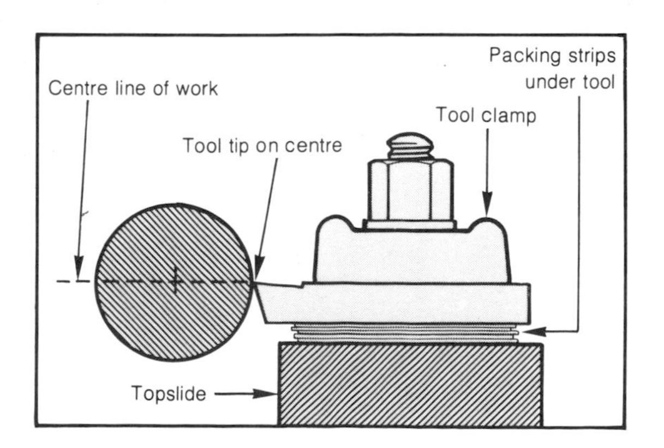

The tool must be presented at the centre height of the work. Achieve this by placing metal packing strips under the tool.

First Cut

You are now ready to set up for a first cut, which will be across the face of the work from the periphery to the centre. All but the very lightest of machines will handle a cut of 0·01in or 0·25mm with ease, so here is how to proceed.

Wind the topslide to about the mid-point of its travel and stop on zero. Wind in the cross-slide until the tool tip is pointing directly at the furthest protruding point of the work (your workpiece may not have been sawn off cleanly), then bring the carriage up until the tool tip just touches the work. At this point you can engage the carriage lock if there is one.

Next, back off the topslide handwheel for about a quarter of a turn, and unwind the cross-slide handwheel until the tool tip lies outside the circumference of the work. Then turn the topslide handwheel back to your original zero, plus 0·01in or 0·25mm.

If the machine has any guards, put them in position now, then press the start button. In a lathe without a clutch, the chuck will start to spin; if it has a clutch, engage it after the motor has started.

With the chuck spinning, start to turn the cross-slide handwheel slowly clockwise, without pauses if you can. You may find it best to use two hands. As the tool engages the work you will see the first swarf coming off. If the end of the bar has been rough sawn it might sound a little 'grumbly', and the swarf will come off in short curly pieces. Keep the tool traversing in towards the centre of the work, and stop when it is just on centre. If the tool is running low you will see a small pimple left at the centre, while if it is running high the handwheel will stiffen as the centre is approached. If it does stiffen, do not force it. Switch the machine off and remove some packing from under the tool. If you get a pimple indicating a low

Setting up for a first facing cut. If the tool tip is advanced so as just to touch the highest point of the sawn face, it can be wound away from the work by turning the cross-slide handwheel.

The tool has now been advanced 0·01in towards the chuck, and the first cut is being taken.

tool, you need to add a sliver of packing that is just half the thickness of the pimple.

Assuming that all is well, switch the machine off and examine the face of the work. If it has a flat finish then you can proceed to the next stage. If there are still some saw marks or irregularities, take off another 0·01in or 0·25mm. A little bright ring showing in the work is a natural phenomenon and nothing to worry about. Circular score marks could indicate a blunt or chipped tool, or the fact that you have wound the cross-slide too fast or in an irregular manner.

That first cut, or series of cuts, are known as 'roughing' cuts. In other words, the material still has a slightly rough finish, and it is a little oversize. To improve the finish, take a last cut of only 0·003in or 0·06mm, turning the cross-slide handwheel very slowly indeed but without actually stopping.

With the end of the work faced to your satisfaction, you can then think about removing material from its circumference. So switch off, unclamp the tool, and reclamp it in a position where it is at a right angle to the bed and parallel with the cross-slide. Also remember to disengage the carriage lock if it was used in the facing operation.

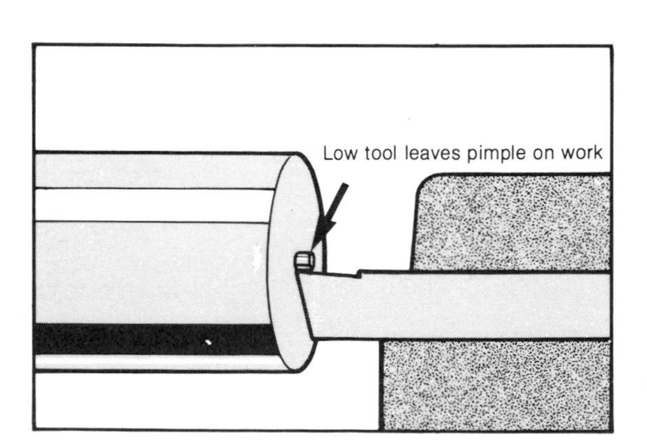

A tool set too low will leave a pimple on the end of the work.

Cuts Close to the Chuck

The next cut you make will take you very close to the chuck jaws, so it is vital that you check for clearances before you proceed. Wind the tool in until it nearly touches the circumference of the work, then traverse the carriage to the left until there is about a 0·25in (6mm) clearance between any point on the tool or topslide and the chuck jaws. Just to be sure, rotate the chuck by hand, and look and listen carefully. As you gain experience you will get the knack of working very close indeed to the rotating chuck, but 0·25in or 6mm is quite close enough until you get some machine time under your belt.

Now you must note the point where the carriage stops to achieve this clearance. Some lathes have adjustable stops that can be engaged to prevent enthusiastic people from moving the carriage into the chuck, but the majority do not have

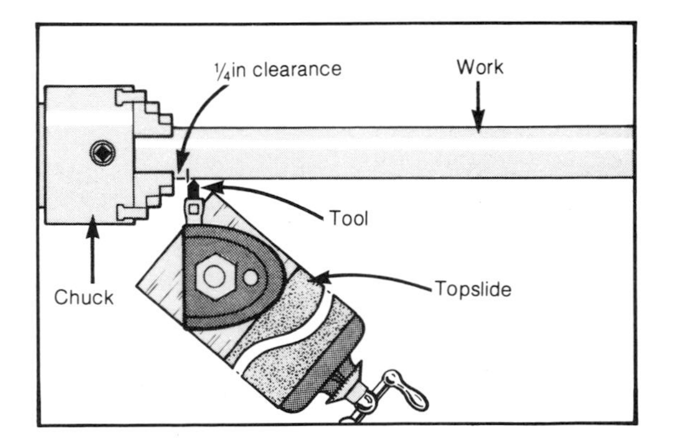

Before you take a cut along the length of the work, be sure that there are sufficient clearances at the chuck end. To make absolutely sure that nothing fouls, you can advance the tool into position and turn the chuck by hand.

such a feature. Until you get used to your machine you can mark the work opposite the tool tip with coloured pencil, and you should be able to see the mark when the work is rotating.

Set the machine up for the cut using the same principles as you used for the first facing cut. This time, however, wind the cross-slide in until the tool just touches the work, and note the reading on the cross-slide collar or return the collar to zero if it is of the adjustable type. Then back off, wind the carriage to the right until the tool is clear of the work, and return the cross-slide handwheel to your original reading plus 0·01in or 0·25mm.

Now, with the chuck rotating, turn the carriage handwheel very slowly and carefully to the left. The swarf should come off fine and curly, but do not be surprised if the depth of the first cut does not appear to be of even thickness. *Very* few three-jaw self-centring chucks run dead on centre; *see* Chapter 11 for the problems this causes and their remedies. Stop when you get to your mark or your memorised position, and switch off. You can now withdraw the tool a fraction so that it does not score the work, and return the carriage to the right before setting up to take a 0·003in or 0·06mm finishing cut.

If you now measure the diameter of the work with a micrometer you may find that you have taken off twice as much as you thought you had. If you started off with an inch bar, the measurement will now be somewhere around 0·974in. If it was a 25mm bar in a metric machine it will be in the region of 24·38mm. The reason is that the calibrations on your machine refer to the radius of the work, not its circumference. One unit of measurement cut from the radius equals two off the circumference, so a 0·01in cut takes 0·02in off the job.

You can now use your new-found knowledge to reduce your inch bar to a diameter of 0·875in, or your 25mm metric bar to 22mm. Take the work down in increments of no more than 0·01in or 0·25mm, checking with the micrometer after every cut. Try to work things so that the last cut is a fine one of no more than 0·003in or 0·06mm. If, on the first effort, you are right within 0·001in or 0·025mm you have done very well indeed.

TAILSTOCK CENTRE

Any work that protrudes more than about 2in (50mm) from the chuck needs supporting by the tailstock centre. This avoids unnecessary strain on the machine and helps you to produce truly parallel work that is unspoiled by vibration of the work or the tool.

Typical Job

A typical job for which the tailstock must be used might be producing a 6in × 0·5in parallel-sided pin from a length of 0·625in bar stock. Those of the metric persuasion can try a 150mm × 12mm component from 15mm stock. Here is the procedure:

1. Find a piece of stock that is at least an inch (25mm) longer than the finished article, and put it in the three-jaw chuck so that only about 0·25in (6mm) protrudes. Face the end until it is clean and free from saw-marks. Then remount it in the chuck so that 6·25in (156mm) is

The end of the work is being bored with a no.4 centre drill, so that it can be located against a tailstock centre.

protruding.

2. For the next stage you are going to need a special drill bit called a Slocombe centre drill, and a no 4 ($^{5}/_{16}$in diameter) is about right for most small lathe work. You can use your centre drill in a drill chuck mounted in the tailstock, or set it into its own Morse taper arbor that will fit directly into the tailstock taper. In fact, making an arbor like this would make a very good first exercise in taper turning.

3. With the machine on about 400 r.p.m., start to run the end of the drill into the work. Take the drill in for about two-thirds of the depth of its taper, then withdraw it.

4. If you have a rotating or 'live' centre, now is the time to fit it to the tailstock taper. If you only have a plain centre, first pack the cone-shaped hole in the work with a good-quality grease with a high melting point, then introduce the centre to the hole. You get a better 'feel' for this with the machine running at slow speed; the centre must be seated just tight enough in the hole for there to be a good bearing surface in the cone, but not so tight as to cause too much friction and unwanted heat. When the tailstock pressure is just right, lock the tailstock barrel.

5. For this job you will need some cutting lubricant, because it is a long cut and you want to keep temperatures down. If the lathe has cutting lubricant equipment, set it up so that it just drips on the tool tip. If it has not, get some soluble oil in a squeezy bottle with a fine orifice, or be ready to apply it from a tin with a small paintbrush.

6. Now you can engage the lathe's feed mechanism, and for a first experiment I recommend a very fine feed because it

Preparing for the first cut, the tool is off the work to the right.

gives the best finish and more time to react if something starts to go wrong. You are looking for about 0·003in (0·05mm) feed for each revolution of the spindle.

7. Set up for taking a 0·01in (0·25mm) cut, as you did in the first exercise, beginning with the tool tip parked in the 'V'-shaped space between the end of the work and the tailstock centre. Engage no higher gear than about 600 r.p.m. on the spindle, start the chuck turning, and engage the feed with the lever on the apron.

8. As the tool engages the work, start to feed soluble oil to its tip with whatever means is available to you. If you do not have any cutting lubricant, you will just have to proceed carefully and watch for elevated temperatures.

9. With a lathe on automatic feed (or 'self act' as it is sometimes known) the temptation is to sit back, relax and watch it do the work. *Don't*: for a start, you may be partly occupied by keeping the cutting area wet with lubricant; you also need to have your left hand hovering somewhere in the region of the stop knob. In addition, if you are using a plain centre in the tailstock, you need to keep an eye on that for signs of overheating and burning. As the tool approaches the chuck, three hands and four eyes would be a distinct advantage because you need to watch all the aforementioned points, and also knock out the feed drive before the tool fouls the chuck jaws.

10. When doing this type of turning, check the tailstock after every cut, because as the work warms up it will expand and increase the pressure. When using a plain centre, withdraw it and repack the

Taking the first cut, the tool is being advanced towards the chuck.

hole with grease every cut or two, and feel it for excess heat after every cut. If it is hot, just stop and let it cool down before regreasing and starting again.

11. Try, again, to arrange your cuts so that the last is a very fine one, and check with the micrometer at regular intervals. When the work is down to the desired diameter, the temptation is to part it from the metal in the chuck with a parting tool. However, I am a great believer in never using the parting tool for a job that can be tackled with a hacksaw. Parting tools do impose a lot of strain on a light machine.

The best method is to remove the job from the chuck and transfer it to the vice, saw the component off the stock, then return it to the lathe for the cut end to be faced. When facing is complete, use the edge of the tool to cut a tiny chamfer on each end. In their freshly-turned state these edges will otherwise be sharp enough to cut you.

The diagram opposite shows several

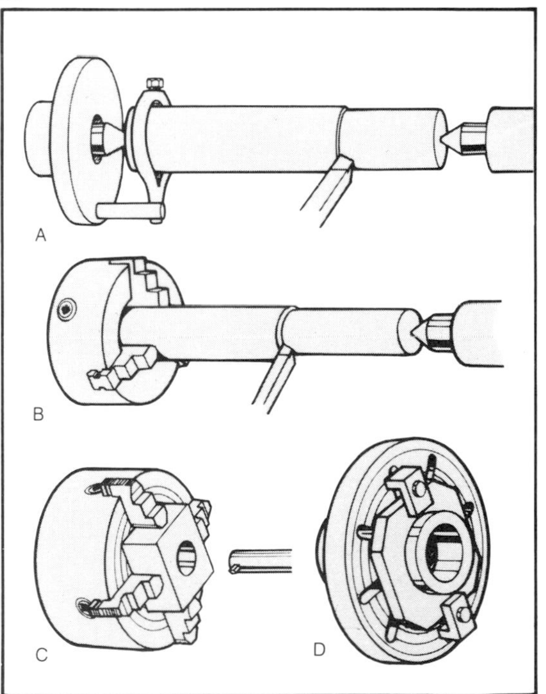

Methods for tackling simple turning jobs. The classic 'between centres' method (A), with catch-plate and driver, is not much in vogue these days. Most of your bar turning will be done as in B. C and D show two methods of holding work for accurate boring.

THE PARTING TOOL

This is a special lathe tool designed for cutting finished work from the part that is gripped in the chuck. It can have a flat end, or be ground with an angled end, so that parting is achieved without leaving a 'pip' on the work.

Parting is always performed at low speed, using plenty of the recommended cutting lubricant. To avoid binding, the tool must be advanced exactly square-on into the work, and on deep parting cuts it is often desirable to cut extra clearance for the tool, as shown opposite.

The operation of parting places a great deal of stress on the machine, and with a light lathe continued parting can cause wear in the top of the front spindle bearing. For this reason, parting is sometimes performed with the tool upside-down in a rear toolpost mounted at the back of the cross-slide. This does not relieve any stresses, but it does apply stress to a part of the machine that does not normally get very much wear.

When parting, the work should not be supported by the tailstock centre when the final breakthrough is made, otherwise there will be a seizure that may damage the tool, the work, and the machine. When heavy workpieces are being parted, make sure they fall on to an offcut of scrap wood rather than on to the lathe ways or cross-slide.

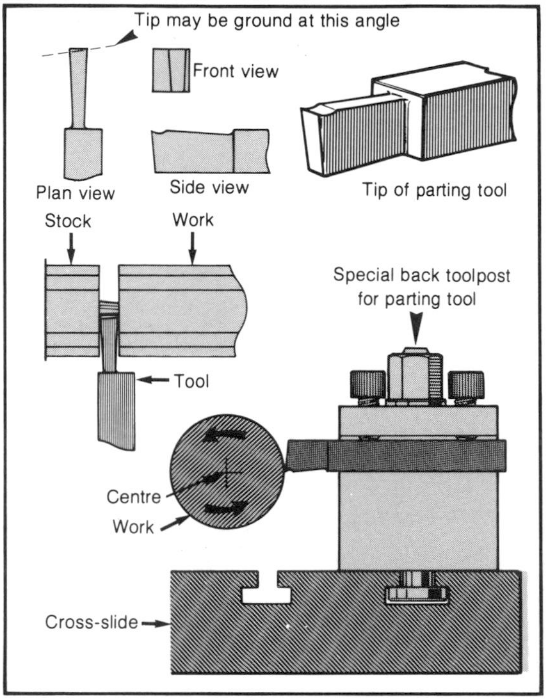

Use of the parting tool. As the tool breaks through, the work must be unsupported at the tailstock end. On light machines the special rear toolpost, with the tool mounted upside-down, is preferred by some metalworkers.

Unless it means re-chucking the work and gripping it in the area of a taper, screw thread, or knurled section, it is better to cut the work from the stock with a hacksaw and face the cut end of the work as a separate operation. Remember: most of the jams and accidents on lathes happen when parting.

lathe set ups which will serve you well for simple turning jobs.

10 Buying a Lathe

Until now you have probably been doing your lathe work on a friend's machine, or perhaps you have joined a local evening class, both to get the use of the machinery and to learn how to use it properly and safely. Let us assume that you now want to buy a lathe of your own, and you cannot afford a new one.

Used machines are to be found advertised in magazines like *Model Engineer* and *Exchange and Mart*, or you might even be lucky enough to locate one through the small ads in your local newspaper. You can also search the Yellow Pages for machine tool dealers, and keep an eye open for factory closing-down sales.

One way or another, always try to see a machine installed and running. You may

Examine the ways for deep scratches. This machine is still accurate in spite of a little horizontal marking. Two deep nicks at lower left were caused by carelessly hacksawing a workpiece held in the chuck - a practice to be avoided. Fortunately, they do not affect the machine's precision.

feel that you can take the word of a reputable dealer that a machine is in good order, but a lathe installed in the corner of a dirty garage or a run-down workshop should be viewed with suspicion. Of course, it is only human nature that anyone selling a lathe wants the best possible price for it, while anyone buying wants to hang on to as much of his brass as possible!

INSPECTING THE LATHE

When examining a lathe, first have a look at the ways. Even the best-kept of machines picks up the odd mark now and again, but if there are a lot of deep scratches and dents, be suspicious. The ways should be oily, totally free from rust, and a dull silvery-grey colour all the way along. Rust, pitting and deep scratches and marks may mean a bed regrind if the machine is to work at all accurately in the future. The same examination criteria apply to the surfaces of the topslide and cross-slides. A few marks and nicks may be nothing to worry about; a profusion of marks and scratches, and broken edges to 'T' slots, spell trouble.

Examine the spindle and tailstock tapers for scoring. Light scoring can be taken out with a reamer of the correct diameter and taper, but a taper that has been really knocked about is beyond repair. Now get the machine running at a medium speed, and leave it for ten minutes or more to let the bearings warm up. Needless to say, during this time keep an ear open for rumbles, squeaks and bangs, and if they are present try to trace them to source. A worn-out motor can generally be replaced cheaply on exchange, and something like a worn bush in a countershaft may only cost a few pounds to put right, but a wobbly spindle bearing in the headstock could mean a major rebuilding job. Worn and noisy belts are no problem; worn-out gear trains spell trouble.

After you have stopped the machine, put a dial gauge on the top of the chuck and try to lift the chuck upwards. Any movement is suspicious, but up to 0·0005in (0·012mm) is acceptable. If you get more than that, adjust the bearings according to the instruction book (if there is one) and try again. If all is still not well it may pay you to enquire about the cost of new bearings before committing yourself to purchase.

Examine headstock and tailstock tapers for marks. This headstock taper is in fine condition, despite a lot of use.

One check for the front spindle bearing is to put a 'clock' on top of the chuck, then try to lever it upwards with a length of timber. Be suspicious of a movement of more than 0•0005in.

Now try a similar check on the tailstock barrel with at least 2in extended and the lock undone.

Now you can try some tests at the tailstock end. Clamp the tailstock to the bed, put the clock on the extended barrel, and try to wobble it up and down with the barrel lock undone. Again, 0·0005in (0·012mm) is the acceptable limit on quite a hard push with 2in (50mm) of barrel showing.

The leadscrew should look clean and should be without lateral movement in its bearings. If some is present it should be possible to adjust it out. Then, with the lathe stopped, engage the leadscrew clasp nut and try to move the carriage up and down the bed. A little slackness is inevitable, but more than 0·01in (0·25mm) could indicate several things: the carriage could be running too loosely on the ways, in which case you can adjust it and try again; the clasp nut itself might be out of adjustment, because there is usually a mechanism to prevent the nut closing too tightly on the leadscrew; finally, the cause could be nothing more than a bit of dirt in the leadscrew and clasp nut threads.

For a further check, look at the backlash in the cross-slide and topslide feed-screws. There is bound to be a bit, but more than ten degrees of free movement on the handwheels could indicate worn feed nuts. On the other hand, it could be no more than the feedscrew shaft moving to and fro in its bush in the slide's end plate. This movement can usually be adjusted out.

The slides themselves should move positively without being too tight. You can check for any wobble with the clock gauge, and adjust it out, and also try to adjust out any tight spots. Do this by regulating the screws along the edge of the slide, until it moves from one limit of its travel to the other smoothly and evenly, with no hint of excessive looseness or binding.

Now run the carriage from one limit of its travel to the other, and check for tight spots. A lathe that has been used a lot for the manufacture of small components will have more wear on the ways close to the chuck, and it will run tight down at the tailstock end. When this problem becomes excessive, there is not a lot you can do short of regrinding the ways.

As a final check, if you can, do some turning. A long, rigid bit of bar is best – something where you can turn a fair length without the use of a travelling steady. Set it up in the three-jaw chuck with the back centre, and cut the full length along it on fine feed. Then do it

With the leadscrew clasp nut engaged, try to move the saddle against a 'clock'. There is bound to be movement here, but an excess may have a variety of causes.

again with a very shallow cut, and get out your micrometer.

Firstly check at each end, and do not be surprised if there is a taper. This does not matter – it can be put right by adjusting the tailstock laterally (usually) or the headstock (rarely). What you are looking for is an uneven taper that could indicate either uneven wear or a twist in the bed. If you get an uneven taper, do not buy the machine. Finally, check that the lathe has the full basic set of change-wheels.

As far as price is concerned, I can give you very little help. Not only do we live in inflationary times, but machine tool values vary so much. A well-used current model that has been looked after by a meticulous amateur may fetch as much as its current new price less about 20 per cent. A machine that has had a hard life in a factory may be worth little more than its weight in scrap iron, yet if it was built to good standards it might be worth buying if spares are still available.

Accessories tend to add quite considerably to the value of a machine. The basic set should include faceplate and catchplate, tailstock chuck, a pair of centres (preferably one soft and one hard), and any unusual tools necessary for the basic maintenance of the machine. Useful extras (roughly in order of importance) include independent-jaw four-jaw chuck, fixed and travelling steadies, vertical slide, tailstock die holder, tailstock half-centre, and assorted tooling.

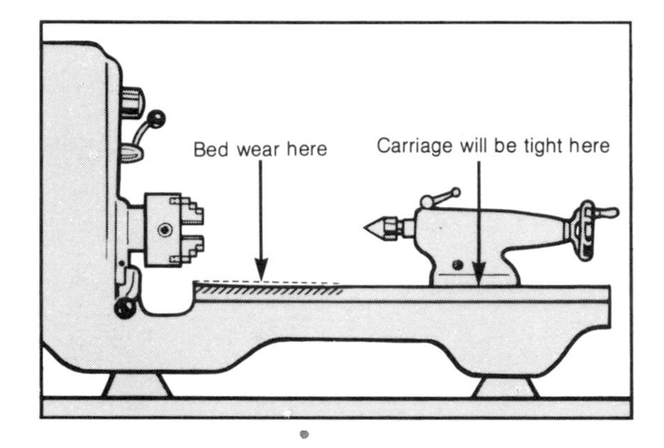

A lathe that has done a lot of work on small components may have bed wear close to the chuck, while the carriage will be tight at the tailstock end. The problem can be remedied by regrinding the bed, but it may prove expensive.

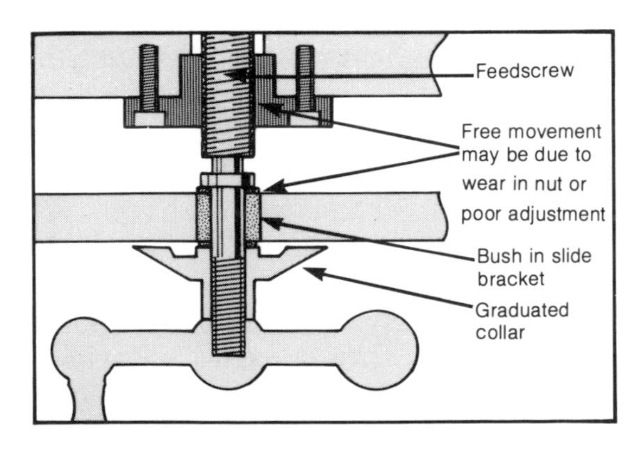

Apparent backlash on feedscrews could be caused by nothing more than poor adjustment. Providing the lathe is still in production, even worn feednuts are not expensive to replace.

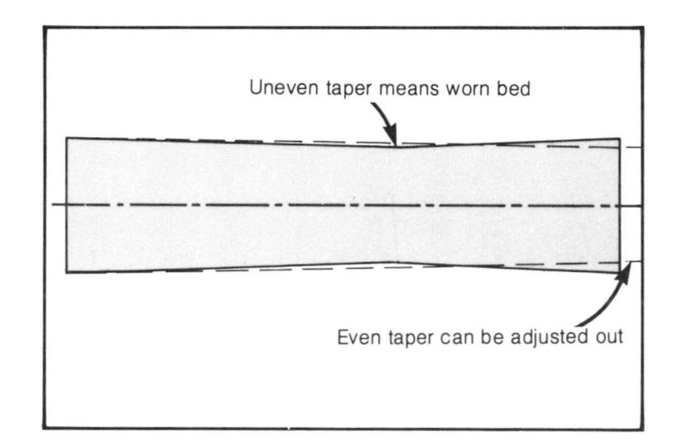

If a lathe produces a straight taper on a test piece, it may be due to nothing more than the tailstock being out of adjustment. A 'compound' taper can be the sign of a worn or twisted bed.

This is just part of the basic Myford set of change-wheels, plus a few 'specials' like the big 100-tooth wheel, and two 21s for metric conversion. Check the wheels present against a screw-cutting and fine feeds chart.

INSTALLING A LATHE

Whether you buy a new or used machine, the chances are that it will be delivered on your doorstep and you will have to install it yourself.

If you buy a 'bench' model, it is best to buy the cabinet stand that goes with it. If there is not one, or your funds do not yet run to it, make a framework from stout angle iron, bolted to a concrete floor, and incorporate plenty of bracing in its structure. Materials like Dexion are not usually rigid enough – go for the thickest, most solid material you can find, and either get it welded together or use the biggest bolts you can find.

The lathe itself should be bolted directly into stout cross-members, with a sheet of steel underneath it to form a chip tray. It will help you clean around the machine if you mount it clear of this tray, on raising blocks about 2in (50mm) high.

Wooden stands or benches are rarely satisfactory. They are not usually strong enough, and even the best respond to atmospheric changes and either warp, shrink or expand. Even the tiniest of movements in the base will destroy the accuracy of the machine, so go for iron or steel, bolted firmly into solid concrete. Even a very lightweight machine, weighing less than 60lb (27kg) will benefit from being mounted firmly on a steel-framed bench, although some of the *very* lightweight models can be operated on a table top with care.

When your base is ready, and level, get a friend to help you lift the machine on to its mounting studs or bolts, and do up the nuts barely finger-tight. For the next operation you are going to need to have the three-jaw chuck mounted on the spindle, carrying a length of stout steel bar that is ideally just short of the length of the bed. You can take the tailstock right off for this operation.

Next, get a clock or dial gauge on a magnetic base, and set it with the foot on the end of the bar with the dial set to zero. Also, lay a spirit level along the bed and, if you have another spirit level, lay it along the cross-slide, at right angles to the bed.

Now, if your prepared base was level in the first place, there is a fair chance that the lathe bed will be level both lengthways and fore and aft too, but it is as well to check. A lathe running out of level can

Many of the change-wheels may be attached to the machine at the time of your examination. This is the Myford set to give a feed of 0•0018in per revolution of the spindle.

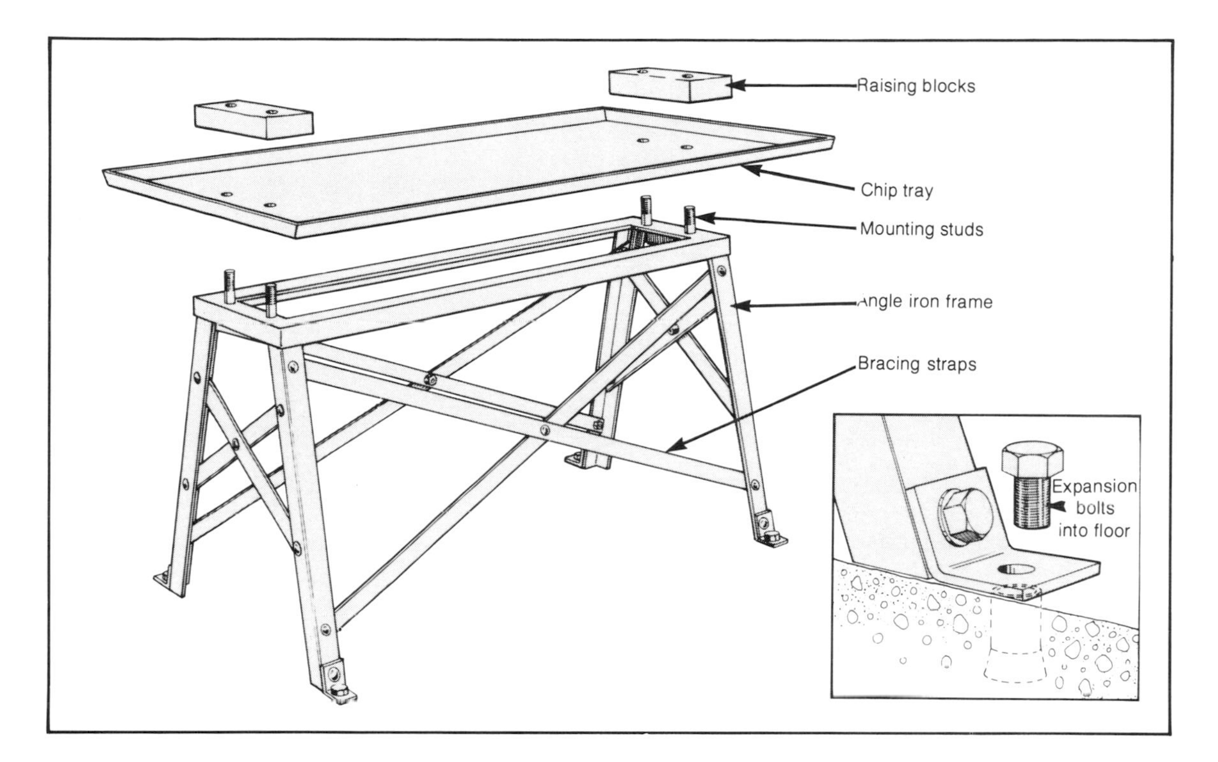

Here are some ideas for making your own lathe stand. Use the stoutest materials you can find, and either get it welded or assemble it with hefty bolts. Raising blocks under the machine will help you to clear swarf away, while a chip tray can be bent from a sheet of galvanised steel.

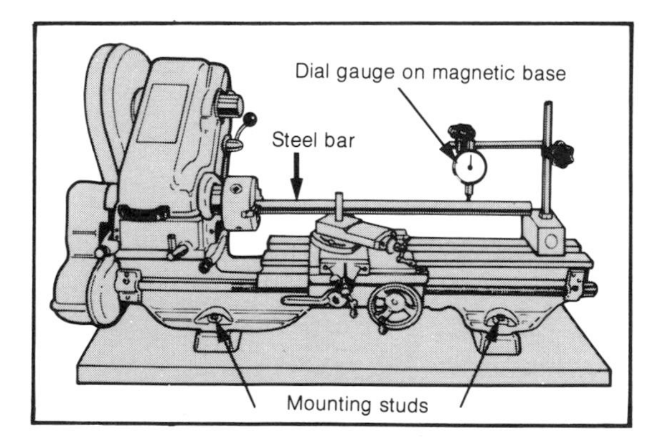

Here is a set up to help you avoid warping the bed as you tighten your lathe down on to its base. Any tiny movement of the dial gauge indicates a problem.

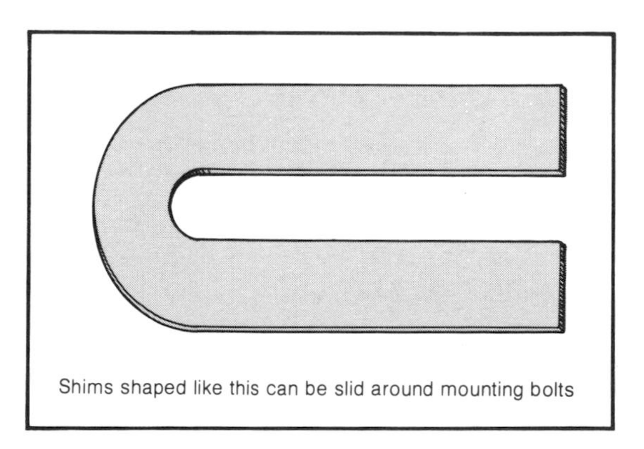
Shims shaped like this can be slid around mounting bolts

If you cut packing shims this shape, they give good support and are easy to introduce and remove.

suffer accelerated bearing wear, so insert metal packing under the lathe feet until both spirit levels read zero. That is the first stage.

The second stage is to bolt the lathe down without warping the bed, and that is where the dial gauge comes in. Any tiny twisting or bending force will read on the gauge, so start turning the nuts down slowly, at the same time observing the gauge carefully. As soon as the gauge moves, slacken the nut that caused it to move, and experiment with the packing under that foot until you can tighten that nut without movement. The aim is to get all four nuts fully tight with the gauge reading zero at the end, and this may take quite a long time. However, it will be time well spent because a lathe that is warped in installation will never produce accurate work.

If you have the proper cabinet stand for the lathe, this bolting down job may be greatly simplified if a thoughtful manufacturer has provided jack screws that run concentric with the mounting studs. With this type of mounting, the same spirit level and dial gauge set up can be used, but instead of using packing you merely adjust the jackscrews up or down.

If you do have to use packing, the chances are that you will need quite a lot – or at least a big selection. Packing must be metal, and steel is best. A pack of shim steel in assorted thicknesses is a good buy before you start, because you will need some very thin pieces that may not otherwise be readily available. For ease of insertion, packing can be cut into 'U' shaped pieces.

The objective of the whole exercise is to finish up with a level and unwarped lathe, tightly secured to a rigid base, which is, in turn, tightly secured to a concrete floor. This ideal situation may take some time to achieve, but a lathe so installed will maintain its accuracy for many years afterwards.

My Myford has stood on its present cabinet stand for more than six years, and it has maintained 100 per cent accuracy for all of that time. It is set up as you see in the photograph on page 75, but one thing that is not apparent is that while the lathe is absolutely level, the cabinet stand is not. The stand has been set up with a deliberate, slight slope to the left, so that spillages of liquids in the chip tray finish up in the region of the drain plug, which is in the extreme left-hand end of the tray. The lathe itself was brought to level by adjustment of the jackscrews.

ACCESSORIES

When your lathe is installed, you will need somewhere to put all the various accessories that go with it. The secret is to have everything easily at hand but not in the way, and in my wooden workshop, which is only heated when I am working in there, I like to have everything on display where I can see it. It has been suggested that this is because I like to show off to neighbours and visitors, but the real reason is that if I can see things, I can keep a visual check on any rust problems.

If you are building shelves, do not clutter up the headstock end of the lathe, because something is bound to get in the way when you want to pass a long length of bar right through the spindle. I do not like reaching over lathes to get at things, because there is always the temptation to lean over when the machine is running. A

This is my shelf of accessories in its usual state of disarray. Note the profusion of tools with no.2 Morse taper shanks, that can be used from either headstock or tailstock.

table or cabinet at the tailstock end is ideal, and you will see that I have built mine on a slope and secured things to it with rails or pegs. Morse-taper accessories are stood in holes. Should you build such a shelf, use old, well-seasoned timber – particularly if you are going to mount taper accessories in holes. Fresh wood sap can be corrosive but old timber, smeared liberally with machine oil after drilling, creates no problems.

Personally, I find that the lathe's own cabinet stand is one of the most awkward storage areas yet devised. This is no fault of the manufacturers, and you may as well use this hollow space for storing something, but I do not like having to bend and reach for heavy metal components. My cabinet stand holds things that I rarely need, like a spare cross-slide, big angle plates, spare bearings, and a large can of undiluted soluble oil. Things which are needed more or less every working day are at a convenient hand level on the shelves.

11 Advanced Lathe Work

So far simple turning work in the lathe has involved only the three-jaw self-centring chuck, sometimes in conjunction with a centre in the tailstock. With the chucks now available, the 'between centres' rig mentioned in Chapter 9 is now little used, although it is one worth remembering if ever you have to work on a long bar that is such a tight fit on the machine that there is no room for a chuck at the headstock end.

KEEPING THE CHUCK ON CENTRE

One problem at this point is the fact that few self-centring chucks close with the jaws accurately on centre. This is of little consequence if the whole turning job can be done with a waste end of the work gripped in the jaws, to be sawn or parted off when all turning work is complete. However, there are some jobs where the work has to be reversed in the chuck jaws and absolute concentricity must be maintained. My best three-jaw has an error in concentricity of 0·002in (0·05mm), which would ruin a job that had to be re-chucked, so what is the answer?

First of all, you need a dial gauge on a magnetic base, or one of the cheaper 'Verdict' types of gauge that mechanically magnifies tiny movements of an arm so that they can be observed. By bringing the foot of a gauge to bear on the work, and turning it by hand, the degree of eccentricity can be observed.

Sometimes you can achieve concentricity with a three-jaw by introducing very thin packing between the jaws and the work. Slivers of aluminium foil are worth a try. There is another trick if your three-jaw has a separate back-plate. The chuck will almost certainly be held on the plate with three bolts that pass through the body from the front, while a recess on the back of the chuck engages with a register on the plate. If you turn somewhere in the region of 0·01in (0·25mm) off the register, you will be able to slacken the holding bolts, tap the chuck body into a concentric position with a small, soft hammer, and retighten the bolts.

This, however, is hard work, and no substitute for a proper four-jaw chuck on which each jaw can be moved independently. With such a chuck you can achieve absolute concentricity, or with the aid of the dial gauge, you can deliberately set work off-centre so that round cams can be turned. The four-jaw also has the

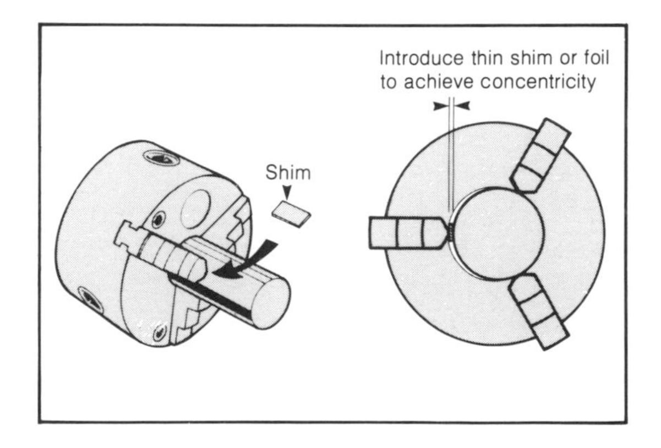

To get a job to run concentrically in a three-jaw chuck that is slightly 'off' you can sometimes pack one jaw with a very thin metal shim, or even a slip of aluminium foil.

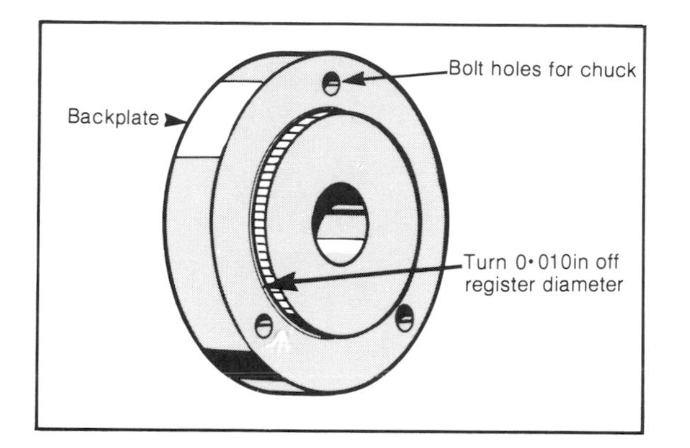

An errant chuck can be made to run concentrically by turning a thin skim off the backplate register, slackening the bolts, and gently tapping the chuck body into position. Do not expect the chuck to remain concentric at all settings.

A robust four-jaw chuck is an excellent tool for gripping workpieces of irregular shape. In this case, an aluminium clamp has been mounted for a boring and facing operation.

ability to grip square or rectangular workpieces – in fact work of any shape where the jaws can get a safe grip. It is the most useful accessory you can have on any lathe.

STEADIES

If you put a long, thin bar in the lathe and take a cut all the way along it from tailstock to as close to the chuck as you can safely work, you will finish up with a bar that is of greater diameter in the middle than it is at the ends. This is because the bar bends away from the tool where it is unsupported. The work may also have vibration or 'chatter' marks in the middle, where it has vibrated as the tool has cut.

The answer to this problem is an accessory called a travelling steady, which is shaped a little like a '£' symbol and is bolted to the carriage on the headstock side of the cross-slide. It has two brass or bronze paws which are adjustable, and which support the work from above and behind while the tool does its work. Once the paws have been adjusted into position, the work should be given a light coating of lubricating oil so that they do not bind or burn.

Another type of steady is for working on the ends of long bars, where they cannot be supported by the tailstock. This accessory is called a fixed steady, and it has three radially positioned paws which rest on the work. The accessory itself is clamped to the lathe ways.

Some steadies have roller-tipped paws, which sound great in theory but do not work too well in practice in home workshops. Small particles of swarf find their way under the rollers, ruin the work, force it off centre, and may damage the machine. Such steadies are really for industrial situations where they can be kept totally free from swarf particles. Fixed steadies are particularly prone to seizure caused by excessive heat generated by cutting, so when they are in use keep the work cool and the paws well lubricated. Worst problems seem to occur when bar material is being drilled through the steady.

DRILLING IN THE LATHE

Anything that can be held in a chuck or otherwise attached to the lathe's spindle can be drilled from the tailstock. The golden rule is that all holes are started with a centre drill, as the point of a standard twist drill is liable to wander off centre as it enters the work.

General rules for drilling from the tailstock chuck are exactly the same as those outlined for use of the drilling machine, with the obvious difference that the work is rotating instead of the drill.

REAMING

When holes of very accurate dimensions are required, drilled holes can be finished with a reamer. Reamers are not designed to remove large amounts of metal, so holes should first be drilled to within a few thousandths of an inch (or 0·1mm) of their finished size.

Reamers come in two varieties. Machine reamers have Morse taper shanks that fit directly into the tailstock taper, while hand reamers usually have parallel shanks terminating in a square so that

The travelling steady in use. Such a rig enables an even cut to be taken from a long, flexible bar.

they can be turned with a wrench or key when used 'freehand'. They usually have a centre drilled into the extreme end of the shank, and this allows us to use what is known as the 'floating reamer' technique in the lathe.

To set this system up, hold the reamer in a two-handed wrench as for hand reaming, and locate the reamer's female centre against the point of a centre in the tailstock taper. The work is set to rotate very slowly, and the reamer is entered into the hole by slowly rotating the tailstock handwheel.

Very great care should be taken when doing this kind of work, as both the work and the machine can be damaged should

The fixed steady enables work to be done on the ends of long bars that will not pass through the spindle. This accessory needs plenty of lubricant where the three bronze paws locate against the work.

When holes are drilled from the tailstock, they must always be started with a centre drill. Otherwise, when a conventional twist drill is entered it will wander off centre.

the reamer seize in the hole. Remember, too, that when the lathe is set at the 30-40 r.p.m. which is right for this work, its torque (twisting force) is enormous. Keep your fingers out of the way when doing this job, and rest one handle of the wrench against an edge of the topslide, while keeping it pulled back against the tailstock centre with your left hand. In order that the hole should be finished truly round, it is essential that the reamer never becomes disengaged throughout the whole operation. The reamer should be advanced very slowly to the desired depth, then slowly withdrawn, with the work still rotating and the centres held tightly in engagement by hand.

Overall this is one of those operations where four hands would be very useful: one to work the tailstock handwheel, one to hold the reamer in engagement with the centre, one to pour a constant stream of cutting lubricant down the reamer's flutes, and one to hover over the stop switch. If your lathe's electrical system features an adjustable overload cut-out, it is wise to set it very finely for this sort of work.

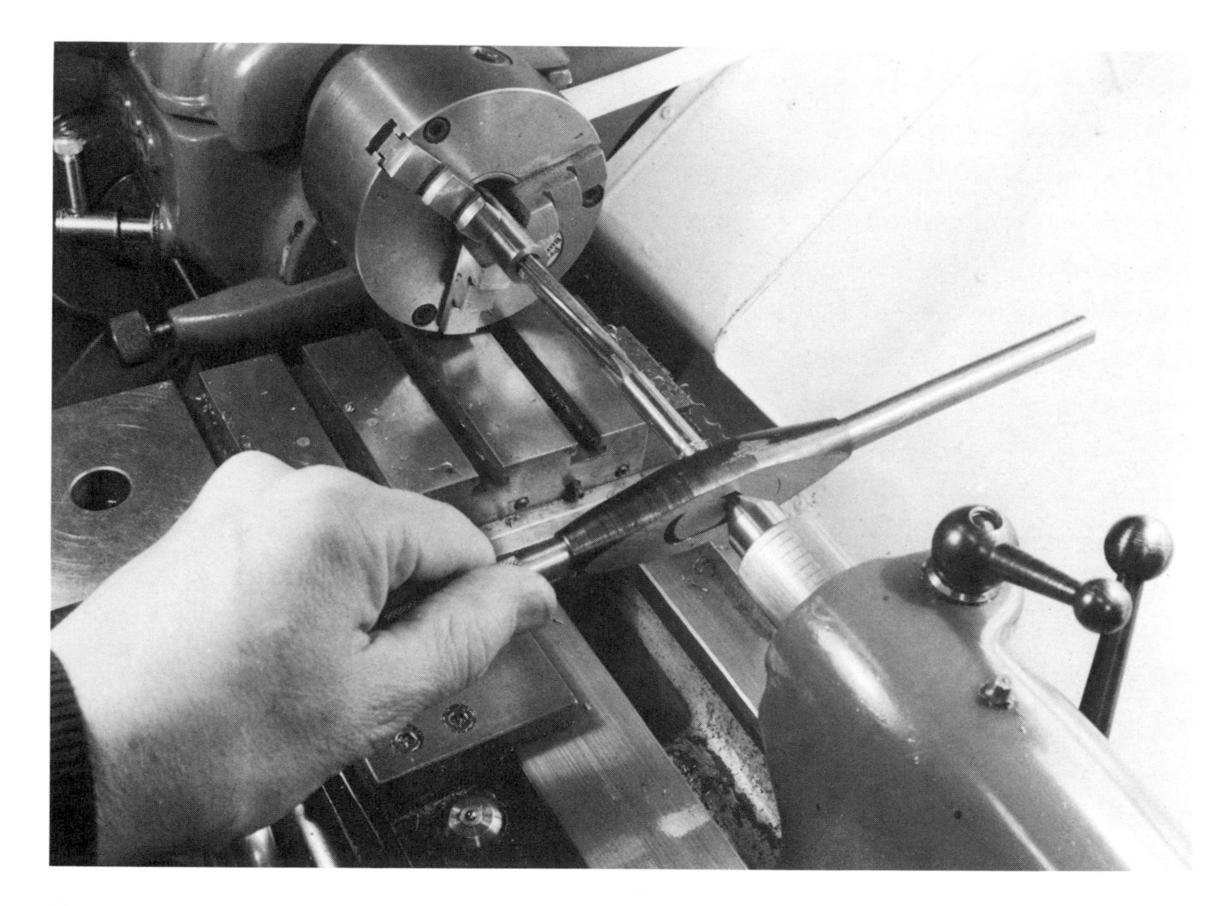

The 'floating reamer' set up, with the female centre in the shank of the reamer located against the tailstock centre. The reamer is held in a large tap wrench, which should be gripped so that the fingers cannot get trapped if the reamer seizes in the hole.

BORING

Big holes, beyond the capacity of your largest drills and reamers, can be bored to very high standards of accuracy on the lathe.

Assume that you want to form an accurate 1in (25mm) hole in your work, and yet your biggest drill is only 0·75in (20mm). Just fit the boring tool into the toolpost as shown opposite, and enlarge your drilled hole by whatever are sensible increments for your lathe. If you engage automatic feed for this operation, be careful when working on blind holes because it is important that the tool should not forcibly 'bottom' in the hole. It is best to mark the boring tool shank at a safe depth with a tiny blob of Tippex typewriter correcting fluid, or fast-drying paint, and disengage automatic when your mark approaches the mouth of the hole. Go the rest of the way advancing the carriage by hand, and work things so that you finish your hole with a very light cut. Progress can be checked with a vernier gauge, or an internal micrometer.

Sooner or later, you will have to mount a great lump of metal like this on a faceplate. This job has been clamped firmly at three points, while the bunch of changewheels act as a balance weight so that the machine is not shaken to pieces. Even with such precautions, such oversize workpieces should be rotated very slowly. (The arrow marks the centre.)

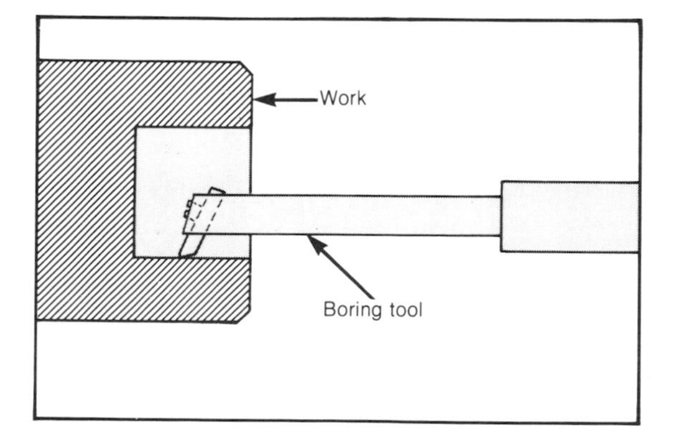

The set up for boring holes that are beyond the ranges of your biggest drills and reamers. Great care must be taken that the tool does not forcibly 'bottom' in the hole.

FACEPLATE WORK

The faceplate is used to hold flat items of large diameter, which are attached to it either by passing bolts through from the back into tapped holes in the work, or with clamps. All sorts of oddly shaped items can be attached to faceplates, and extremely awkward mountings can often be simplified by drilling and tapping an extra hole in the plate. Although this may sound like sacrilege to some, a few extra holes will not do too much harm.

It is with faceplate work that the turner

usually first encounters the problems of balance. If you do mount a job that is so off balance that it causes the machine to vibrate, you will never be able to finish it accurately and in extreme cases you could damage the machine. You can first try reducing speed considerably, but this makes for tedious work on a long job. It is better to bring the plate back into balance by bolting weights to the light side of the plate. Big nuts, or even the lathe's smaller change-wheels, are fine. Do not do what I once did and try to use a large pot magnet; centrifugal force slung it across the workshop like a missile, and I was lucky not to have been hurt.

With complicated faceplate rigs, very great care should be taken that balance weights, clamps, bolt heads, or parts of the work not to be machined all run clear of the tool and the topslide. A few minutes spent rotating the faceplate by hand and observing carefully can save you a great deal of trouble. Faceplate work is also a very good example of the problem of balancing set up time with working time: a cut may take about twenty seconds to complete, but the set up to achieve it may take an hour of head-scratching and experiment. That is one of the frustrations – and pleasures – of lathe work.

MILLING IN THE LATHE

The basic lathe works in two axes or dimensions – along the bed and across it. If a third, up and down, axis can be added the lathe can be converted into a small milling machine. The cheapest way of obtaining this third axis is to buy a vertical slide which can be fixed to the cross-slide by 'T' bolts. This vertical slide, like the cross-slide, is controlled by a hand-wheel and feedscrew so that it can be moved up and down accurately. Work is attached to the vertical slide by clamps, or held in a machine vice which is attached to the slide by 'T' bolts.

Rotary milling cutters can either be held in the chuck (a four-jaw is best, with the tool set with the aid of a clock gauge), or held in collets which are inserted

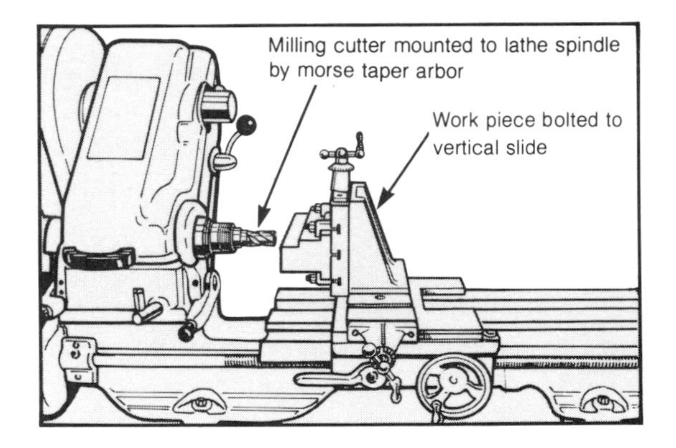

The addition of a vertical slide adds a third axis to the lathe. Work is generally bolted to the slide's T-slots, while the cutter is held in the lathe spindle.

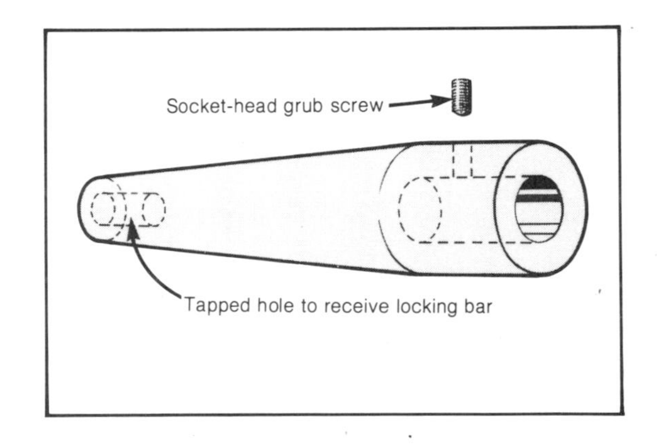

A simple cutter arbor can be made from a length of scrap steel bar, turned to suit the spindle taper. There *must* be provision for locking the cutter arbor into the spindle, otherwise it may jump out.

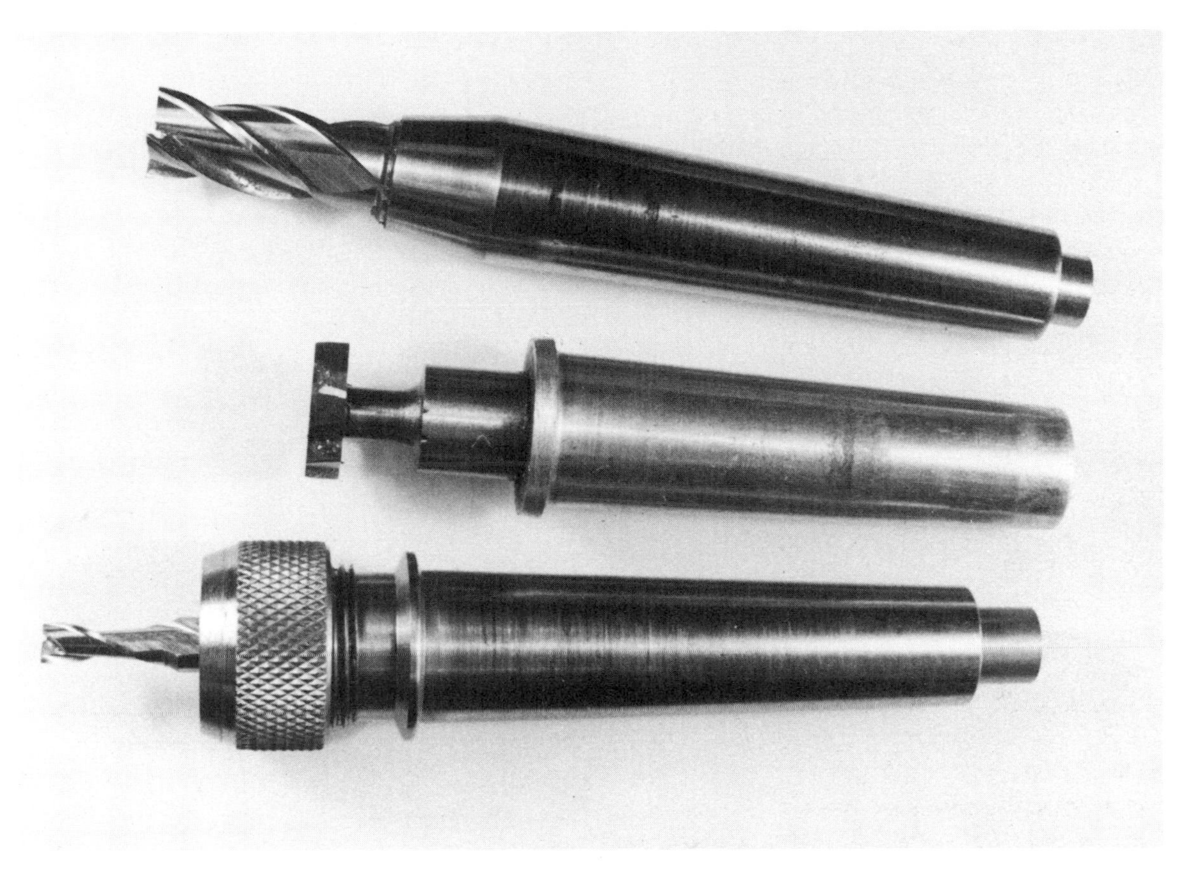

Cutters held in morse-taper shanks. Top is an end mill, while a T-slot cutter is in the centre. The slot drill at the bottom is held in a collet in the morse-taper arbor.

into the spindle taper, or mounted in their own individual Morse taper arbors which fit directly into the spindle taper.

In a small workshop with a few cutters this latter course of action is best, as Morse taper arbors are easily turned from lengths of scrap steel. Cutters are inserted into reamed holes in the arbors, and held in place either with a set screw or a tiny smear of Loctite 270 engineering adhesive.

With this system, cutters must be locked in position by passing a length of threaded rod right through the spindle. The thread should engage in a tapped hole in the tail of the arbor, while a nut of suitable dimensions takes care of the other end. Milling cutters not secured in this way can (and in fact, usually do) 'walk' out of the taper, shatter, and ruin the work. The presence of the threaded rod makes it easy to remove the arbor from the taper: just screw the nut right to the end of its thread, and give it a tap with a soft hammer.

Cutters themselves come in a wide variety of shapes and sizes, but for plain slotting and a limited amount of general shaping either slot drills or end mills are favoured. Both of these tools are like short, stubby twist drills with the ends ground flat and cutting faces on the forward edges of the flutes so that they will cut sideways as well as forwards. The slot drill has two flutes, the end mill usually four. Slot drills will generally take a slightly larger bite out of the work than do end mills, but they leave a poorer surface finish.

Another useful milling tool, to be

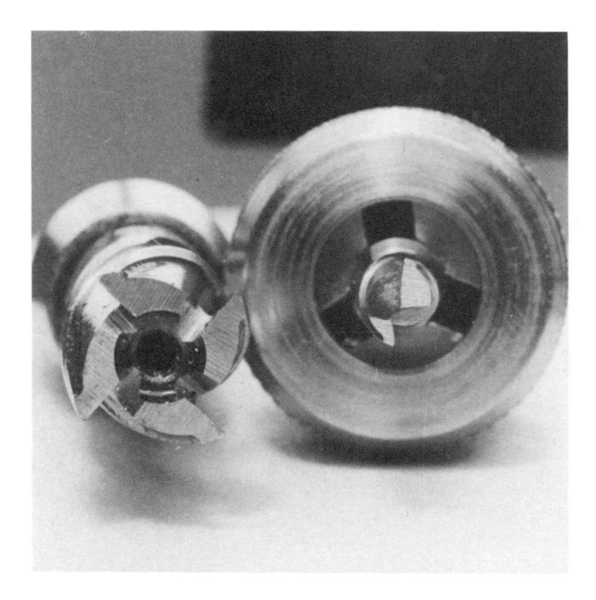

The end mill (left) has four flutes, while the slot drill (right) has just two. Generally, slot drills can be used to take coarser cuts.

This fly cutter, which I made myself, utilises worn-out centre drills as cutting tools. Mounted on a small iron backplate, it can be screwed direct to the spindle nose while the two cutting tools traverse work clamped to the cross-slide.

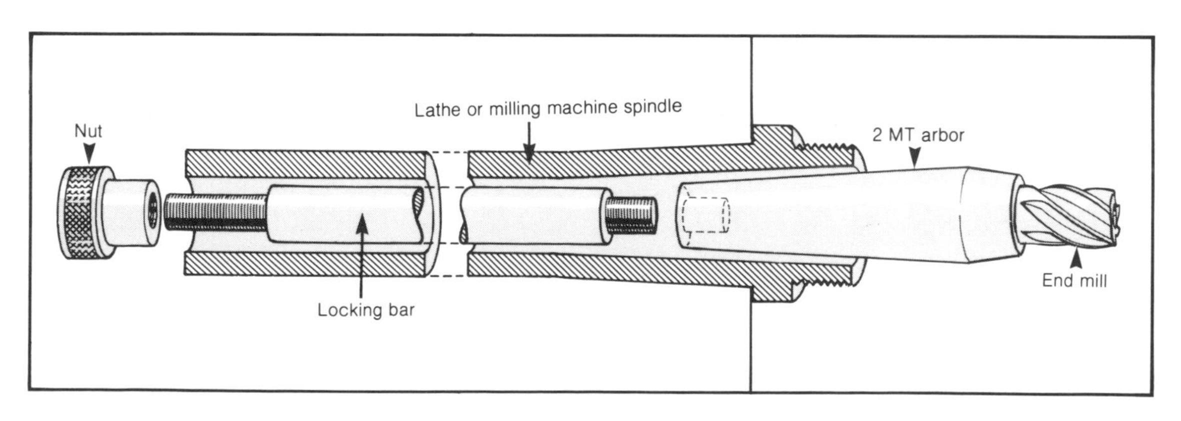

Here is the simplest way to lock in tapered arbors. If you have both a lathe and a milling attachment, the same locking bar may do for both machines.

brought into operation when large flat surfaces have to be milled, is the fly cutter. Various commercial cutters are available, but a satisfactory one can be built on to an unwanted chuck backplate which is then screwed directly on to the spindle nose. Mine has two cutting tools which are ground from old blunt No. 4 centre drills.

The Milling Attachment

This device is like a little, vertical milling machine that sits on the lathe bed, while work is clamped to the cross-slide. Some milling attachments are powered from the lathe's spindle, while others have their own motors. These attachments get rid of one of the main problems associated with the vertical slide – vertical slides are not rigid enough for anything other than light work. With an attachment, capacity is usually increased, too. For lathes in the Myford 7 series you can get a special long cross-slide – 10·75in (273 mm) – against the standard item's 8·5in (216mm) length. This is a further aid to greater capacity.

When buying a milling attachment, try to get one with a spindle nose and taper compatible with that on your lathe. If you do not, you might find yourself having to observe two sets of standards in tool mounting. My Amolco attachment has an identical spindle nose to the Myford lathe, and all that is required is a different length of locking bar to hold arbors in the spindle taper.

This is the British-made Amolco milling attachment, which is available to fit a wide variety of lathes in place of the tailstock. This machine uses tools mounted in Morse-taper arbors, locked into the taper by a screwed rod that passes right through the spindle.

THE KNURLING TOOL

This is the tool used to impress those criss-cross 'grip' patterns on nuts intended to be tightened with the fingers, or with tool handles, for example. The tool works by impressing two extremely hard metal wheels against the work, each wheel carrying the imprint of half the pattern. The tool is traversed along the work in the toolpost, leaving the pattern behind it as it travels. Usually several passes backwards and forwards along the work are necessary to produce a pattern of satisfactory depth.

There are two types of knurling tool. In one, the wheels are impressed into the work by rotating the cross-slide

This is the best type of knurling tool to use in a light lathe. Stresses on the machine are kept to a sensible minimum due to the tool's 'clamping' action.

handwheel, while on the other, each wheel is mounted in one half of a clamp, which is tightened on the work with one wheel on top and the other beneath. This latter type is superior on light lathes, because it imposes less strain on the cross-slide feedscrew and the spindle front bearing.

12 Screw-cutting in the Lathe

BASIC CALCULATIONS

The lathe's spindle can be geared to the leadscrew to achieve a wide variety of feed rates; it therefore follows that, if suitable gear ratios are chosen, and a tool that corresponds to the thread form is used, the lathe will cut a screw thread on a bar of suitable diameter.

Let us start with a simple assumption. If the gearwheel on the back end of the spindle has 20 teeth, the leadscrew has 8 threads per inch, and the leadscrew also carries a 20 tooth gearwheel which is engaged with the spindle gearwheel by a series of idler gears, then the leadscrew will rotate at the same speed as the spindle. If the machine is then suitably tooled, the thread that it cuts will be the same as that on the leadscrew – 8 threads per inch. Those of the metric persuasion can assume that their leadscrew has a 3mm pitch, which is exactly reproduced on the work.

Now let us alter the gearing by putting a 40-tooth wheel on the leadscrew. On the imperially-calibrated machine the thread produced will be 16 per inch, while the metric machine with the 3mm leadscrew will cut a pitch of 1·5mm. The leadscrew will be rotating at half the speed of the work, so the pitch of the thread will be halved.

From this point it is not difficult to work out all sorts of possible pitches with simple gearing. For example, on the imperial machine we can get 20 threads per inch with a 50-tooth wheel on the leadscrew: $[50 \div 20] \times 8 = 20$. On the metric machine, if we put a 60-tooth wheel on the leadscrew, we get a pitch of 1mm: $[60 \div 20] \div 3 = 1$.

We can further expand the range with simple gearing by putting different gearwheels in at the spindle end of the train. For instance, on the imperial machine if we put a 40 on the spindle and a 60 on the leadscrew we get 12 threads to the inch: $[60 \div 40] \times 8 = 12$. On the metric machine, if we put 40 on the spindle and 30 on the leadscrew we get a pitch of 4mm: $[40 \div 30] \times 3 = 4$.

Fortunately, you will not usually have to do these tortured mathematics for yourself, because the lathe should have a screw-cutting chart with it. Just look up what you want, and follow the instructions.

There are further possibilities for screw pitches: instead of employing idler wheels between the machine's spindle and the leadscrew, introduce compound gearing by locking two gearwheels together, driving one, and driving off the other. In this system, the wheel driven by the spindle is referred to as 'driven', while the wheel locked to it is referred to as the 'driver'. Also, as very small wheels cannot usually be accommodated directly on the spindle, the gear train usually begins with a driver wheel that revolves at spindle speed, mounted directly below the spindle and driven by the spindle through a tumbler reverse mechanism. If this sounds complicated, *see* the illustration opposite. There are usually two studs on which compound gears can be mounted.

Thus, the screw-cutting chart on an imperial machine, assuming you want a thread of 19 threads per inch, will read like this:

T.P.I.	19
Driver	40
1st Stud	Driven 38
	Driver 20
2nd Stud	Idle 55
Leadscrew	50

Put another way, this can be expressed as:

$$\frac{38}{40} \times \frac{50}{20} \times 8 = 19$$

Remember that 8 is the number of threads per inch on the leadscrew, and that an idle wheel plays no part in the overall gear ratio.

On the metric machine, you can try a pitch of 0·9. The formula is:

Pitch	0.90
Driver	45
1st Stud	Driven 50
	Driver 20
2nd Stud	Idle 55
Leadscrew	60

Or, put another way:

$$\frac{45}{50} \times \frac{20}{60} \times 3 = 0{\cdot}9$$

Do not let the maths bother you, because you will only need these calculations if you get an old machine that has become parted from its screw-cutting chart. Even then, you may be able to acquire a chart, or a photocopy of one, by writing to the manufacturer or advertising in an engineering magazine.

Even more pitches are available by introducing a second compound gear driven by the first. The screw-cutting chart will then look like this on the imperial machine:

T.P.I.	64
Driver	35
1st Stud	Driven 40
	Driver 20
2nd Stud	Driven 60
	Driver 30
Leadscrew	70

On the metric machine:

Pitch	0.55
Driver	55
1st Stud	Driven 50
	Driver 35
2nd Stud	Driven 60
	Driver 20
Leadscrew	70

All of the preceding figures assume that the imperial lathe has an 8 threads per inch leadscrew, and the metric machine has a leadscrew of 3mm pitch. These figures all correspond to Myford leadscrews, but other machines have leadscrews of different pitches. However, the principles are the same. You can even make imperial lathes cut metric pitches – Myford use two 21-tooth wheels in the

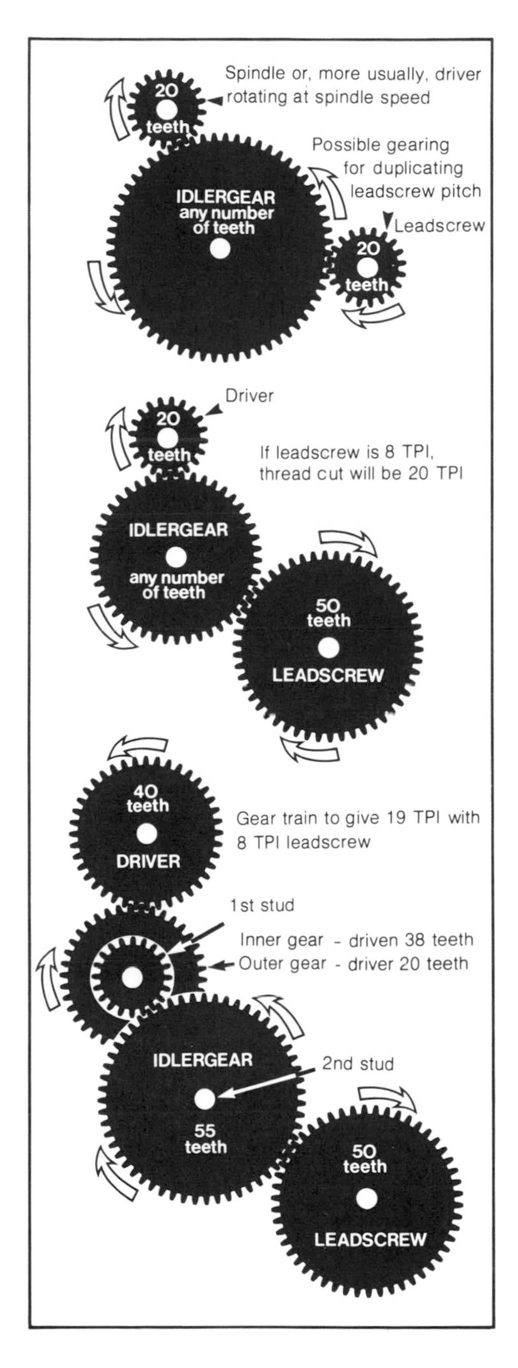

Here are some change-wheel set ups for screw-cutting. The top set up duplicates leadscrew pitch, while the middle diagram gives 20 threads per inch with an 8 threads per inch leadscrew. At the bottom is an example of compound gearing to give 19 threads per inch with an 8 threads per inch leadscrew.

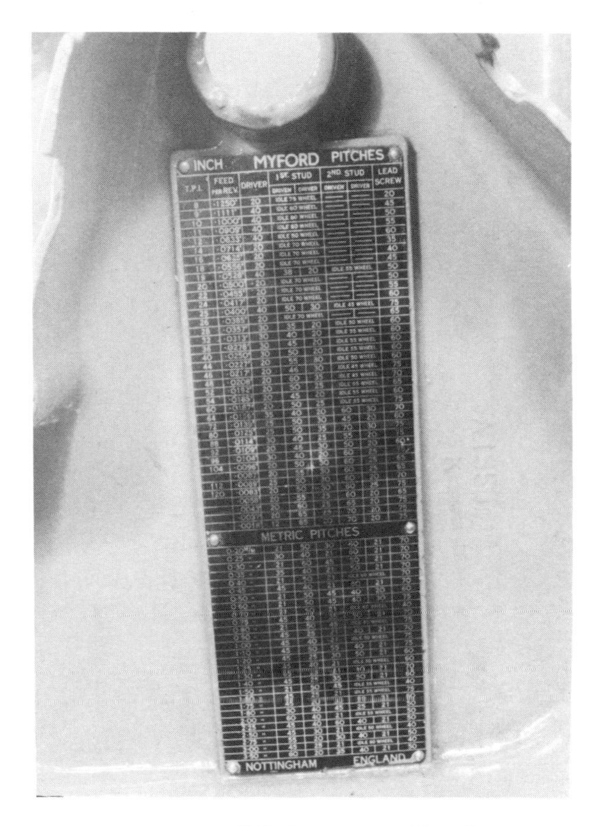

On most lathes you will find a screw-cutting chart like this, attached somewhere on the machine.

train, while others convert with a single wheel of 127 teeth. On some machines, conversion from metric to imperial is achieved with a 63-tooth wheel on the leadscrew.

Of course, if you have managed to afford a machine with a screw-cutting gearbox built into the left-hand end of the leadscrew, much of what has just been discussed will be superfluous knowledge for most common screw pitches. However, sooner or later you will encounter an odd pitch that will mean setting up gear trains of your own.

At this stage it is best actually to practise on the machine, setting up the change-wheels for a few selected pitches just to get the feel of it. You can always check that you have got things right by engaging all the gearing and turning the chuck by hand, with a dial gauge bearing against the toolpost. Check the advancement for one complete turn of the chuck against the quoted pitch of the thread. Convert threads per inch to pitch by dividing 1 by the number of threads per inch. For example, 8 T.P.I. = 1 ÷ 8 = 0·125in.

When you have done that, it is a good idea to set the machine on a low speed with the carriage up the far right-hand end of the bed, engage the leadscrew clasp nut, and just get used to the rate at which the carriage travels for a given spindle speed. When you are screw-cutting you will have to engage and disengage the clasp nut with great precision, often working very close to the chuck, or to a part of the work which is not to be screw-cut, or a shoulder on the work.

SCREW-CUTTING TOOLS

Screw-cutting tools must be ground to conform exactly to the form of the thread to be cut. For example, if you wish to cut a Whitworth or BSF thread, your tool must be ground to a 55 degree angle, while a 60 degree angle is necessary for metric threads, and a 47·5 degree angle for BA. Many pitch gauges provide a suitable template for tool grinding, or you can mark the angle on a small piece of sheet steel and cut a template of your own. In general rake and clearance angles for screw-cutting tools are the same as for general turning work, but for coarse pitches a little more side clearance is desirable so that the side of the tool does

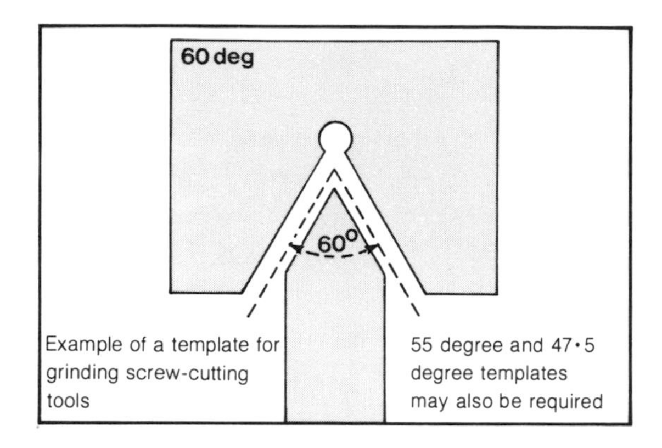

A template like this will help you grind screw-cutting tools accurately.

not rub on the walls of the thread being cut.

PREPARATION OF WORK

Material to be screw-cut should be turned to the correct overall diameter for the thread to be cut, and provision must be made for the tool to run clear of the work at the end of the threaded section. The easiest way of achieving this is to undercut the thread (*see* opposite, above). The diameter of the undercut should be very slightly less than the core diameter of the thread, which can be found from screw thread tables. Before starting screw-cutting, establish that the tool is presented at a true right angle to the work.

CUTTING THE THREAD

Do not try to cut even the finest thread at one single pass of the tool. First look up the thread depth in your screw thread tables, and with the machine switched off, advance the tool until it just touches the work. Then either return the

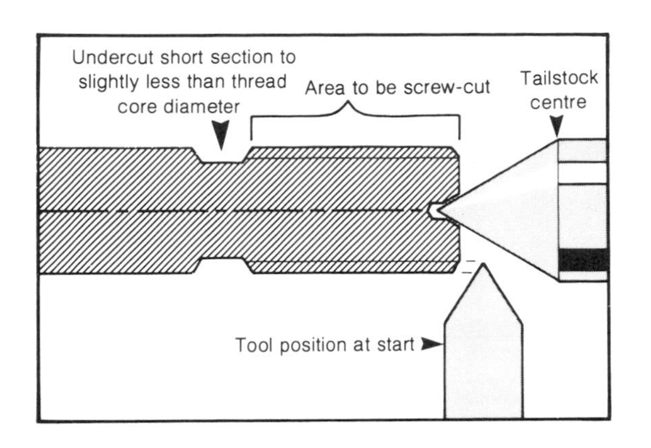

This is a good set up for screw-cutting the end of a bar – for instance when making a stud. At the end of its traverse, the tool runs clear in the undercut area.

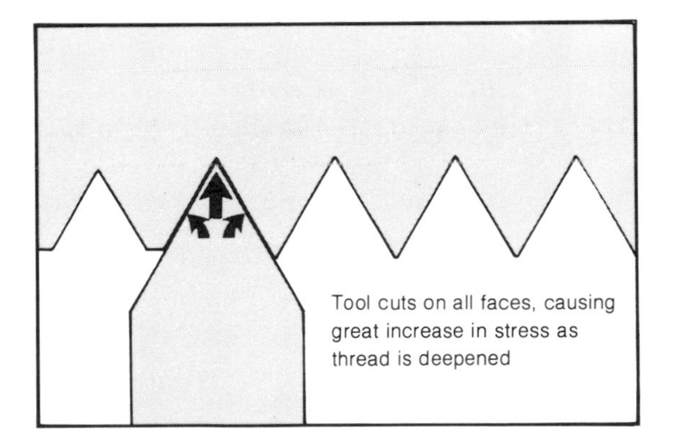

If the tool is advanced directly into the work via the cross-slide, stresses increase enormously as depth increases. As depth increases, cuts have to become increasingly shallow.

graduated collar on the leadscrew handwheel to zero, or if you cannot do that on your machine, note down the reading. The first cut can be whatever you know to be well within the capacity of the machine, but as the tool advances into the work on successive cuts, the cut depth will have to become shallower and shallower, and you must be prepared to make the last few cuts very shallow indeed – perhaps no more than 0·002in (0·05mm) at a time. This is because, as the tool advances, the front on which it is cutting broadens and a 0·01in (0·25mm) cut may overstrain the machine, or even break the tip off the tool. There is a way of alleviating this problem, discussed later in this chapter.

The objective, then, is to make successive cuts until the full depth of the thread is reached, and this must all be done without disengaging the gearing between the spindle and the leadscrew. How this is achieved will depend on the pitch of the thread being cut compared to the pitch of the leadscrew. For a simple thread, that is, either of leadscrew pitch or a direct multiple of it, proceed as follows:

1. Having noted the start position of the cross-slide handwheel, or having returned the graduated dial to zero, put on the first cut and let the tool traverse across the work, disengaging the carriage clasp nut at the end of the cut. The tool can then be wound back, and the carriage returned to its start position in preparation for the second cut.
2. Advance the cross-slide feedscrew to its position for the first cut plus about half as much again, engage the clasp nut, and traverse the tool across the thread for a second time. Continue this procedure with ever-shallower cuts until the full thread depth is reached.
3. As a final check before you take the last cut or two, you can test the thread with a known accurate nut of the same thread.

That procedure is fine if the pitch to be cut is a direct multiple of leadscrew pitch. With other gearing, the leadscrew will present you with more than one theoretical start point for the thread, and if you engage the clasp nut at random you may find the second cut runs between the correct thread grooves. To pick up the correct start point on the leadscrew, your lathe must be fitted with a thread dial indicator. This is a device that keeps a small gearwheel in constant mesh with the leadscrew, and a shaft connected to the gearwheel is attached to a rotating dial. Marks on the dial can be compared to a fixed mark on the indicator's casing.

With the indicator fitted, it will be noted that the dial rotates when the leadscrew is rotating but the carriage is stationary. The dial is stationary when the leadscrew is rotating and the clasp nut is engaged.

If, therefore, the clasp nut is always engaged against the same numbered mark on the dial, a wide variety of compound-gear threads can be engaged at the same start point. Not all of them can be engaged, however, so beware, and consult your lathe's handbook before starting a thread that requires a complex gear train.

This is the thread dial indicator – a vital accessory for most screw-cutting operations.

An example of this last problem occurs when an imperially-calibrated lathe is geared to cut a metric thread. The golden rule with these threads is never to disengage the clasp nut throughout the whole operation. When this is done, the tool has to be returned to its start point by running the machine in reverse, if it has a reversing switch. If it has not, a small lathe can be wound backwards by turning the chuck by hand.

The details above form a very simplified explanation of the use of the thread dial indicator, and there is no space here to mention all the possibilities. For further reading on the subject, I suggest L. H. Sparey's *The Amateur's Lathe* (Argus Books), or suitable literature put out by the manufacturer of your lathe.

DEEPER CUTS

There is a method of avoiding the necessity to take very shallow cuts as a thread-cutting operation advances. This is done by advancing the tool by the topslide rather than the cross-slide.

Method

First of all, halve the angle of the thread form: for Whitworth and BSF you have 27·5 degrees, and 30 degrees for most other triangular form threads. Then turn the topslide so that it makes this angle with the axis of the cross-slide. (*See* diagram opposite).

Now, if all tool advancement is done with the topslide rather than the cross-slide, all cutting will be done by the tip and the leading edge of the tool, while the trailing edge will just be rubbing the work. In this way, stresses on the tool will be considerably relieved, and the tool will perform a greater work rate without straining the machine.

There is, however, one disadvantage. As the tool is not advanced straight into the work, but at an angle to it, it will have to be advanced further to produce a completely formed thread. Think of it as the difference in length between the hypotenuse and the next longest side of a right-angled triangle.

This is where schoolboy maths is involved again, because when we know all the angles of a triangle, and the length of one edge, there are well-established formulae for establishing all the other information about that triangle. In this case we know that the most acute angle of the triangle is either 27·5 or 30 degrees, while the depth of the thread is also known from consulting tables. The formula for finding the depth of topslide cut to apply is therefore the true depth divided by the cosine of the angle. Here is a simple example:

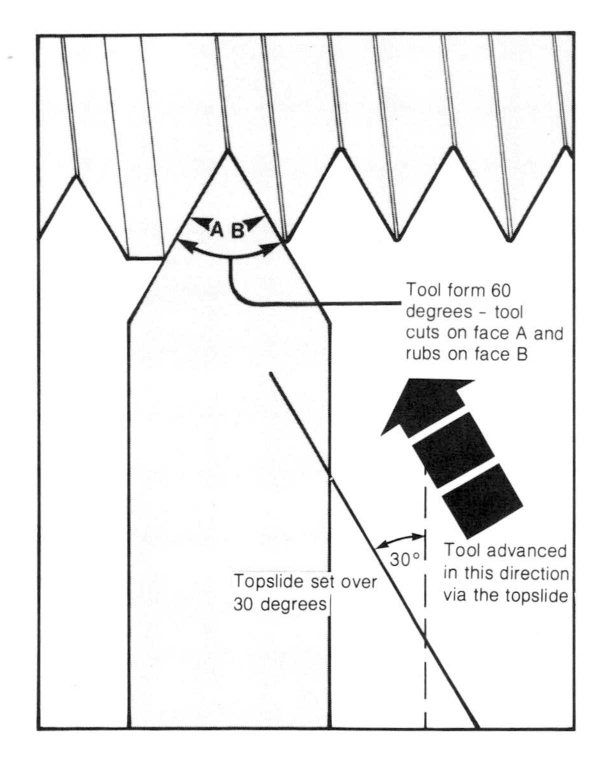

If the topslide is set over to half the thread angle, and advancement is made via the topslide feedscrew, stresses are considerably relieved because the tool is cutting on only one face.

Imagine you are cutting a metric 60 degree thread with a depth of 1·5mm. Your topslide angle is 30 degrees, and the cosine of 30 is 0·86602. 1·5mm divided by 0·86602 is 1·73mm, so that is somewhere near the depth of the cut to take.

I say 'somewhere near' because the calculation assumes the thread form to be a true triangle lying in exactly the same plane as the bed of the lathe. In fact, the triangle has a slightly rounded apex and it lies at the helix angle of the thread, which both increases as pitch gets longer and diameter decreases. However, this is all rather theoretical for practical screw-cutting work, and in the home workshop the best guide to depth is still comparison with a known accurate nut, or the female component into which the thread will fit.

INTERNAL SCREW-CUTTING

The same general principles applied to external threads can be applied to internal, although you start with a hole that is simply a running clearance on the core diameter of the thread, and work outwards instead of inwards.

Internal work is, however, less easy than external work for two reasons:

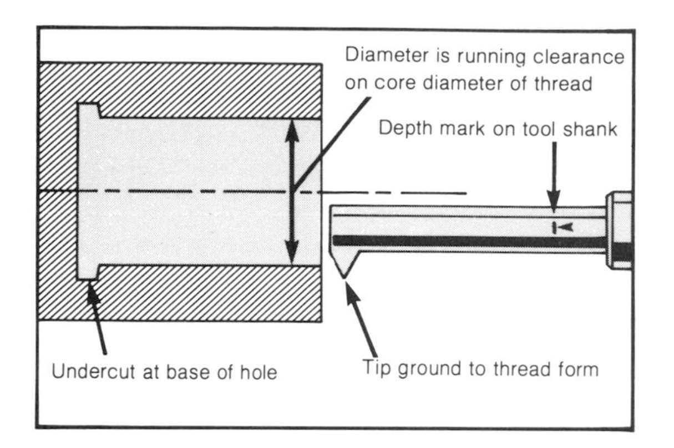

A set up for internal screw-cutting.

unless the hole is very wide and shallow you cannot observe the tool tip as it cuts, and a boring tool ground to thread-cutting form may need to have a long and therefore flexible shank in order to reach the bottom of the hole. This means a slightly frustrating time taking lots of light cuts.

You also have to use good judgement to prevent the tool from fouling the bottom of the hole. The trick to this is to machine as generous an undercut as possible at the bottom of the hole, and use your ears as well as marking the tool shank. With most materials you can actually hear when the tool stops cutting as it passes

This is the tailstock die holder. When using it, hold the handle so that your fingers cannot get trapped if the die seizes on the work.

the end of the thread. If you mentally lose track of the tool's position, then switch the whole machine off. Whatever you do, do not disengage the clasp nut from the leadscrew – you will ruin the thread you have cut, and you might break the end off the tool, too.

THE TAILSTOCK DIE HOLDER

This is a half-way stage between die-cutting threads and true lathe screw-cutting. On a light machine it is not suitable for threads of very large diameters (above 0·25in or 6mm) even in reasonably soft metal.

The tool consists of a parallel shank which terminates in a taper that fits the tailstock taper. A barrel slides on the parallel shank, and the mouth of the barrel is machined to accept dies of standard diameter. For regulating the dies there is an arrangement of three screws similar to those on a plain die holder.

When the tailstock die holder is used, the work is set to revolve at a very low speed (usually the lowest speed available) and the die holder is advanced by hand until the die's cutting faces engage with the end of the work. Once the cutting faces engage, you simply hold on to the holder until the die has cut the length of thread you require – the practical limit being the length of the parallel shank minus about an inch. The leadscrew is not involved in the operation. Before you begin, it helps the die's cutting faces to engage evenly if you cut a slight chamfer on the end of the work.

The same rules apply as when die-cutting threads by hand, except that you cannot back off to clear the swarf. You should also remember that in bottom gear the torque of the lathe is enormous, so in the event of a seizure between the die and the work, you must let go very quickly.

The only advantage the tailstock die-holder offers over a hand operation is that you can be sure the die is presented exactly square to the work. If you do not like doing this job under power, disengage the lathe's drive and turn either the chuck or the die-holder by hand.

For threads of a large diameter for which you have dies, the threads can be formed by a normal screw-cutting procedure except for the last cut; this is done with a tailstock die-holder, with the relevant die used for a final, finishing cut. This way, you get the best of both worlds.

GENERAL ADVICE

Never be in a hurry. Always work slowly and carefully, and double check before you start. Few metals suffer from being cut very slowly; indeed, more often than not, very slow turning with a light cut gives a superior finish.

Keep screw-cutting tools very sharp, and use a cutting lubricant, particularly for the finishing cut. Do not be disappointed if you do not get a perfect thread on your first effort: experience will teach you a 'feel' for the job.

13 Projects

BARBECUE OR TOASTING FORK

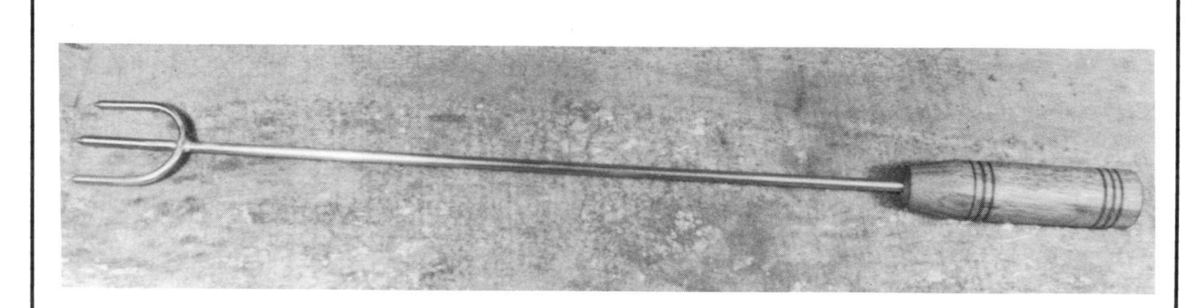

A fork like this is easily made with a minimum of tools and a small gas torch. The handle can be carved if you have no lathe.

Materials

About 20in (500mm) of steel rod (preferably stainless), approximately 3/16in (4·5mm) diameter.
Off-cut of wooden dowel, approximately 3·5in × 7/8in (90mm × 22mm).
Small piece of silver solder (with a high melting point) plus flux.

Tools

Hacksaw
Flat file or grinding wheel
Small round file
Gas torch and fire-brick
Drill, same diameter as steel
Short off-cut of steel bar, approximately 1·25in (32mm) diameter, or any tough cylindrical material of the right dimensions
Vice
Soft hammer
Fine emery paper and sandpaper

Method

1. Cut the steel bar into two pieces, one approximately 15in (380mm), the other 5in (127mm). Exact dimensions are not critical. Smooth the saw marks and burrs off one end of the long piece, and file or grind the other end to a sharp point.

2. Using the vice (with smooth jaws or soft jaw covers), the short off-cut of thick steel bar or any tough cylindrical material, and the hammer, bend the short piece of rod into an accurate 'U' shape. The legs of the 'U' can be trimmed to even length with the file or saw. When this is done,

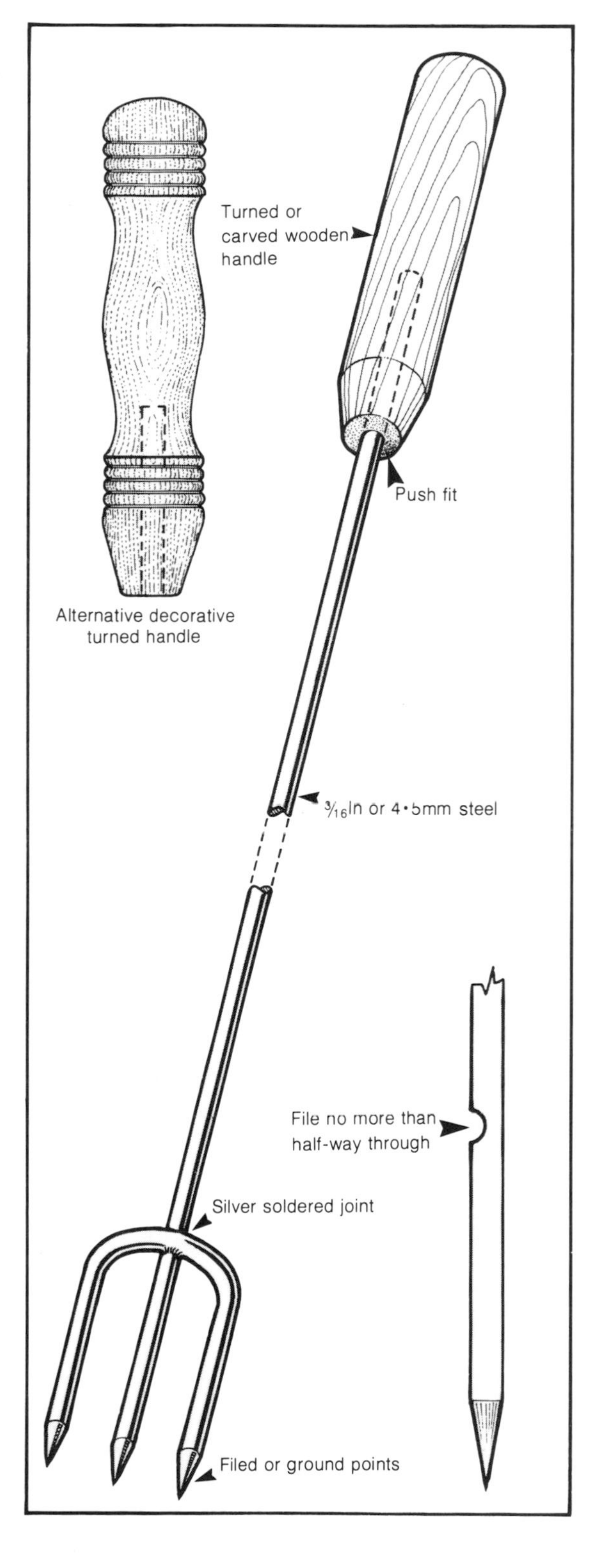

Here is how the barbecue fork is assembled. You do not need a lathe, but if you have one you can add any decoration you like to the handle.

sharpen the points with the file or grinding wheel.

3. On a flat surface, lay the 'U' over the long piece of rod so that the points are exactly level, and mark the crossing point on the long piece with a little file nick. Then transfer the long piece to the vice, and at the marked point, file no more than half-way through with the small round file.

4. Clear the workbench of all inflammable materials, and lay the work on the fire-brick. Mix a small amount of flux (no more than about the volume of a pea) to a paste with a drop of clean water, and apply it to the area of the joint only, being sure that the touching faces have a thin coat of flux between them. Clean flux away from other areas with a bit of rag. Apart from the coat of flux, the area of the joint must be clean, bright metal.

5. With the job laid out neatly on the fire-brick, light the torch and play the flame on the area of the joint only. As heat rises, the flux will steam and dry out, and eventually it will vitrify and flow as a liquid. When the area of the joint is dull red, touch the end of the stick of silver solder against the fluxed area of the joint, keeping the flame going, but melting the solder against the work rather than letting it fall in blobs from the flame. You will see the solder flow into the joint like melted butter. A tiny dab of solder is enough, so take the stick away before a large blob builds up.

6. Turn the torch out, and let the job cool in its own time. Do not accelerate cooling by quenching in water. While the joint cools, you can work on the handle.

The first stage of forming the U-shaped prongs in the vice, with a former and a soft hammer. If you use a socket spanner as a former, pick a good tough one.

7. Clean up the wooden dowel with sandpaper, and drill a concentric hole about 1·5in (40mm) deep in one end. If you have a lathe you can turn and drill the handle in the machine. With no lathe, drill as close to the centre as you can, and do your best to keep the hole straight.

8. Return to your fire-brick, and be sure that the job has cooled fully before you pick it up. The blackened or blued area where you applied the heat will polish back bright with the fine emery paper. Be particularly careful to clean any flux away from the area of the joint, and if it does not come off easily with emery paper, give it a good long soak in warm water. The flux at this stage will have a hard, glassy appearance – not white and powdery as it was when you began.

9. You can now unite the fork with the handle. If the handle is not a tight fit on the rod, put a little epoxy resin adhesive down the hole, and let it cure. If you wish you can finish the handle with varnish, linseed oil, or furniture polish.

Comment

Your fork should save you a lot of burnt fingers and singed cuffs when you turn your barbecue sausages and steaks. Do not leave it directly over the charcoal grill, or use it to poke the embers, otherwise you will overheat it and melt the

Forming the final bend in the U-shaped prongs.

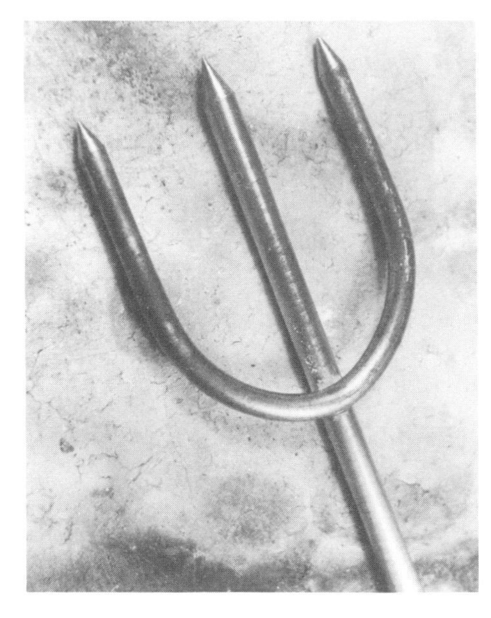

This fork is ready for silver soldering or brazing.

solder out of the joint.

If you want a fork that will stand higher temperatures, make it from plain carbon steel rather than stainless, and either braze the joint or get it welded.

SHEET METAL VICE

My sheet metal vice shows signs of hard use.

Materials

Two lengths of steel angle 26in × 1·75in × 0·125in (660mm × 45mm × 3mm). A scrap bed frame yields ideal material.
Two 0·375in bolts, any thread, at least 3·5in long, or 10mm bolts at least 90mm long; nuts to suit.
4in (100mm) of thick-walled metal tube; bore to allow the bolts to pass through.
Six 1·5in (40mm) countersunk wood screws.
Soft solder and flux, or epoxy resin adhesive.

Tools

Hacksaw
Flat file
Clearance drill for bolts
Clearance drill for woodscrews, small drill for screw holes.
90 degree countersink bit
Wood-boring bit of clearance diameter for nuts, or small, half-round chisel
Centre punch and hammer
Gas torch (if using solder)
Steel rule and scriber

This item is easily made in the home workshop, and it will prove invaluable when you have a large and awkward piece of sheet material to file, cut, or bend. The dimensions quoted are based on the sheet metal vice in my workshop, but the size is largely up to you. You can scale it up or down as you wish, but if you make one larger than the size quoted you must get steel angle of much heavier section, otherwise the material will be too flexible.

Method

1. Trim the two pieces of steel angle to length, and file off any burrs or sharp edges.

2. Mark the centres of all the holes with small, scribed 'x' marks, then punch mark them with the centre punch.

3. Drill the two holes for the big bolts first, with both halves clamped together in the vice. If you are using a vertical

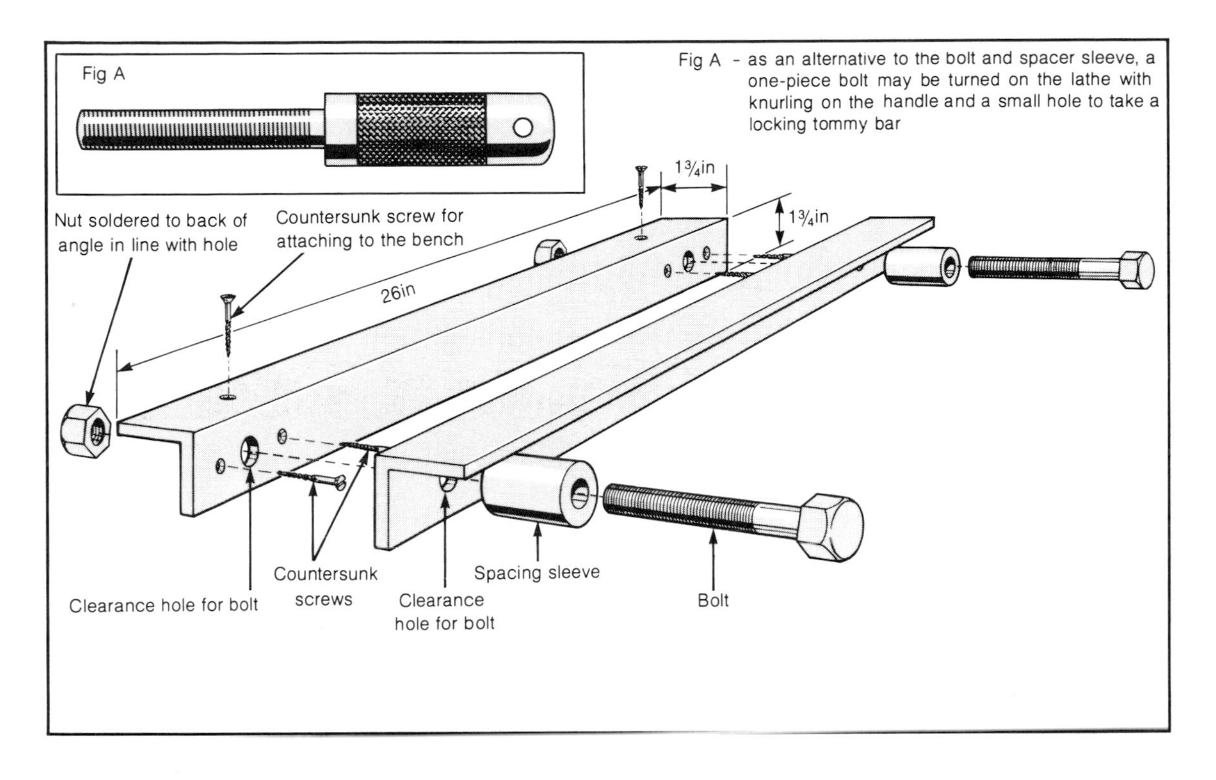

Here is how the sheet metal vice is assembled. Dimensions are only a suggestion, but if you make a very big one, very heavy gauge steel angle is recommended.

drilling machine, the two halves can be held together with G-clamps while being supported in the machine vice. The operation will be eased if you go through with a small drill first, then enlarge the hole with the 0·375in or 10mm drill.

4. Drill and countersink the holes for the woodscrews, being sure that, when fitted, the screw heads will lie either flush with the level of the surrounding metal, or slightly below it.

5. Clean and de-grease the nuts, and clean the metal to which they will be joined. If soldering, lightly coat both the surface of the metal and the nut with flux, being careful that no flux runs up the thread. To solder, heat the whole job

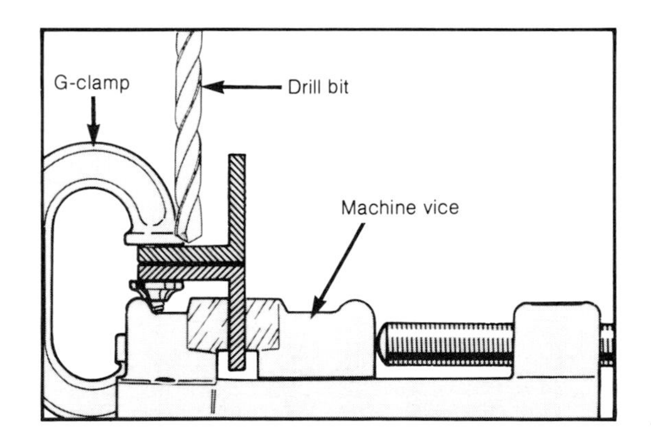

The vice jaws can be made to come together exactly by drilling them simultaneously. This is a suggested set up.

with the torch from underneath, and allow the heat to be conducted to the area of the joint. Melt the solder against the work, not in the flame. If using epoxy, follow the instructions on the pack.

Whether soldered or stuck with epoxy, this will be a low-strength joint in engineering terms. Do not worry – it will be subject to mainly compressive stresses in use.

6. Mark your bench for where the bolts go through and the nuts will be recessed. This can be done by offering the back part of the vice up to the bench and passing a punch through the nut. If you have a wood-boring bit, use that first, then follow on with the bolt clearance drill. If you are using a chisel, drill the hole then enlarge its mouth.

7. Mark and drill the woodscrew holes, using a drill that is slightly less than the core diameter of the screw. Then insert the screws and do them up tight.

8. Take your thick-walled tube, and cut the two spacing pieces that are to fit on the bolt shanks. File the ends flat, and remove any burrs. Thread the tubes on to the bolts, and assemble the front half of the vice.

Comment

As the vice stands, it will have to be tightened with a spanner. If you like, you can cross-drill the bolt heads so that they can be tightened with a short length of steel bar. If you have a lathe, you might want to make the bolts and spacing pieces as a first exercise in screw-cutting.

This nut has been soft soldered to the back of the steel angle. On this example, a slight excess of solder has been used.

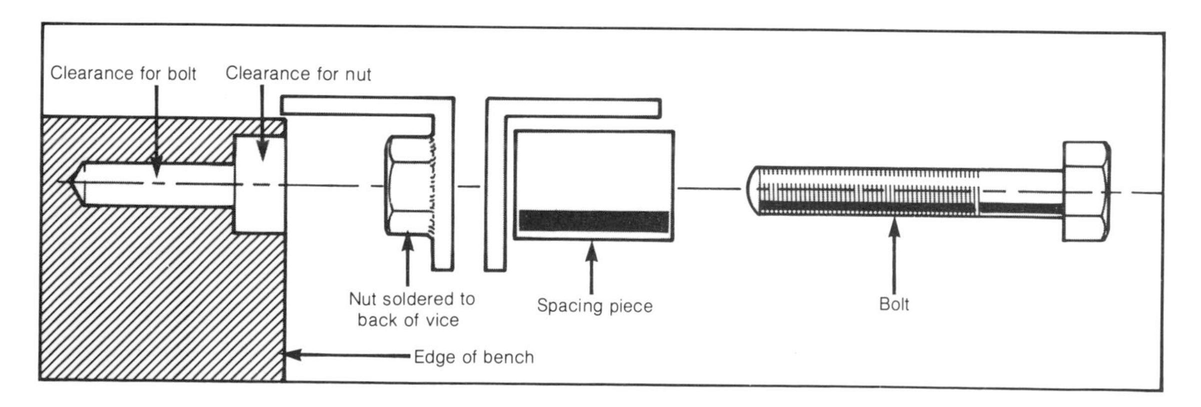

This is the way the vice goes together on the bench edge. A spot of grease down the hole in the bench will help keep the bolt threads lubricated.

SCRIBER

This is the simplest project in the book in its basic form, but you can add complications if you like. For instance, if you have a lathe you can turn the main taper on the machine, and knurl the shank for an easier grip. However, the scriber works just as well in its plain form, and its manufacture will introduce you to the heat-treatment of steel.

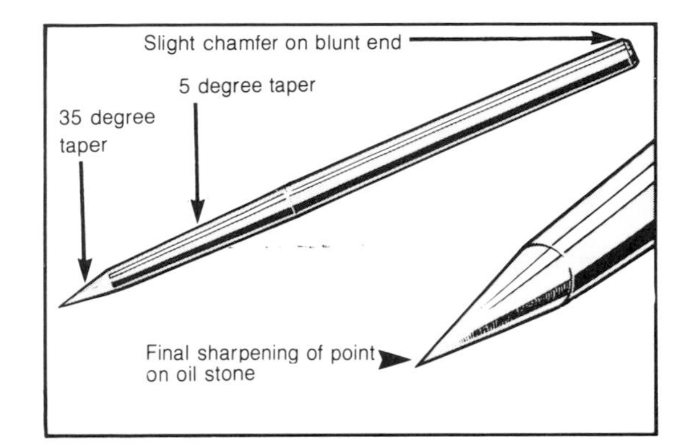

Suggested tapers for making the scriber. It does not matter if they are not exact, but hardening and sharpening are all important.

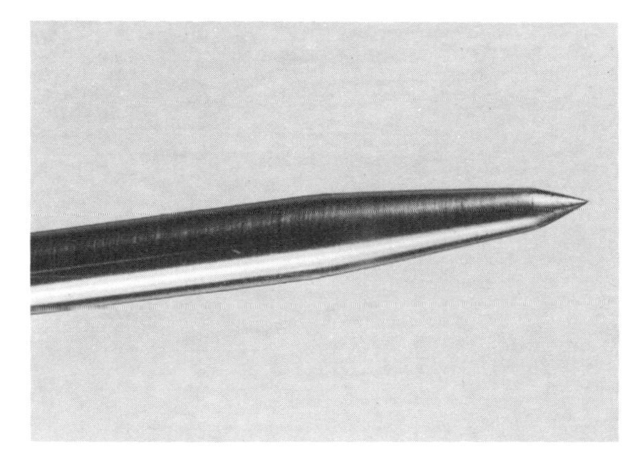

The end of your scriber should look like this. Total length is about 5in (130mm).

Materials

About 5in of $^3/_{16}$in round silver steel, or 130mm of 5mm diameter.

Tools

Vice
Flat file
Small, fine sharpening stone
Heat source (gas torch or domestic gas cooker)
Fine emery cloth or wet-and-dry paper
Cup or tin of clean, cold water

Method

1. Hold the piece of silver steel in the vice, and file one end flat. Then file on a slight chamfer. This is so that you do not cut yourself on the 'blunt' end.

2. File the 'sharp' end to a blunt point, producing a taper of about 5 degrees. The length of the taper does not matter too much. Then bring it to a sharp point, by filing the very tip end to an angle of about 35 degrees.

3. Smooth and polish the tapers with fine emery cloth.

4. Heat the tip of the point until it is cherry red when viewed in normal light. This will represent a temperature of a little over 800 degrees Centigrade. While it is still at this temperature, quench it by plunging it vertically into the cold water. Small objects cool fast, so you will have to have the water very close to the flame. This operation will bring the steel to a fully hard condition, in which it will easily cut into most common metals. It will not,

however, withstand any blows without shattering, so never use a scriber as a punch.

5. Remove any blueing from the tip by polishing with emery. Bring the tip to full sharpness by stroking it with your sharpening stone. Do not do the final sharpening on a rotary grinding wheel – the heat generated will render the point soft.

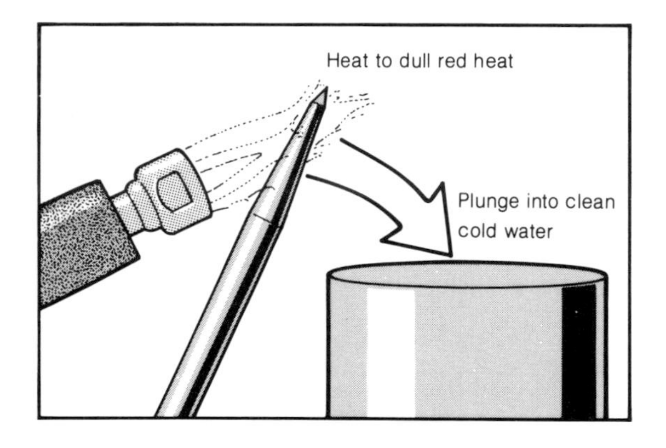

The scriber point is hardened by heating to dull red heat and plunging it into clean, cold water. This produces a condition known as 'glass hard'.

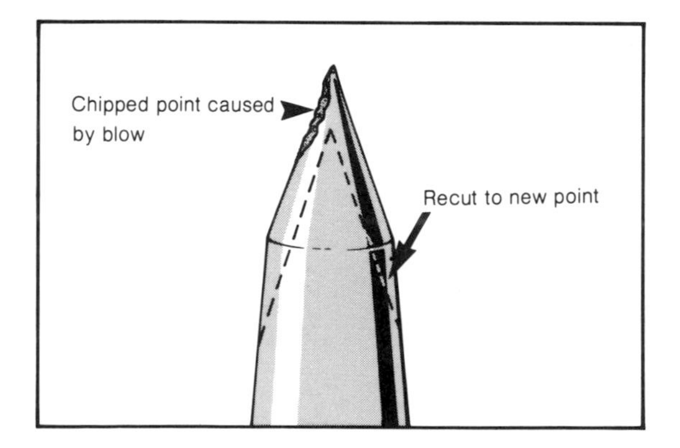

If you ever chip a scriber you can regrind it on a stone, but you will have to soften it by heating it and letting it cool slowly before you work on it with a file. Afterwards, it must be rehardened.

Comment

This little scriber will be very sharp indeed, so you might like to stick it in a cork, or protect its tip when not in use with a sleeve of rubber or plastic tube.

If you do ever break a splinter off the tip (for instance, if you drop it on a hard floor) you will have to soften the tip before you work on it with a file. To do this, heat it to red heat and let it cool slowly. When you have refiled the tip to the correct profile, you can reharden it by heating and quenching.

SCREWDRIVER

This is a good first exercise on the lathe, because it introduces you to a lot of the machine's features without the need for working to very precise limits. You will do plain and taper turning, drilling, and knurling. If you do use the screwdriver as a first exercise, try to keep as close as you possibly can to the quoted dimensions just for practice.

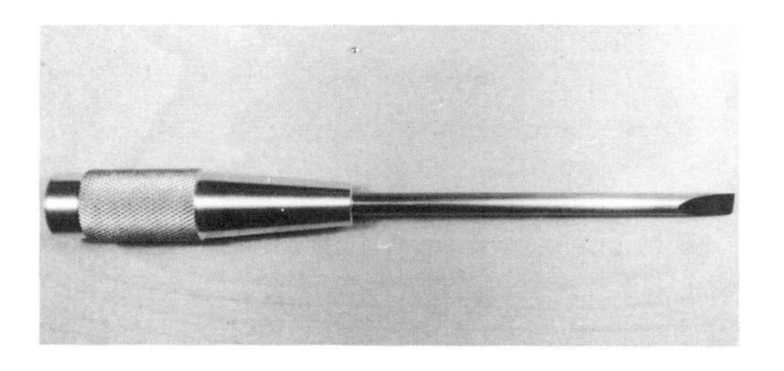

Your finished screwdriver will look something like this. Note that this example has the desirable hollow-ground point.

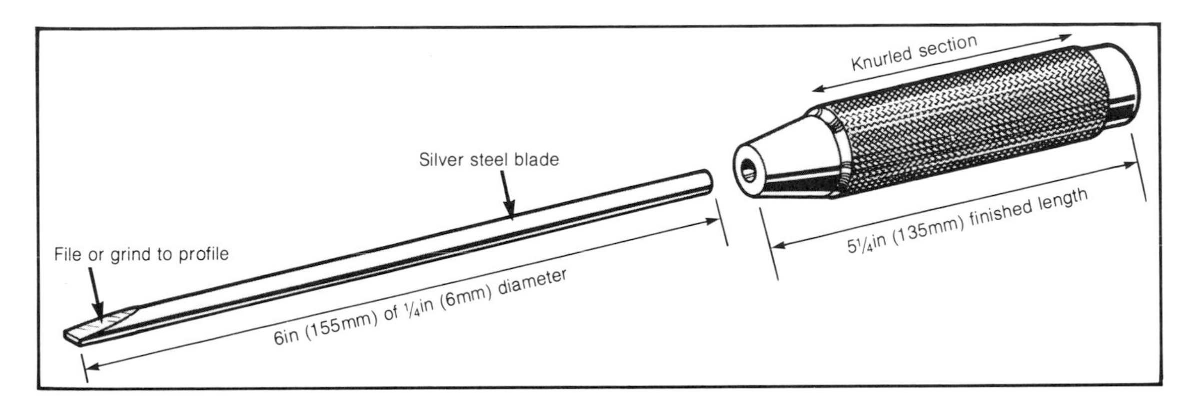

General layout of the screwdriver.

Materials

About 6in of ¼in round silver steel, or 155mm of 6mm material.
About 4in of ⅞in diameter aluminium or aluminium alloy bar, or 100mm of 20mm material.
Loctite 270 engineering adhesive.

Tools

Centre lathe with the following accessories:
- **Three-jaw chuck**
- **Tailstock centre**
- **Tailstock chuck**
- **Round-nosed turning tool (see page 87)**
- **Knurling tool**
- **0·25in or 6mm drill bit**
- **Turpentine or white spirit**
- **Centre drill**

Hand tools:
- **Flat file or rotary grindstone**
- **Hacksaw**
- **Fine emery cloth**
- **Heat source (gas torch or domestic gas cooker)**

Method

1. Enter the alloy bar in the lathe chuck as far as it will go, and face the end. If the lathe spindle taper does not allow you to completely 'swallow' the bar and leaves a long overhang, you will have to take many light cuts.

2. Extend the work in the chuck so that you are gripping it by 0·75in (20mm) at the end. Centre drill your faced end, and support it with a tailstock centre – a running or 'live' centre if you have one. A plain centre must be lubricated with grease.

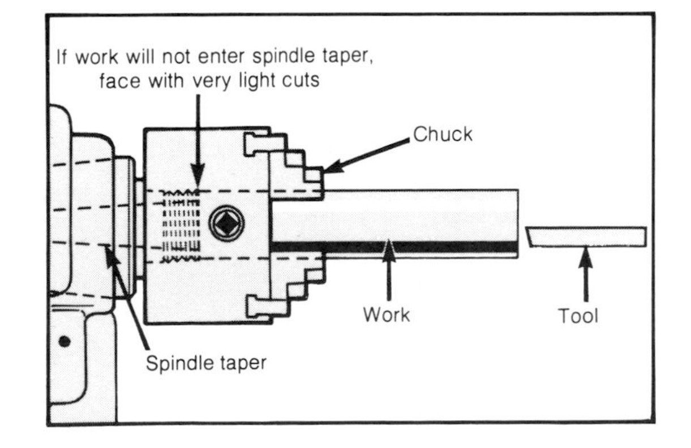

If your chuck and spindle will not 'swallow' the handle piece, you will have to face it with very light cuts.

3. With the machine in a fine automatic feed, take a fine cut along the full length of the work, finishing as close to the chuck as you can safely go. The cut should be just deep enough to render the workpiece truly round. Check with the micrometer, and reduce your 0·875in bar to exactly 0·8125in. Take the metric bar down to 18mm.

4. Further reduce 1·25in of the tailstock end of the bar to 0·75in (32mm to 20mm), then do the same to 0·5in (12mm) of the bar immediately in front of the chuck. The central 'barrel' that you have left will eventually carry the knurled pattern.

5. Swing the topslide over 5 degrees and cut a taper on the tailstock end of the work. For the topslide handwheel to clear the tailstock you may have to increase considerably tool and tailstock overhang. Cut the taper so that it terminates about 0·125in (3mm) from the 'barrel' section.

6. Return the topslide to a position roughly parallel to the bed, and fit the knurling tool. Run an even knurl the full length of the barrel section, going deep enough to form a good grip pattern, but not so deep that you crush the tips off the little metal pyramids the knurling tool forms. For knurling, you will have to reduce considerably the machine's speed.

Taking the first cut off the diameter of the handle material.

Turning the taper. Note that the tool has been moved to the right side of the toolpost to facilitate clearances between the handwheel and the tailstock casting on this particular lathe.

Knurling the main part of the screwdriver handle.

7. Using the round-nosed tool you used for general turning, form a groove about 0·093in (2mm) deep at the point at which the handle will be cut or parted from the piece that remains in the chuck.

8. Place the relevant drill in the tailstock chuck, and drill a hole about 1·5in (38mm) deep.

9. For this job you can use a parting tool, if you have one. The tip should be ground at a slight angle, with the acute angle on the right, and the tool mounted with the tip dead on centre. Use a low speed and plenty of lubricant, and enter the tool so that half of the groove you have cut near the chuck face forms a slight chamfer on the end of the work. With no parting tool, remove the whole job from the lathe, and use the groove as a guide for sawing. Then wrap the knurled section in two or three layers of ordinary writing paper, and grip the job lightly in the chuck, sawn face outwards. The paper prevents chuck-jaw marks on the knurl. Face the sawn end, and the handle is complete.

10. Take your length of silver steel, and tidy one end with the file. File or grind a screwdriver blade profile on the other end, and finish it with fine emery cloth. If

The parting cut has just been begun. Note that this operation is performed with the tailstock removed, otherwise there could be a nasty bang when the tool breaks through the centre.

you use a grinding wheel, you can easily form the desirable hollow-ground point, or you can achieve the same effect with a half-round file.

11. Heat the blade tip to cherry red, and quench it in clean, cold water. The tip will now be glass-hard and brittle. Polish it bright with emery.

12. Now return the blade to the flame, and heat it until it turns a dark straw colour. Do not play the flame directly on to the thin tip as it will become overheated, but allow the heat to be conducted to the tip by heating a point about 0·75in (20mm) away from it. The moment the dark straw colour is achieved, withdraw the work from the flame and plunge it into cold water. This is known as 'tempering', and it should give you a screwdriver with a point tough enough not to distort when you put heavy pressure on a screw, yet not so hard that it chips or shatters.

13. Check that the screwdriver shaft is a free sliding fit in the handle. Clean out both the hole and the shaft, and drip a little Loctite 270 into the mouth of the hole and on to the end of the shaft. Enter the shaft down the hole to the bottom, turning it as you go to distribute the Loctite evenly. In a warm atmosphere, you should be able to use the screwdriver in about an hour.

Comment

Had you been making this screwdriver a few years ago, it would have been necessary to make the shaft of the screwdriver an interference fit in the hole in the handle. It would have been assembled by

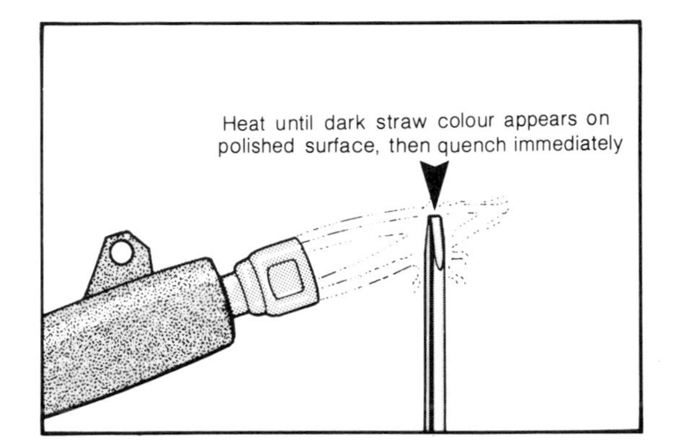

After hardening, the blade must be tempered. To do this, polish it bright, then heat it until it turns a dark straw colour. As soon as this colour appears, quench it very quickly in clean, cold water. It is only necessary to harden and temper the tip.

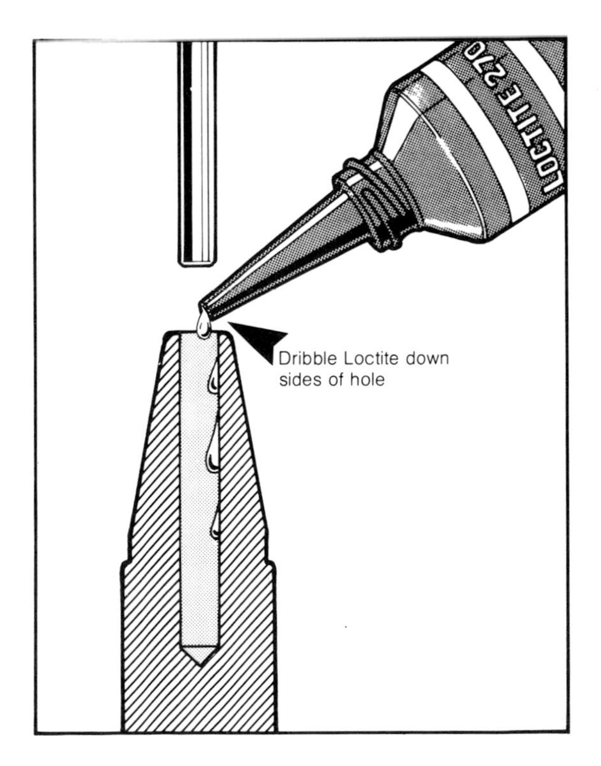

A few drops of Loctite will hold the blade firmly in the handle. If you ever need to get the blade out, the adhesive bond can be broken by heat, but you will need to get it very hot indeed.

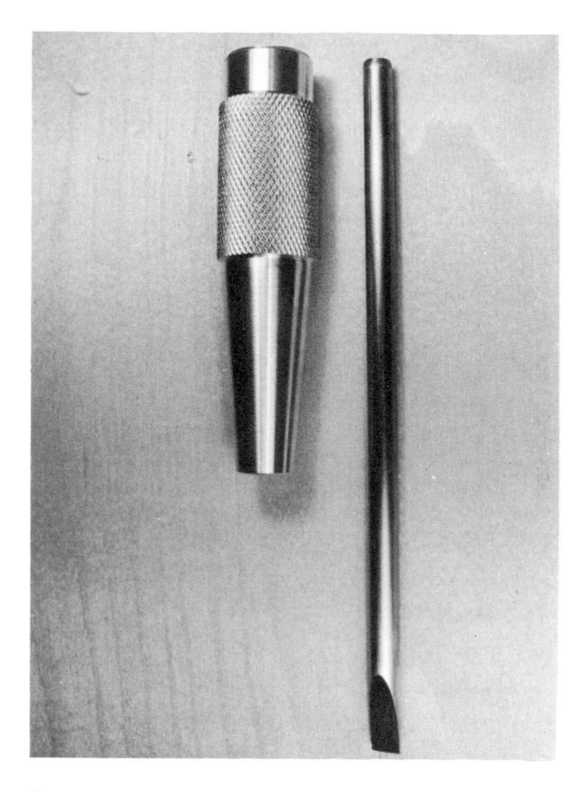

The two components of the screwdriver ready for assembly.

heating the handle to expand it, sliding it on quickly, and waiting for it to cool and contract and therefore grip the shaft very tightly. Loctite is quite expensive, but it has thousands of uses in the workshop and you only use a few drops at a time. It is a curious chemical composition which sets and forms a tight bond when deprived of air. In a home workshop it is superior to press and interference fits, which require the ultimate precision in machining. A tiny bottle lasts a long time.

The screwdriver should give you years of use in your workshop, and if you damage the tip you can heat-soften it, recut it, then harden it and temper it again. Remember, however, that it is completely electrically conductive, so do not use it on electrical work.

SMALL SOFT HAMMER

The tool to be described is very light, in fact it weighs only 3oz (85g), including the handle. It is not so much a 'hitting' hammer, as a tool for tapping lightly-clamped work into position on faceplates and milling slides. With such a hammer it is possible to move work 0·001in (0·025mm) at a time – just what you need when tricky work has to be set exactly on centre or in a precise position for milling.

You do not have to stick to the materials or the dimensions quoted. The original was made with one lead face and one copper face, but a copper face and a plastic face might be better, as plastic does not

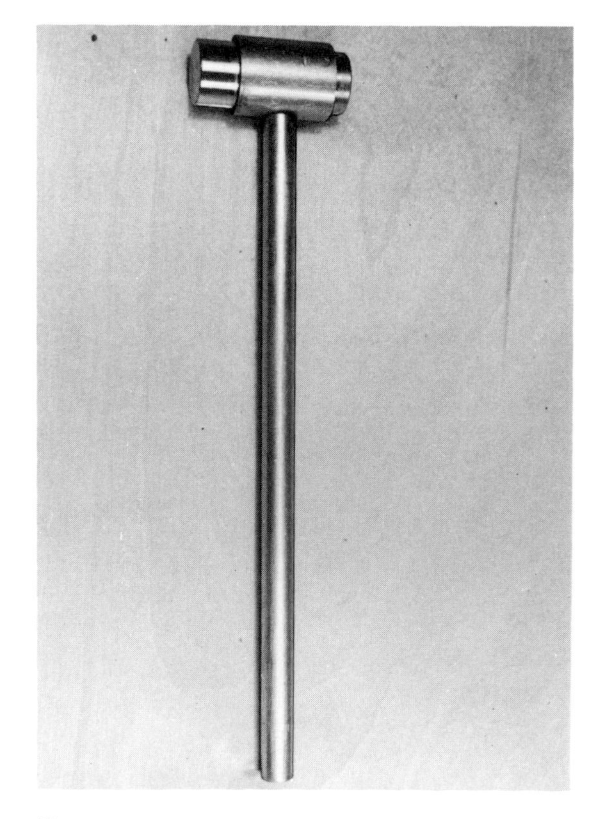

The small soft hammer made by myself. This tool has had a lot of use, so the lead face is somewhat worn.

distort so much as lead under blows. When you look at my hammer, you will see that the lead face has been trimmed back to shape so many times that it is now due for replacement.

Materials

$^7/_8$in (22mm) of 0·75in (20mm) aluminium bar
6·5in (165mm) of $^5/_{16}$in (8mm) aluminium rod
$^5/_8$in (16 mm) of $^5/_8$in (16mm) copper bar
$^5/_8$in (16mm) of $^5/_8$in (16mm) plastic (soft nylon or PVC is suggested, but any plastic that does not crack under blows will do)

Tools

Centre lathe with the following accessories:
Three-jaw chuck
Tailstock chuck
Plain turning tool suitable for facing cuts
Small boring tool
Big drill bit of slightly less than $^5/_8$in diameter
$^1/_4$in (any thread) or 6mm taps and die
Relevant tapping drill
Tailstock die holder (optional)
Centre drill

Method

1. Trim both ends of the aluminium rod flat by facing in the lathe. Then reduce about 0·375in (10mm) of one end to 0·25in (6mm). Thread this end right down to the shoulder either with the tailstock die holder or with the die held in a hand wrench.

2. Face both ends of the short, thick piece of aluminium bar and, beginning with the centre drill, enter the sub-$^5/_8$in drill about $^5/_{16}$in (8mm) into each end.

3. Using the micrometer, carefully check the diameters of the copper and plastic that are to form the hammer's faces. They might be slightly more or less than the nominal diameters, so check and write the figures down.

4. Using the boring tool, enlarge the sub-$^5/_8$in holes to the exact diameters of the facing material. The finished holes should be $^5/_{16}$in (8mm) deep, and flat bottomed.

5. Clamp the workpiece to the toolpost, introducing packing underneath it to bring the centre of the work exactly to centre height, and mount it so that it lies exactly at right angles to the lathe bed. If this is not possible on your lathe, the next operation will have to be done with a hand drill or in a drilling machine.

6. Beginning with a centre drill in the lathe chuck, produce a hole of tapping size for the $^1/_4$in or 6mm thread that enters where you wish the hammer shaft to be fixed. Do not take it in further than $^1/_2$in (12mm), and produce a slight chamfer in its mouth with the coned part of the centre drill.

7. If the hole has been drilled in the lathe, you can use the lathe chuck as a guide for entering the tap. Switch off and disengage the clutch or drive mechanism, and enter the taper tap down the hole for two or three full turns. These threads around the mouth of the hole will form a

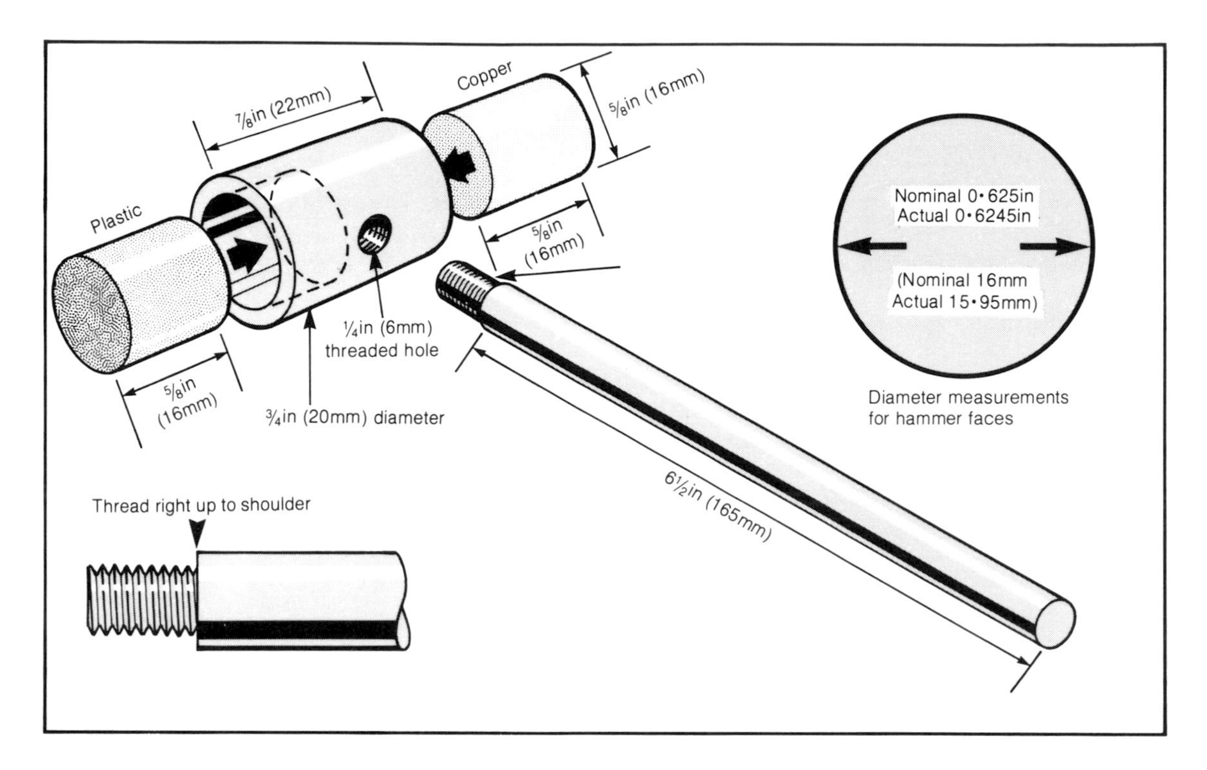

Details of the hammer. It is very difficult to thread the end of the shaft right up to the shoulder, but a neat appearance can be gained by countersinking the threaded hole into which it fits. For the face material always measure the diameters - they could be slightly undersize.

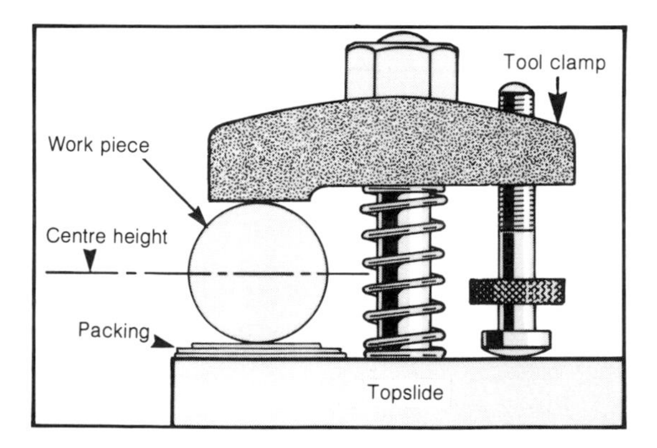

The tapping hole in the hammer body can be bored on-centre and straight by mounting it in the tool clamp on the lathe topslide, with suitable packing underneath.

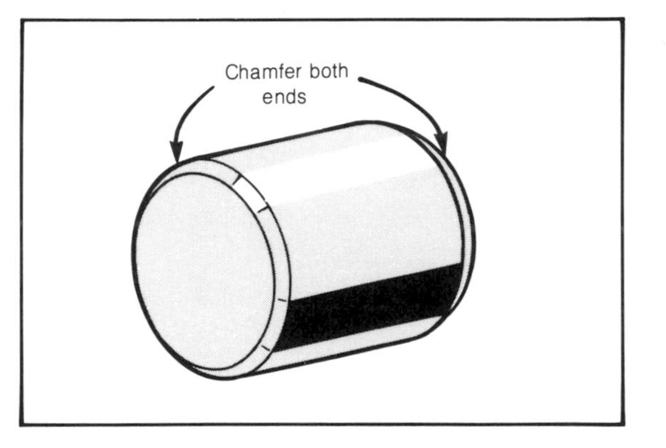

Before fitting, the hammer faces should be lightly chamfered on both ends.

guide for completing the thread with a conventional tap wrench off the lathe. The finished hole must bear a full thread for at least $^3/_8$in (10mm).

8. Face both ends of the material which will form the hammer faces, and lightly chamfer both ends with the edge of the turning tool.

9. This is where you discover how accurate your boring and measurement have been, because the hammer faces should be a tight press fit into the hammer body. You should have to press them in, using a smooth-jawed vice. However, if they are a loose fit they can be stuck in with Loctite engineering adhesive or a smear of epoxy resin.

10. Screw the handle into the completed head.

Comment

At all stages in this job the relevant cutting lubricants should be used. If adhesives are to be used, joining faces should be carefully cleaned first. A good wash in hot water and washing-up liquid is as good as anything.

SMALL WOODWORKING PLANE

I made this little plane many years ago, when I was building and racing model aircraft. It was designed for the accurate planing of soft balsa wood, but over the years it has been used for trimming a wide variety of timbers and plastic laminates. It can be made entirely with hand tools, but if you have a lathe you can add some ornamental nuts like those on my plane.

Materials

About 15 square in of sheet steel with a long edge of at least 4in (97 square cm, long edge 100mm). Minimum thickness 0·09in or 13 standard wire gauge (2·3mm)
$2^1/_4 \times {}^1/_2$in countersunk screws (any thread) with nuts and washers to fit (60mm × 12mm)
1 short $^3/_{16}$in BSF or 2BA (5mm) socket-head cap screw
10in of $^3/_4 \times {}^1/_8$in (255mm of 20mm × 3mm) aluminium strip
1 worn-out HSS hacksaw blade
Silver solder and flux

Tools

Scriber, ruler and set square
Centre punch
Hacksaw
Flat file
Round file, approx 0·25in (6mm)
90 degree countersink bit
Drills for $^1/_4$in (6mm) clearance
$^3/_{16}$in BSF or 2BA (or 5mm) taps, plus relevant drill
Gas torch
Fire-brick
Short end of scrap steel bar approx 2in (50mm) diameter
Grinding wheel

Method

1. Mark out the shapes shown in the diagram, using the scriber. Try to make the most economical use of the metal, but leave a gap a little more than the width of a saw blade between items.

2. Saw out the shapes, keeping to the

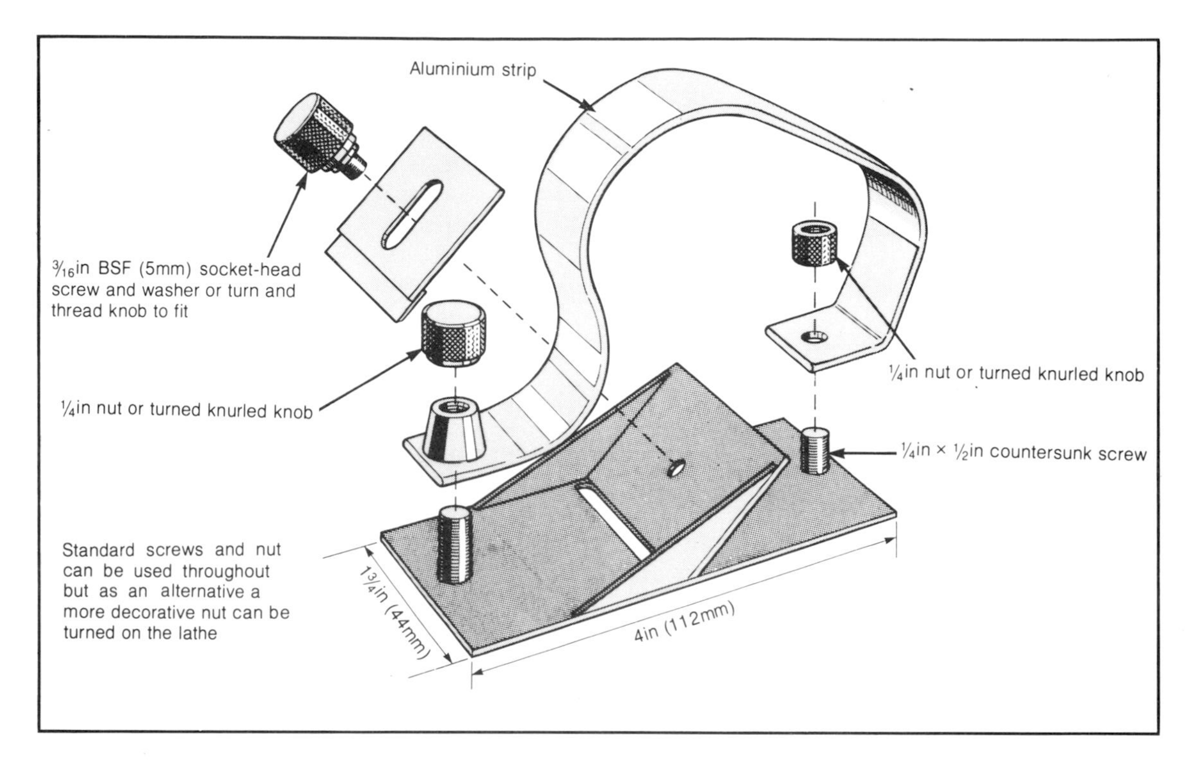

Here is how the woodworking plane goes together. You can make it as big as you need, but if you exceed the quoted dimensions you will have to use thicker plate.

waste side of the scribed lines. Smooth all edges down to the scribed lines with a file.

3. Drill all the holes, starting each hole on a punch mark. Drill a 0·25in (6mm) hole at each end of the blade slot in the base, and at each end of the slot in the blade. Countersink the two holes in the base, being sure that the countersink is deep enough to bury the screw heads completely.

4. Form the slots in the blade and the base with the round file. For this job, you can use hard vice jaws as a guide, or an off-cut of hard steel strip.

5. Mix a little silver soldering flux to a paste with clean water, and coat all edges to be joined. Clear the bench of all inflammable materials, get out your fire-brick, and set up the job on its surface. This tedious job will be helped if you have some little square and wedge-shaped pieces of broken fire-brick to use as props and supports. You can also use little blocks of scrap steel, providing you are careful not to solder them to the job. Be sparing with the silver solder, but try to build up a little fillet in the acute angle behind the blade support. If you get the occasional blob where it is not wanted, do not worry – you can remove it later with a file.

6. Take the scrap hacksaw blade and, using the vice, snap off a piece a little longer than the length of the blade.

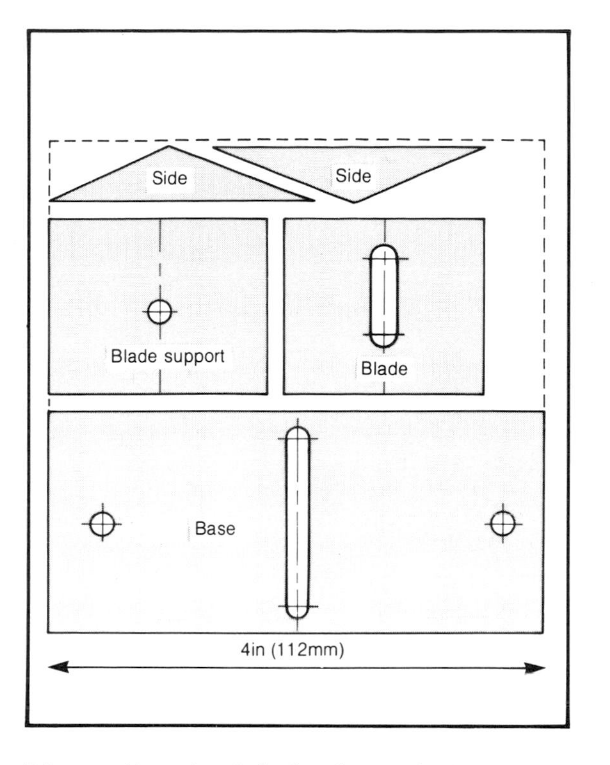

When marking out parts for the plane, make the most economical possible use of the piece of plate that you have, but remember to leave gaps to accommodate the width of the saw blade and to allow for finishing with a file.

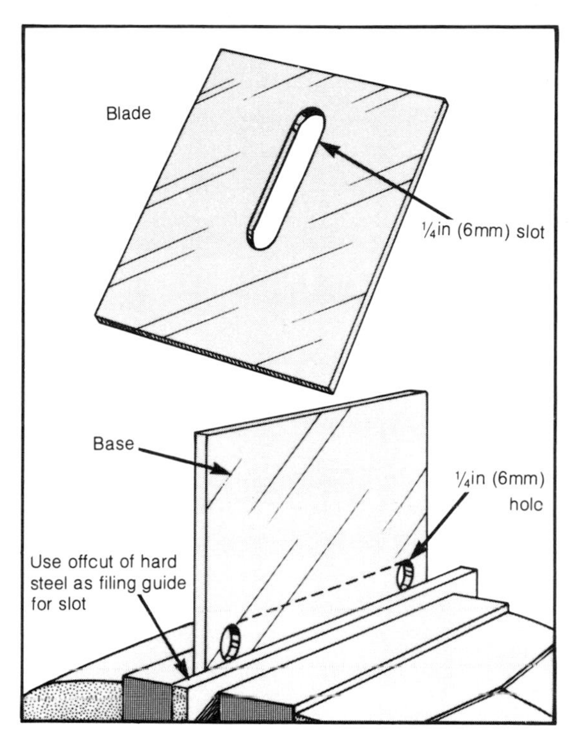

If you can not cut the blade and base slots on a mill, you can file them with a round file using a bit of hard steel strip as a guide. To make life easier, you can drill several holes along the length of the slot.

Square up the ends exactly to length on the grinding wheel, and grind off the teeth. Remember which side the teeth were, because this will be the 'hard' side of a composite blade. Remove any paint from the blade with fine emery cloth.

7. The cutting edge can now be silver soldered to the blade. If you do not take it beyond dull red heat you will not spoil its hardness. When the job has cooled, sharpen the blade, from the back only, on the grinding wheel.

8. Tap the hole in the blade support, and fit the blade using the small socket-head cap screw with a washer underneath it. Establish that the blade has a sufficient range of adjustment, because now is the time to correct things by further filing the slot if all is not well.

9. Square off the ends of the aluminium strip with a file, and bend it to a comfortable handle profile using the length of scrap steel bar as a former for the curves. To save the material from cracking when you form the sharp angle at the back end of the handle, first heat and quench the bar to soften it, remembering to hold it in pliers or tongs as you handle it when hot, because heat will be conducted rapidly from one end to the other. After bending, drill the holes for the mounting screws.

10. Your plane is now ready to be completely assembled, but first give it a good clean to get rid of any flux, and gently file away any silver solder that has run beyond the limits of the joints. The base and the blade should be left as bright, polished steel, but the rest of the plane can be painted any colour you wish. Matt black makes a nice contrast with bright metal.

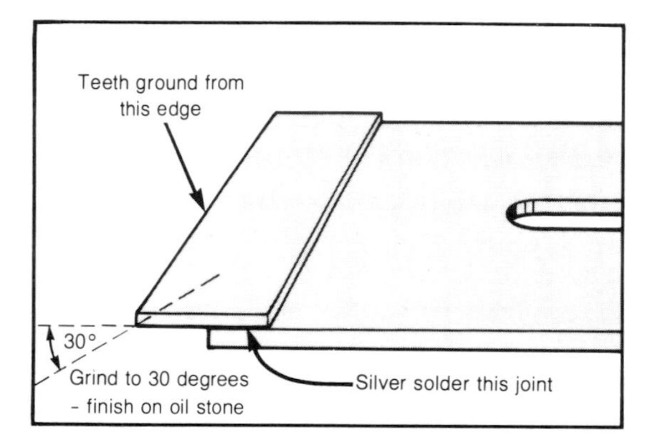

The blade edge is made from a length of high-speed hacksaw blade, and is held on with silver solder. Always make the toothed edge the sharp edge - some blades are of composite construction and the backs are of softer steel.

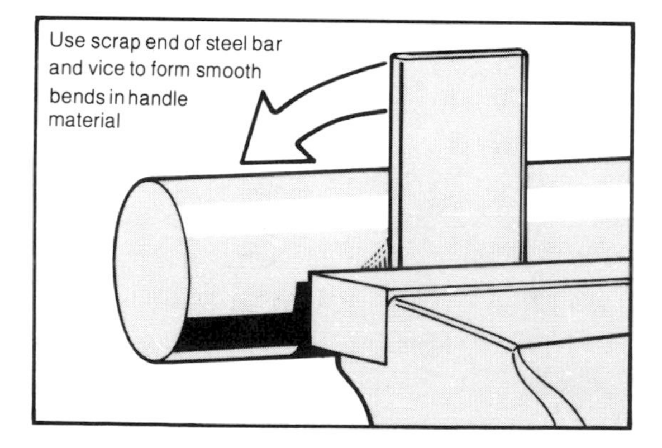

When bending the aluminium strip for the handle, use lengths of round steel bar as formers for the curves.

Comment

If you decide to scale this little plane up, you will have to make it from much thicker metal. The original was built from stainless steel, although almost any workable grade of steel will do. An example made of polished brass would be a nice exhibition piece.

ORNAMENTAL JUG

The original of this jug was made from a scrap end of 23swg (0·61mm) galvanised steel sheet left over from covering a bench top, and the most difficult part of the whole construction appeared to be the marking out, to cut the sheet of steel that would be bent into a truncated cone, forming the jug's body.

A completed jug made by myself to the dimensions mentioned in the text.

Materials

A thin sheet of soft metal that can be soft soldered, at least 15in × 9¼in (for the body, spout, and handle), plus a piece to make a disc 4 11/16in diameter (381mm × 235mm, plus 119mm disc).
Soft solder and flux.
Paint and metal primer, colours to taste.

Drawing Requirements

A sheet of paper at least 20½in × 16in (521mm × 407mm). Several smaller pieces stuck together will do.
Ruler
Straight edge at least 21in (534mm) long
Giant compasses, or trammels, with 20in (508mm) reach
Protractor
Set square
Sharp pencil

Tools

Metal shears or sheet-metal cutter
Half-round file (fine)
Sheet-metal vice, or conventional vice with two 8in (204mm) lengths of steel angle
Metal or wooden cylinder approximately 2¾in diameter by 8in long (70mm × 185mm)
Gas torch or very big soldering iron
2 small G-clamps or bulldog clips
Soft hammer

In fact, there is a very easy way of doing this, but you need some drawing instruments that can be found in the average schoolboy's geometry set, and a will to improvise. The size of the original jug was 4·75in across the base, 7·25in high, and 3in across the top (121mm × 184mm × 76mm). These dimensions give a cone shape that is pleasing to the eye, although you can scale up or down as you wish. Do not try to build a jug out of thick, hard plate or you will have difficulty in forming the shape without proper plate-bending tools. In fact, the softer the metal the easier the job is.

Materials listed here are for a jug the same size as my original.

Method

1. This is the drawing stage. Take your sheet of paper and lay it down with the short edge towards you. Draw a horizontal line across it from edge to edge, about ¼in (6mm) up from the bottom. From the centre of this line, draw a

This diagram gives a good idea of the proportions of the finished jug.

vertical line that goes right to the top of the paper.

Using your horizontal line as a base line and the vertical line as the centre, draw an elevation of the jug body. This should appear like a truncated cone drawn at its centre section.

Now project the two lines that mark the sides of the jug upwards, until they converge on the centre line. This will happen at a point about 20in (508mm) above the base line, near the top of the paper.

Next, using the protractor, measure the included angle formed by these two converging lines. It will be near enough to 15 degrees. Multiply this angle by pi (3·1416), this being the relationship between the diameter of the jug and its circumference at any given point along its

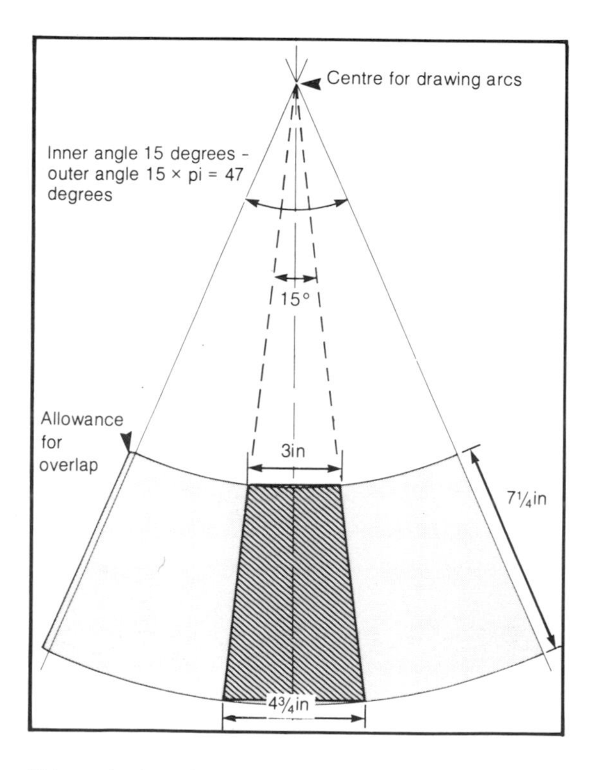

This method can be used to project the shape to be cut for the jug body.

height. The answer is 47·12389 which for practical purposes can be rounded down to 47 degrees. So, construct an angle of 47 degrees, centred around the vertical centre line of the jug, from the point where the lines converge, and project these lines down to the base line. The drawing at this stage looks like the elevation of a Red Indian tepee.

In fact, the area between the last two lines you have drawn represents the shape of a piece of metal that could be bent into a true cone of the correct taper for the jug's body. However, as you cannot solder plate edge to edge and expect the result to be both strong and waterproof, allowance has to be made for a small overlap. So, along one edge of the triangle (it does not matter which one) draw a parallel line about $\frac{3}{16}$in (5mm) away.

Now the arcs have to be drawn which will represent the top and bottom diameters of the jug. If you do not have compasses or trammels big enough, you can improvise by tightly binding one leg of your dividers and the spiked leg of your compasses to a bit of metal rod. Tightly wound plastic insulation tape makes a firm job.

Using the point at the convergence of the lines as the centre, draw an arc that passes through the bottom corners of the jug's section, and is wide enough to join the outer lines that you have drawn. Then draw a second arc that passes through the top corners of the jug's elevation.

The area between the arcs and the side lines, when bent into a circle, will form the truncated cone of the jug's body, including the overlap. If you cut the shape out with scissors you can use it as a template for cutting the metal. Also, if

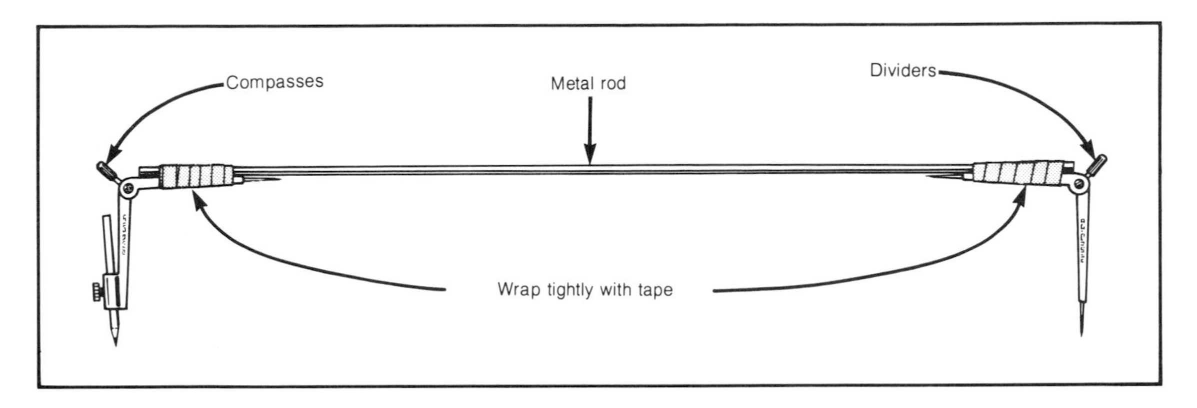

If you do not have giant compasses or trammels, you can use this method to improvise with the components from a 'schoolboy' geometry set.

To be sure that dimensions are correct before you cut the metal, you can first make a template from paper or thin card and stick it together with adhesive tape.

you have doubts at this stage, you can bend the paper and stick it together with masking tape. This exercise should confirm that you have a free-standing, evenly-proportioned truncated cone.

2. This is where you start cutting the metal. If using the paper as a template, stick it to the metal with wallpaper glue, or any adhesive for which you have a solvent. Cut around the edges with metal shears or a sheet metal cutter.

At this stage you can also mark and cut the base disc ($^{11}/_{16}$in or 17·5mm diameter, while the waste from the jug body should yield a strip 9in × 1in (230mm × 25mm) for the handle. File all the cut edges smooth, and the cutting stage is complete.

3. This is where you will need your big wooden or metal former, the soft hammer, the sheet metal vice, and some patience.

Take the piece of metal for the jug's body, and first form the stepped overlap. This is done either in the sheet metal vice or between two lengths of steel angle held in a conventional vice, and it is not as difficult as you may think. Once one right angle is formed, the metal will work-harden along the ridge and will be very reluctant to bend at that point again, so the second angle should come relatively easily. Do not worry if you do not get two sharp right angles – any tiny gap will be filled with solder.

Next, using the cylindrical former, the vice and the hammer, form the metal into a cone. Take it gently, in easy stages, and do not form any sharp bends. Getting it just right without proper bending rollers will take a lot of patience and fiddling, and sharp creases put into the metal are very difficult to get out. When the cone is complete, set it aside and work on the handle.

All you need to do on the handle is to fold the edges over for about $^{1}/_{8}$in (3mm) each side. If this presents difficulty, grip the job in the vice and make the folds over the back edge of a scrap hacksaw blade.

4. The first soldering job is the long seam along the jug body. First make sure the edges to be joined are spotlessly clean, then give them a light coat of flux. If after you have bent the body to shape the edges do not meet exactly, hold them together at top and bottom with small G-clamps or bulldog clips. If using a gas

This shows the seam side of the jug. The seam can be partly hidden by soldering the handle over it.

torch do not heat the joint directly or you will burn the flux. Play the flame a little way away from the joint, and allow the heat to be conducted in. Avoid extreme local heating at any point along the joint, otherwise the metal may distort.

If you use plumber's solder you will find that it goes through a long 'pasty' stage as it cools, and this will allow you to wipe the joint with a thick pad of cotton rag, removing any excess solder and forming a very neat finish to the joint. Otherwise, any excess solder will have to be removed the hard way, with a file.

When this solder joint is complete and cool, stand the jug body on its base and observe it carefully to be sure that it stands square. Tiny mistakes can be corrected by filing the base but do not be tempted to take big cuts with metal shears, otherwise you may eventually finish up with a 2in (50mm) jug that still does not stand level!

5. Press the base into the bottom of the cone of the jug body, and tap it gently with a tiny hammer or a bit of scrap wood or metal until it lies level. Run a tiny fillet of flux around the inside rim, and wrap the jug body in wet cotton cloth, except for a ½in (12mm) strip around the base. This will keep the seam joint cool while the base is soldered in.

When making this joint you will have to work very carefully otherwise, in spite of your precautions, you will melt the seam joint. In fact, if you have solders of two different melting points, make the seam joint in your hardest solder, and use the soft stuff for the rest of the job.

When this base joint has cooled you can fill the jug up with water and see if it leaks. Big leaks have to be resoldered, but you may decide that a tiny 'weep' will be

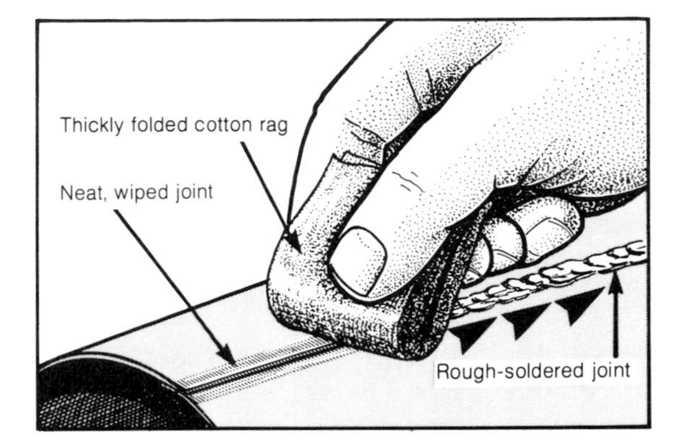

Proper plumber's solder has a long pasty stage as it cools, so if you work quickly you can produce a very neat 'wiped' joint along the jug's main seam. If you do not have a proper plumber's moleskin, use cotton rag, not a synthetic material, and be careful not to burn yourself.

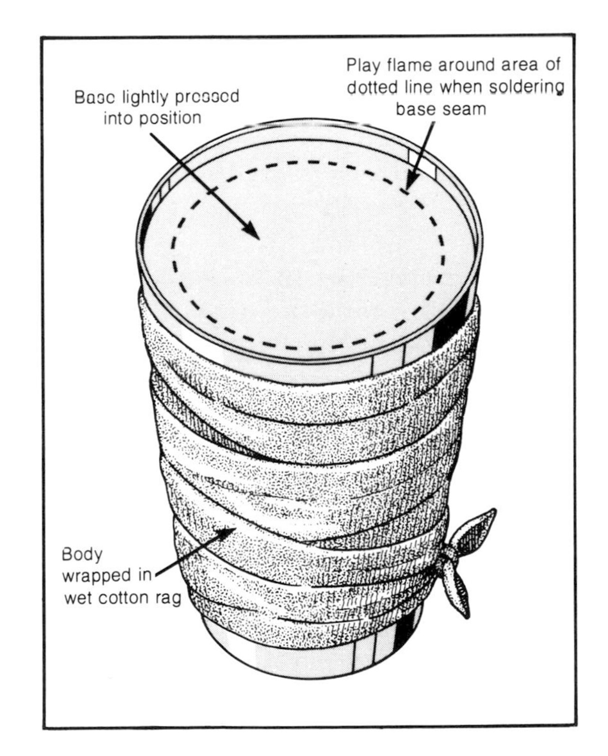

Producing several soldered joints in one component is always a bit of a nightmare, because the heat required to make one joint can unsolder another. When soldering in the base you can combat this by wrapping the body in wet cotton rag.

sealed by subsequent painting or a tiny smear of sealing compound.

6. Solder the folded edges of the handle and bend it to shape, using the vice and the cylindrical former you used for the body. Soldering the handle on is another tricky job. You can protect much of the seam with wet cotton rag, and one of the best methods is as follows: flux the joining faces, and wire the handle into position with some tiny flakes of solder trapped between the joining faces; heat the handle gently, and remove the heat source as soon as the solder has melted.

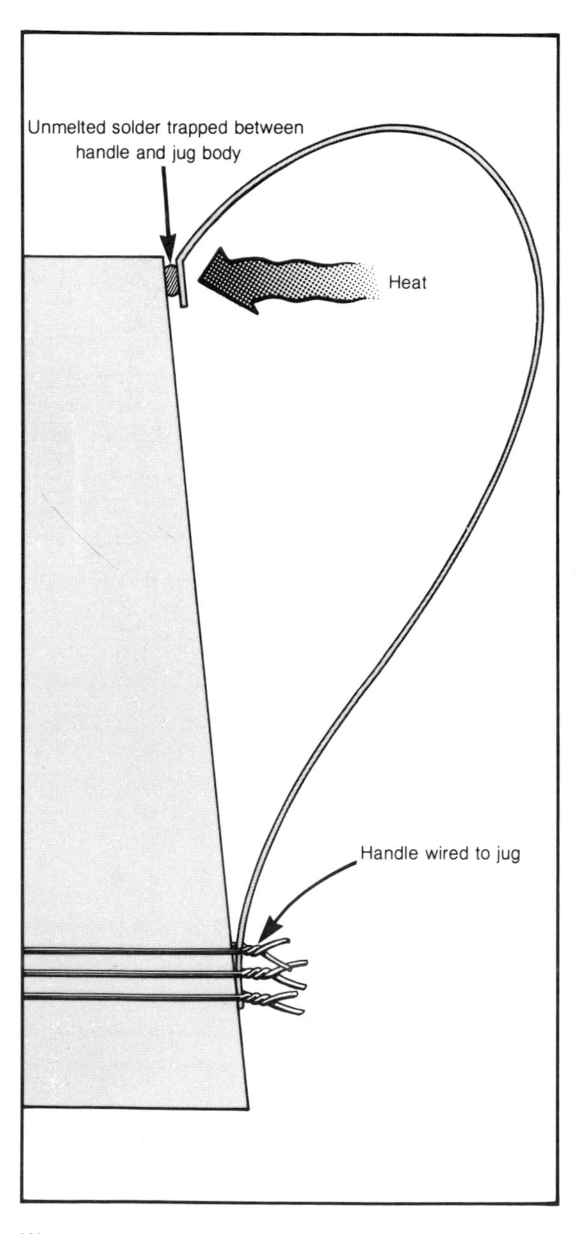

When the handle has been bent to shape, this is a good method for soldering it on.

7. The spout has been left until last because, if you follow this pattern, the spout and the handle will look best if they are set at exactly the same angle. The spout blank is cut in the shape of the tip of a broad leaf, and folded along its centre line.

Offer the cut and folded spout up to the jug body to ensure that it looks right, then mark round it with a pencil or scriber. Cut the 'V' shape out of the jug body, being careful not to distort the metal. You may have to bring the cut out section to its full form with a lot of patient filing.

Soldering the spout in is one of those jobs for which you will wish you had three hands, one tipped with steel

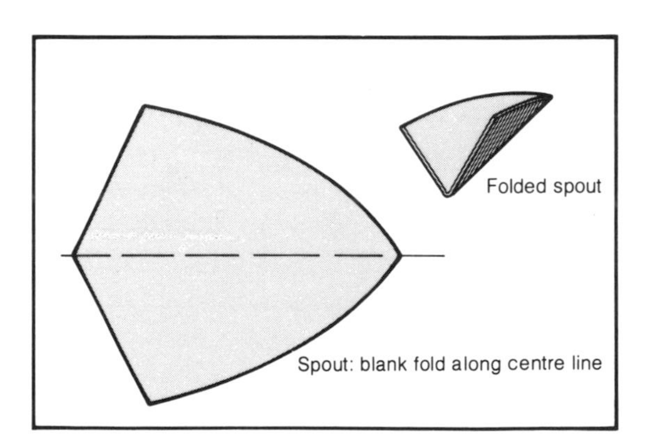

The jug spout is cut from flat material and folded to shape, using a bit of flat steel bar as a former to get a clean, sharp fold.

fingers. One way is to support the jug horizontally, handle downwards, by using the vice, and spring a curved strip of scrap plate into the mouth of the jug. This strip is very lightly greased, so that solder will not stick to it, and the spout is balanced on it for soldering.

Do not worry if there is a bit of a lip between the spout and the jug body on the inside – it can be filed off later. Try to build an even fillet of solder between spout and body on the outside.

8. The metalwork is now finished. Before painting, clean the jug thoroughly inside and out, being sure to get rid of any flux. Cellulose thinners, although dangerously inflammable, are one of the best flux removers known.

Comment

My jug was originally made for mixing soluble oil and water in the workshop, but it finished up as a container for flowers on the dining room table. In this mode, its life will be considerably extended if the water is held in a jam jar inside the jug. I would be wary about using the jug to contain anything you are to eat or drink – solder contains poisonous lead, and the residues of paint probably do not do you any good, either.

HOME SECURITY 1

Unless you are prepared to spend many thousands of pounds, you cannot make your home secure against someone who is determined to rob you; however, you *can* do a lot to deter somebody who fancies a bit of casual house-breaking and is going to try somewhere else if your house presents a few difficulties.

In fact, most houses are illegally entered in just the same way you would get

This is one of the simplest things you can make in your workshop. All you need is an angle section made from any metal, a hacksaw, a file, and a drill.

Materials

About 2in (50mm) of steel angle.
Three countersunk wood screws.

Tools

Hacksaw
Flat file
Drills, including countersink drill
Mallet and wood chisel

in if you had forgotten your key – in other words, by forcing the door or a window. Remember, too, that if a burglar first gets into your workshop, he will have access to tools that may provide the means of entry to the rest of the house.

Here are two little security projects that you can tackle in an afternoon, and the first is to prevent anyone from working the credit-card trick on your Yale-type locks.

Method

1. Cut the steel angle so that it has one long flat side and one short one – about ½in (12mm) measured internally. File the ends square.

2. Drill three clearance holes for the wood screws through the long flat of the angle. Countersink them from the inside of the angle.

3. This will depend on the nature of your door frame. You may have to cut a little recess for the device, using the wood chisel. Position it so that when the door is closed the forward edge of the door in the region of the lock is a tight fit in the angle.

Comment

The presence of this little piece of steel angle means that anyone trying to slide

The steel angle in position on a door frame. Its presence makes it very difficult to open a Yale-type lock with a plastic credit card.

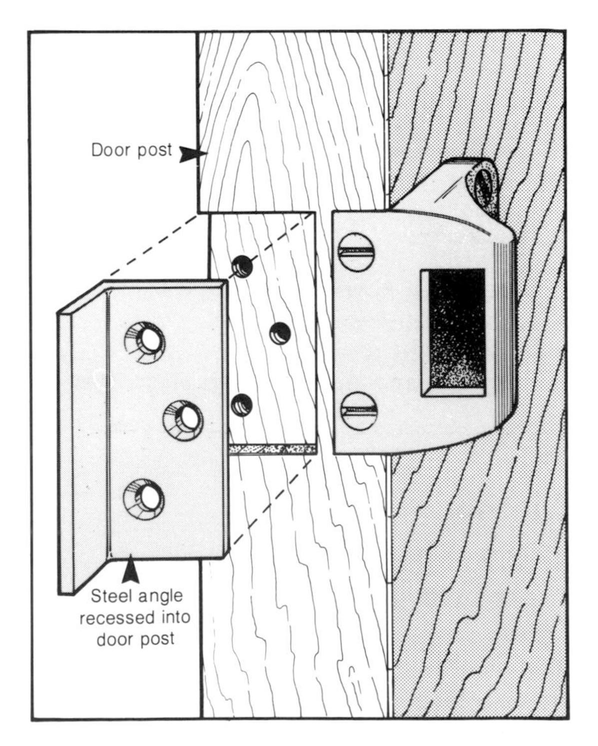

This is how the little piece of steel angle is fitted to the door post. When in place, it stops someone opening a Yale-type lock with a plastic credit card.

the tongue of the lock back by introducing a strip of plastic into the crack is going to be confronted with a very sharp angle through which the plastic will not slide. This means that your casual burglar may now try to find a window that he can spring off its catch, so you will now want to defeat that trick ...

HOME SECURITY 2

Materials

One short length of steel angle (2in or 50mm)
Equal length of metal strip approximately $\frac{1}{4}$in (6mm) thick
4 countersunk wood screws
Epoxy resin adhesive
One socket-head cap screw, approximately $\frac{1}{4}$in (6mm) diameter, any thread

Tools

Hacksaw
Flat file
Clearance drill for wood screws
Countersink drill
Tap to suit screw thread
Tapping and clearance drills for thread

Method

1. Trim the steel angle and the strip to the same length and file the ends square.

2. Drill two wood screw clearance holes in one face of the steel angle, and two more in the strip. Countersink all four holes.

3. Drill a clearance hole for the thread in the as yet undrilled face of the angle.

4. Drill and tap a hole through the middle of the strip.

5. File the head of the socket-head screw to a domed shape, so that it cannot be gripped with pliers.

6. Assemble the two halves to the window frame so that the screw clearance hole lines up with the tapped hole. Fill the screwdriver slots in the mounting screws with epoxy, and paint over.

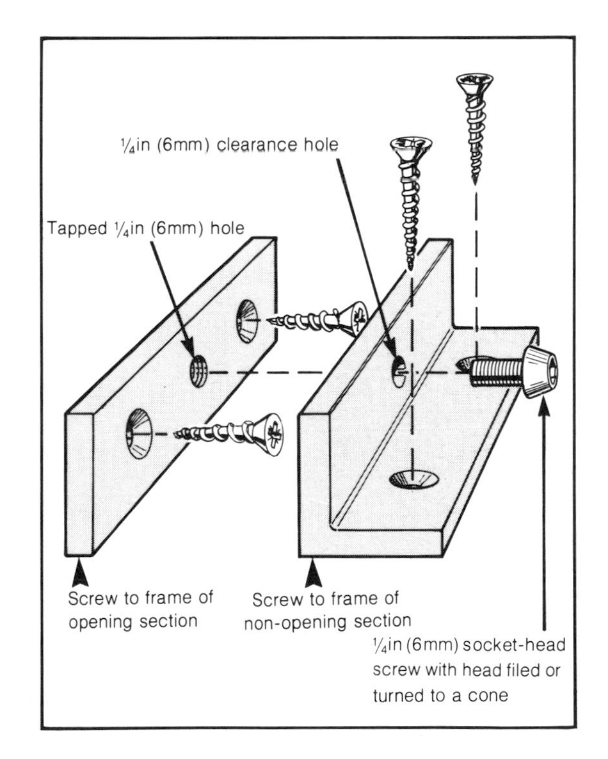

This is the window lock. If the head of the socket-head screw is filed or turned to a cone, it can only be opened with the correct key – something a casual housebreaker is unlikely to carry with him. Woodscrew heads that secure the angle should be filled with epoxy resin or thick paint.

Window lock components before fitting.

The window lock in position. Note that the screw head has been turned or filed to a cone so that it cannot be gripped with pliers. If the wood screw slots are filled with epoxy resin, the only tool that will open it is a hexagon key of the correct size.

Comment

The efficiency of this lock is probably better than some available commercially, for which anyone can buy the keys from hardware shops. The chances of a burglar having the right Allen key in his possession are extremely remote.

Glossary

Most of the technical terms used in this book are explained in the illustrations. However, in cases of confusion the following glossary of engineering terms should prove useful in the interpretation of both this book and of your general engineering reading.

Allen screw A screw manufactured with a hexagonal socket in the head. It is turned with a hexagon key, or Allen key.
Alloy Any compound of metals (for example, brass is a compound of copper and zinc). Commonly mis-used to signify an aluminium-based alloy.
Anneal Bring metal to a fully soft, unstressed condition – usually with a process utilising heat.

Backlash The slack or 'dead' movement between male and female screw threads, usually caused by wear or poor manufacturing standards.
Barrel (micrometer) The cylindrical moving part of a micrometer.
Blind hole A hole that does not pass right through a component.
'Blue' A dye compound used for marking-out, and for checking surfaces for accuracy against known accurate surfaces.
Brazing Joining metal components (usually steel) with the use of melted brass.

Centre drill A rigid, short drill bit with a 60-degree point, usually used from a lathe tailstock.
Clearance drill Any drill bit chosen to cut a hole of slightly greater diameter than the stud, shaft or screw that will pass through it.
Clearance angle The angle formed between the front face of a lathe tool and the vertical, when the tool is in a horizontal plane.
Collet A device for holding a cylindrical workpiece within the taper of a machine-tool spindle.
Comparator A name often given to any accurate measuring device.
Countersink A cone-shaped depression machined into the mouth of a hole.
Counterbore A parallel-sided depression machined into the mouth of a hole – for instance, to hide a screw head.

Dial gauge A circular gauge on which a pointer rotates against a calibrated dial when a plunger or 'foot' is brought into contact with work.
Die Commonly signifies a device for forming a male thread on a shaft or rod. Otherwise, any tool in which metal is formed by compression.

Epoxy resin An adhesive consisting of two viscous constituents which, when mixed together, react to form a solid mass.
End mill A cylindrical milling cutter with cutting faces on its end, and usually on its sides as well.

Fastening An engineer's term for any mechanical device used for joining two or more components together. Examples are nut and bolt, rivet, wood screw.
Female thread A thread formed on the inside face of a hollow, cylindrical component, for example the thread on a nut.
Ferrous Literally 'of iron'. A metal, the main constituent of which is iron.
First tap A tap with a long taper at its nose, used for forming the first stage of a female thread.
Flutes Straight or spiral grooves between the cutting faces of a tap, reamer or drill bit. The flutes provide for the clearance of swarf.
Flux A chemical substance used to prevent surface oxidisation of materials being brazed, soldered or welded. Some fluxes also have a cleaning action.
Fly cutter A cutter attached to the spindle nose of a lathe or milling machine, usually used for generating large flat surfaces.

Forge To form metal by blows with a press or hammer. The equipment on which such operations are carried out.
Foundry A workplace where cast components are produced.
Four-jaw Short term for a four-jaw, independent-jawed chuck.

Galvanised Metal covered with a thin layer of zinc which has been deposited by an electrolytic process.
Green wheel A very hard grinding wheel used for sharpening tungsten-carbide tipped tools. The name comes from its distinctive colour.

High-speed steel A special alloy tool steel which retains its hardness and cutting edge at relatively high temperatures.

Imperial measurements Measurements based on the inch standard.

Knurling The diamond-chequered 'grip' pattern formed on cylindrical components such as tool handles and round nuts designed for finger tightening.

Lathe features:
- *Apron* The vertical face in front of the saddle.
- *Back-gear* A set of low-ratio gears that can be brought into operation for very slow turning.
- *Bed* The base of the machine on which the carriage and tailstock run.
- *Carriage* The component which slides along the bed, carrying the cross-and topslides, toolpost, etc.
- *Change wheels* Variable gears which can be interposed between the spindle and the leadscrew.
- *Centre height* The vertical measurement from the bed face to the centre of the spindle.
- *Counter-shaft* On a belt-driven lathe the shaft which is driven by the motor, and which transfers the drive to the spindle.
- *Cross-slide* The main slide which moves through a horizontal plane at 90 degrees to the bed.
- *Faceplate* A flat, circular work-holding plate which can be attached to the spindle nose.
- *Feedscrews* The screw threads which control the movement of the top and cross-slides, tailstock barrel, etc.
- *Handwheel* Any wheel used for manual control of the machine.
- *Headstock* The heavy metal component at the left-hand end of the bed which carries the spindle.
- *Leadscrew* The master feedscrew which runs parallel to the bed and can be driven by the spindle through change wheels.
- *Saddle* The top part of the carriage which straddles the bed.
- *Spindle* The main rotating component of the lathe, carried in the headstock bearings.
- *Steady* A device used, usually, when turning long cylindrical work, to prevent bending under cutting stresses and to damp vibration.
- *Stud* A small spindle on which change wheels are mounted.
- *Tailstock* The component mounted on the right-hand end of the bed, used to support work or as a base for drilling.
- *Toolpost* The fixture on which turning tools are mounted.
- *Topslide* The small slide on top of the cross-slide on which the toolpost is mounted.
- *Vertical slide* A component, mounted on the cross-slide in place of the topslide, to convert the lathe into a milling machine.
- *Ways* The faces of the bed.

Letter drills A series of 26 drills, ranging in diameter from 5·94 to 10·49mm.

Male thread A thread on the outside of a cylindrical component, for example, the thread on a bolt.
Metric measurements Measurements based on the millimetre standard.
Micrometer A precision measuring device based on an accurate screw thread.

Milling A method of removing metal in which the workpiece is brought into contact with a tool mounted on a rotating spindle.
Morse taper A series of standard tapers for holding tools in the mouths of rotating spindles, tailstock barrels, etc. (Named after the inventor.)

Number drills A series of 80 drill bits, ranging in diameter from 0·34 to 5·79 millimetres.

Pilot hole A small hole drilled as a guide for a larger drill bit.
Pitch The measurement between peaks, for instance of a thread or saw teeth.
Plug tap A tap for cutting a female thread right to the bottom of a blind hole.
Protractor A device for measuring angles.
Pulley A grooved wheel used in belt-drive systems.
Punch A tool designed to be struck, usually forming a hole or a depression in the work.

Quenching The rapid cooling of metal by plunging it into a liquid - usually water or oil.
Quill The rotating shaft of a drilling or milling machine which can also be moved in a vertical plane.

Rake The angle formed between a lathe tool's top cutting face and the horizontal axis of the shank.
Reamer A tool for fine-finishing a hole to accurate dimensions.
R.P.M. Revolutions per minute.

Second tap A tap used to cut a female thread, after the thread has been begun with a first tap.
Scriber A pointed metal instrument used for marking lines on work.
Slot drill A drill bit designed to cut sideways, to form a slot.
Solder An alloy of metals that can be melted to form a joint between metal components.
Soluble oil A specially formulated oil which has been treated with an emulsifying agent so that it can be diluted with water. Used as a cutting oil or coolant.
Spelter The brass used for brazing.
Stellite A hard metal alloy sometimes used for tool tips, or to face components subject to a high wear rate.
Swarf The metal shavings formed by machining operations.

T-slots The slots in cross-slides and milling machine beds, shaped like an inverted T, through which work can be held down with T-bolts or conventional bolts and T-nuts.
Tap A tool for forming a female thread.
Thimble-screw The ratchet screw at the end of a micrometer barrel.
'Thou' One thousandth of an inch (0·001in).
Tungsten carbide A very hard material sometimes used for tool tips.

V-belt A drive belt of blunted 'V' section which transmits drive through its angled faces rather than its base.
Vernier gauge A precision measuring device of the caliper type.

Index